Under the Wire

Under the Wire

THE WORLD WAR II ADVENTURES
OF A LEGENDARY ESCAPE
ARTIST AND "COOLER KING"

William Ash
with Brendan Foley

Thomas Dunne Books
St. Martin's Press 🐟 New York

THOMAS DUNNE BOOKS.
An imprint of St. Martin's Press.

UNDER THE WIRE. Copyright © 2005 by William Ash and Brendan Foley. All rights reserved. Printed in the United States of America. No part of this book may be used or reproduced in any manner whatsoever without written permission except in the case of brief quotations embodied in critical articles or reviews. For information, address St. Martin's Press, 175 Fifth Avenue, New York, N.Y. 10010.

www.stmartins.com

Design by Phil Mazzone

ISBN 0-312-33832-5
EAN 978-0-312-33832-9

First Edition: October 2005

10 9 8 7 6 5 4 3 2 1

From Bill to Ranjana

and from

Brendan to Shelly

Contents

Preface

In a modern world where heroes are generally either nonexistent or else two-dimensional media fabrications, there is an understandable search for something or someone better. In many years of covering feature stories ranging from banking to bomb disposal, I have only ever met one genuine hero, and that is Bill Ash.

Bill would laugh at such an idea, but then he is virtually unique in that he can find something funny in any situation. He even managed a smile through broken teeth while being beaten by the Gestapo in Paris, answering their demand to betray "just one name" of those who helped him by delivering up the name of his French teacher back in Texas.

His ability to laugh at himself in the middle of wartime life-or-death situations runs through all of his adventures like a watermark of honesty. Yet Bill is not just the master of seeing the funny side. His humor in the face of the carnage and cruelty of World War II is simply the most obvious and constant reminder of something bigger—the sense of shared humanity that brought him into the war while his country was still neutral.

Bill's instinct to defend those less capable of defending themselves seems to have been present almost from birth, just like his fascination for escaping. What started with battles against playground bullies in Depression-hit Texas ended in his volunteering to fight possibly the greatest bully of all time—Adolf Hitler. He is a modern Huck Finn, transplanted from the Mississippi to Occupied Europe, his raft replaced by a Spitfire.

In Britain, Bill stood out among the fearless but mainly upper-class young Englishmen who risked their lives as wartime fighter pilots. By contrast, he was a constantly hungry, resourceful American son of the Great Depression, fighting on his own terms, even though doing so cost him his citizenship.

His position as an outsider gave him a unique perspective. He witnessed the bravery of the French resistance first hand as they tried to keep him from capture, but when the Gestapo finally did seize him, he had a chance to see the darker side of humanity. Bill claims he organized his war badly. If he had started off in the hands of the Gestapo, he would have been a bit clearer on why he was there in the first place.

His mix of grit, humor, and humanity make his story unique, illuminating world events through small, person-sized adventures. Through his eyes, we share the feelings of 1930s America as it teeters on the brink of war, and understand in a far more profound way than in any dry history book how the Nazis were stopped, and just who defeated them.

While most prisoners of war would assist others' escape attempts, only a minority risked death as active escapees. Fewer still became serial escapologists like Bill. Most did not live to tell their stories, and those who did paid a high price. The fictional character played by Steve McQueen in the film of *The Great Escape* captured the imagination of millions. Bill Ash is one of the few real-life "Cooler Kings" of the war, fact rather than fiction. Each time he was released from solitary confinement, he would restart his escape plans within days, sometimes within hours, under the wire in a tunnel, through it with cutters, or vaulting over it to freedom like some ungainly flightless bird.

Bill's one-man war touched the lives of hundreds, from Depression America to flight training in Canada, then from Blitz-hit London to Occupied Europe and the streets of Paris. As an escapee he moved through France, Germany, Poland, and Lithuania like a roadrunner, destination unknown. As his incredible wartime journey evolved, he realized his own instinct for freedom was simply an articulation of a desire felt by millions. His own unique war, whether in the air or on the run, was a microcosm of that great struggle.

To have survived so much and yet be willing to risk his life on one last escape attempt from inside a raging battlefield in the dying days of the world's most terrible conflict, partly to save sick comrades and partly just for the hell of it, says something special about Bill. To me, it says he is that rarest of things, a good friend and a genuine hero.

Brendan Foley, London, 2005

Under the Wire

1. An Apprenticeship in Escapology

More than sixty years ago, in March 1942, I was a young warrior—a rare creature in the form of an American Spitfire pilot, flying a magnificent, gleaming machine in the skies over Occupied France. I had joined up to fight the Nazis while America was still neutral. That action had cost me my citizenship, and in an ill-considered burst of gratitude, the British had put me in charge of a Spitfire.

A Spitfire cockpit is small. It smells of metal and leather, of raw horsepower and excitement. Once in the sky a Spitfire pilot is alone, a hunter, an acrobat, and a warrior king. The only trouble in my case was that the king was about to be beheaded.

I looked down at a small French village, looming closer by the second. Then I looked up at half a dozen enemy aircraft, Focke-Wulf 190s, circling and taking leisurely turns trying to blow me out of the sky. For the first time, I began to wonder if the British were about to regret entrusting me with their magnificent flying machine. My plane was shot up. My gun button was jammed and useless. I had just switched off my coughing engine, which was full of cannon holes and threatening to burst into flames.

As the Luftwaffe planes roared in for the kill, I turned to face them, minimizing myself as a target, and stared directly into their cannon fire. I knew that it was time to end one career as a Spitfire pilot and to start a new one. My career choices were limited: I could become a prisoner, an escape artist, or a corpse. How, I asked myself as I looked for a field in which to crash-land, did an American, flying for the Canadians, fighting for the British, come to be blown out of the sky by a German, somewhere over France?

People seeking an answer to that question, or those who know a bit about my first wartime career as a Spitfire pilot and my second rather longer stint as a prisoner of war and escape artist, sometimes ask me about my early life. They are apparently looking for clues to why a young American would go halfway across the world to fight for the British against the Nazis while the United States was still staunchly neutral. Sometimes they also ask me if there was anything in my childhood in Depression-hit Texas that pointed me toward a career as an unlikely escapologist on what turned out to be a somewhat bumpy unauthorized tour of Occupied Europe. To them, and to you, all I can say is that from my earliest memories I have always disliked bullies, and from just as early, I have always loved running away.

I was born in 1917, at about the same time as the Russian revolution, but into the slightly less tempestuous world of Dallas, Texas. My father was into ladies' hats. Not that he wore them himself; rather, he was a traveling hat salesman, though for all the hats he sold he might as well have worn them himself. He was the quietest, gentlest soul you could imagine in the toughest, most brutal of professions. He had a great baritone voice and used to sing while my mother accompanied him on the piano, up to the day when several stern-faced men came and repossessed it.

My father was also a very talented artist who would spend his evenings quietly sketching or with his head buried in a newspaper, but the 1920s and '30s were tough times in which people made their living any way they could, rather than thinking much about what they would like to do. In another time and place my father's creativity would have taken him far, but as it was, it took every bit of his fortitude and optimism to face a world of flinty-faced shopowners who would greet him or any salesman bearing his cherished samples with a cheery "Whadda you bringing that crap in here for?"

My formative years were a succession of ups and downs dictated by the precarious fortunes of my father's work. We would move from place to place, usually to a smaller cheaper apartment as times got tough, not so much white collar as frayed collar.

Our family car—upon which my father's job and our capacity to eat depended—was just as changeable, and he was always having it carted away when he could not keep up with the payments, like a cavalryman having his horse shot from under him during a rout. Just as changeable as my address and my father's mode of transport was the school I attended as we moved about to stay one step ahead of the rent collector.

I attended numerous grammar schools, mostly in the poorer, rougher parts of Dallas, and being a newcomer on a regular basis led to what seemed like an endless string of fights and schoolyard battles. I've never liked fighting, but despite my passion for running away from places, I've always been stubborn about not running away from battles.

At James Bowie School, when I was about six, I remember that the local kids had found a better amusement than beating each other up. They would force two smaller kids to fight and bet on the outcome. A gang of boys, so big and sophisticated that they must have been all of eight years old, had captured my friend George and were holding him like a victim destined for human sacrifice. Two other big boys grabbed me and told me that I could easily beat my friend. Even then I was quite a tough little soul, with a wiry build that later led me to be quite a handy boxer, and a tuft of hair that stood up as if it was looking for a fight even if I wasn't. To impress the point that my victory was assured, they said that if I lost the fight they would batter me as well.

As a crowd formed, they held us from behind like fighting cocks, urging us to hammer each other while massive wagers of pennies and bubble gum were placed on the outcome. Then something strange happened. George looked over at me and burst into tears. A red mist came down on me at the thought of those bigger boys bullying my friend, and when we were released like reluctant gladiators, instead of charging at George, I made a beeline for one of his bigger tormentors and belted him on the jaw. George turned around and started in on another of them. I'd like to say that we polished off the lot of them, but life, as I was to rediscover during the war, is not like that. Still, we did shut down the tote for the day.

My mother regarded such events as occupational hazards of boyhood, and was determined that her son would rise to president of the United States at the very least. She was a handsome, determined woman who diverted all her exasperation at her easy-going husband's lack of success into a misplaced attempt to propel her only son into the financial stratosphere.

Perhaps that's why I can never remember a time from being old enough to walk that I did not have at least one job. When I was hardly past the toddling stage and certainly could not read, I was selling magazine subscriptions door to door, egged on by free gifts for the best salesperson such as tiny paper-tissue model airships that were in vogue in the 1920s, just like the real thing. Unfortunately, like their larger counterparts, when the toys were filled with hot air, they had a propensity to burst into flames, a fact that crept back in to my mind many years later as I was being shot from the sky in my sputtering Spitfire over northern France.

Dallas in the 1920s and 1930s was a tough, boisterous town with one foot already heading for its oily boomtown future, but the other one stuck firmly in its Western past. Just down the road, Fort Worth in the 1920s was even more of a cattle town and I grew up in the noisy crossroads between an ever-changing city landscape and the changeless scenes of the old West.

Not that Dallas in the 1920s would have thanked you for reminding it of the Wild West. It was hurrying into the future for better or worse. A few years before I was born there was a huge flood that killed several people and destroyed millions of dollars worth of property in the town and the good burghers of Dallas decided it was a good excuse for a new town plan. The following decades saw new buildings, parks, and hundreds of small companies emerging, many of them linked to the oil business that was just starting to take off in the surrounding areas of Texas. Things were so speeded up; it felt a little like living in one of the silent Buster Keaton movies of the time. Other businesses were turning from local stores into national institutions, like Nieman

Marcus, whose first store was doing booming business in the downtown Dallas of the 1920s, or the 7-Eleven chain that started life in the city in 1922. I added the role of shelf stacker to my childhood résumé.

Perhaps it was to escape the endless array of jobs and chores, sandwiched between our precarious domestic existence and the nonstop battles in ever-changing school yards, but somewhere along the way I developed a taste for running away from home in search of adventure. I had been inclined to wander off from the earliest time I can remember, but by the age of seven or eight this had evolved into full-fledged escapes.

At about that age I was walking to school one day when I decided to just keep walking, past the school, and all the way out of town to the road that led to Fort Worth. Once on the road, I flagged down a passing Model T Ford and explained that I had to reach my parents, who were gravely ill in Fort Worth. The driver peered at me and asked me which parent was ill. I told him both of them, and confided that I suspected food poisoning. Just as he was getting justifiably suspicious, I produced an envelope addressed to a hat factory in Fort Worth and ordered him to make haste to their place of employment. It seemed good enough for the driver, and we zoomed out of town. The envelope was one of hundreds my father would send looking for work, but in the height of the Great Depression, he might as well have saved the stamp, as it turned out he did, with his young son thoughtfully delivering it by hand.

When we reached the Fort Worth hat factory, I thanked the driver, walked in the front door, deposited my father's letter, and walked out the back door. I spent the day seeing the sights, then exchanged my lunch money for a trip to the movies, and by the

evening decided it was probably time to head home. I turned myself in to the local police and inquired whether there were any reports of search parties looking for small boys from Dallas. They
said there were not, but were kind enough to drive me home,
where, as always, my mother would administer a stern punishment but dine out on an ever-growing store of anecdotes about
her little boy's adventurous streak.

It might seem strange in these much more dangerous times
that a child could survive such escapades unscathed, but there was
still something of a sense of innocence and adventure in the air in
the 1920s. The freewheeling history of the Wild West was recent
enough for some of the old-timers from that era to still be walking around, capable of inspiring young minds with a thirst for adventure. I remember befriending one old codger during a
childhood vacation in New Mexico. As I sat beside him on the
warm red earth, he told me stories of gunfights and galloping, of
jail breaks and burning barns. He turned out to be George Coe,
who rode with Billy the Kid during the Lincoln County War.
George had his trigger finger shot off in the battle of Sawyers
Mill in 1878, yet even without it, he seemed able to beckon me
into a world with more adventure than the one we are forced to
inhabit. I soon became known as Billy the Kid.

George filled me with such a love of tales of the Old West that
years later when I was a pilot I used to hurry home from aerial
battles over France in order to find out what happened in some
Western potboiler novel I had left unfinished at the base when
the order came to scramble.

Back in the Dallas of the 1920s, the city still pined for a long-
dead dream that it might somehow become a river port and the
center of life in the Midwest, but the Trinity River proved hard

to navigate. It was only when the army made Camp Dick in Dallas a hub for their newfangled flying machines during World War I, at about the time I was being born, that a different possible future presented itself. The same ambitious eyes that oversaw the local business world saw new alternatives in the form of the boom in motorcars and the birth of aviation. Both events got into full swing just as I was growing up.

"Let the automobile be our wagon and the air be our ocean," the city fathers declared, sincerely, if slightly pompously, and set about building a big commercial airfield at Love Field that was bought by the city in 1927.

My memory of these great business and architectural changes is clouded by the fact that a young boy with a sense of adventure has much more important things to think about. Our proximity to so much flying may have given me my first yearnings to become a pilot, but in the meantime there was always something crashing or burning down or someone being shot that seemed much more interesting. I remember feeling that we were hurtling into the future when I stared in wonderment at the age of six at Dallas's latest claim to fame—the city's first electric traffic light, attracting crowds of spectators outside the vaudeville theaters and new movie palaces springing up along Elm Street. It was invented by a quirky old Dallasite called Henry Dad Garrett, who ran the local fire station. There must not have been too many fires, since he also had time to invent one of the first car radios and install the first police and fire emergency radio system in the country at about the same time. He could also be said to have invented public radio in America. When there were no fire or police signals to send out, he used to play his own classical record collection for anyone with a crystal radio set who happened to be listening in.

The feeling of growth, change, and possibilities continued throughout the 1920s. When I was ten, in 1927, I and forty thousand other kids rejoiced in escaping from school for a day. We were given the day off to go see Charles Lindbergh, the celebrated aviator, who was flying to Dallas in his plane the *Spirit of St. Louis* on part of his victory tour following his solo flight across the Atlantic that year.

That cold September day it rained constantly, but every one of us children and about another sixty thousand grown-ups formed the largest, soggiest crowd in the city's history, lining the streets of his parade route through downtown Dallas. People climbed trees, they clung to lampposts, they crowded onto balconies and wriggled dangerously along rooftops for a better view. When Lindbergh arrived, the city residents went wild, cheering and waving as he passed by in an open automobile. This must have been his hundred-and-first victory parade, and he seemed a bit less excited than the rest of us. The local newspaper reported that "a glassy stare and a mechanical lifting of his hand to his bare head were his only reactions to the cheering of his admirers." Still, once again the thought crept into my head: It must be great to be able to fly. Ironically, while I went on to become one of the earliest American Spitfire pilots, Lindberg become a cheerleader for U.S. isolationism in the late 1930s.

Even in the supposed boom times of the Roaring Twenties, things were quite tight for me and my family, so my range of part-time jobs proliferated. In a few years my efforts to sell magazine subscriptions door to door had been joined by a paper route, then shelf stacking at local stores, so by the time I was about ten I had amassed the considerable fortune of $200 as the only possible means to bankroll my future education. Then, in

1929, a family friend who worked for General Electric pointed out to my parents that it was a crime not to have that money working for my future in the form of stocks and shares. He even gave them a tip on American Commonwealth Power. No sooner had my personal fortune gone into their coffers than the entire American banking industry collapsed in the crash of October 1929 that heralded the start of the Great Depression. I found myself a ruined tycoon, just in time for my twelfth birthday. The family friend who worked for General Electric took me to one side and warmly explained that the financial lesson this event taught me would stand me in good stead for the rest of my life and was worth far more than a paltry $200. Speaking personally, I still miss the $200.

By the early 1930s my father's business was in real trouble, and after so many adventures of moving home and running away from home, home finally ran away from me. When I was twelve, my mother decided that she should join my father on the road, where the hatchet-faced hat shop owners would have a harder time pushing her around than my gentle, amiable father. My only sister, Adele, was sent to live with relatives in Ohio, and I took a room close to my high school. Adele was beautiful, kind, and very smart. In another time and with more opportunities she would have had an amazing career. Instead of that, in those early years she sometimes had to make do with very little. I remember that when she was out with a date who tried to impress her with a flashy tip to the waiter, she would forget her hat or bag accidentally-on-purpose so she could scoot back in to redistribute the wealth between the undeserving waiter and herself to fund future breakfasts for her ever-hungry brother. I'm proud to say that Adele and I were not just siblings, but became best friends. In comparison to many Americans in the newborn "hungry thirties," we were not badly off, but they were certainly tough times, and more about survival than lofty aspirations. It makes me smile when I read history books that claim Dallas was not affected by the Depression.

As the hard times bit deeper, employers instituted wage cuts in many industries, from the department stores to the clothing manufactures. Not everyone took such treatment meekly. At the time, one of my many occupations was chasing copy and advertising for the *Dallas Morning News*, so I frequently found myself somewhere close to the action, whether it was just a bent fender after a car collision on Elm Street or staring silently at the bullet-riddled bodies of Bonnie and Clyde, our homegrown Dallas bank robbers, when the law had finally caught up with them in 1934. No one seemed to have told them that the Depression was not so bad locally.

Not everyone who protested against the poverty of the times used tommy guns. At about the same time there was a strike among the skilled lady dress cutters of Dallas, whose pay was chiseled down to less than ten dollars a week when they were getting up to forty dollars elsewhere in the country. When some of them joined a union they were sacked and victimized, but the strike quickly spread to fifteen factories in the town. The police were ordered to escort scab labor into the factories until the striking ladies descended on them, scratching, biting, and bashing both the police and their charges. The strikers entered two of the factories and ejected the women who had been brought in to do their jobs after first removing all of the strikebreakers' clothing. This proved very popular with us local office boys and made headlines all over the world as the insurgents were dubbed "the stripping strikers." Within two years the strikers had been quietly given their pay increase and union rights, and the weapon of clothes removal disappeared once more from the staid streets of Dallas.

The number of part-time jobs I took to support myself continued to rise as I worked my way through high school, so that by the time I reached Texas University in the state capital of Austin, I was working half a dozen of them. Not that they were all conventional jobs—at one stage while being a gas pump attendant and full-time student, I was also publishing an ersatz version of Who's Who for the more egotistical students on the campus, charging them five dollars each to be listed in this exclusive tome, with the only entry qualification of course being the ability to give me five dollars. Simultaneously I was running a scam to write essays on behalf of the richer, lazier students for a small fee, working as an assistant librarian, operating a small dance hall in downtown Austin, and still chasing advertising copy for the local newspapers. Somewhere along the line I managed to read enough books and write enough essays of my own to get a reasonably decent degree—the first in my family.

At about that time in the later 1930s I was reunited with my wonderful sister Adele, and in my last year at the university we rented a little place together. The never-ending Depression still had us eternally searching for our next meal, no matter how many jobs we worked or scams we attempted, but we did develop some creative ways of making our money go farther.

Every week when we got our paychecks, we would instantly cash in two dollars for twenty dimes. No matter how carefully we tried to make our meager money last all week we knew we would be utterly broke and hungry before the next payday, so we devised a way to make sure that we did not spend it all at once. Standing in the center of the room we would hurl the dimes in all directions. Over the week we would pick up and use the ones that were easiest to spot, but by the end of the week when we were starving and had run out of money, we would be able to turn the room inside out and usually find a thin dime hiding under a piece of furniture or lodged in a crack in a floorboard, and at that time a dime was the difference between breakfast and coffee for two and going hungry. The searching took our minds off rumbling stomachs, and the jubilation at finding a dime and heading for the diner was about the same as if we had won the lottery.

Despite our lack of funds, we embraced every form of culture and entertainment we could find. I remember one particular night, returning to my digs from one of the half-dozen jobs that barely kept me fed and housed. I was so tired I was almost sleep-walking when I heard the strains of music coming from a church hall. It was Beethoven's Fifth Symphony, and it was the first clas-sical music I can ever recall hearing. The magnificent sound floated out of the church into the Texas night, stopping me in my tracks. I stood and listened until the very last notes had died away. It was a love affair with music that was to run like a silver thread through the rest of my life, from my precarious days in the De-pression, to airfields in Britain, where the same notes would mix with the sound of Spitfires taking off, and later in the darkest days of life in a German POW camp—but that was another world.

Music, playing on the phonograph, on the radio, or just inside my head, helped to keep me sane despite the myriad dull jobs and the ever-present twin anxieties of completing the next essay as-signment and finding next week's food and rent money. One other thing also helped to keep me on track during the Great Depression, which most of us thought might never end, and that was my ability to escape normality. By the late 1930s my runaway childhood had given way to occasional bouts of youthful madness that would see me abandon my work and studies long enough to disappear into the wilderness, paddling a canoe up a wild river or riding a borrowed horse through unspoiled western territory.

I remember summer days when I pondered what I might do with my future as I lazed with a fishing pole on a remote riverbank. As I looked up I saw groups of Texas robins, much bigger than normal ones, as are most things in Texas, gorging themselves on wild berries. The summer was ending, and the fruit had started to ferment on the branch, so there were scores of drunken robins, wheeling and flapping in wobbly arcs in the sky, trying not to collide with each other. It made me think how great it would be to fly. In my head I was still listening to Beethoven's music, and from that moment on, I realized that music, flying, and successful escapes were three of the great loves of my life, and that all three could allow me to soar away from gravity, from hard times, and from imprisonment of the body or, worse still, imprisonment of the mind.

2. Discovering America

By early 1939 I had left Austin as a young, restless Texan with an urge for adventure and not much hope of getting a real job in the depths of the Great Depression. Along with ten million unemployed people, I drifted from place to place all over the Midwest for the best part of a year, mostly hitching rides in battered cars, but sometimes riding the rails and avoiding the railway bulls who were employed to knock nonpaying passengers off the freight cars they were clinging to. In truth, though, by the end of that tumultuous decade the bulls had almost given up. The volume of men hoboing from one place to another looking for work was so great, usually matched by an equal number coming in the opposite direction for the same reason, that the train bullies lowered their expectations. Instead of attempting to eradicate their entire species, they concentrated on keeping the hobos out of stations and cracking a few heads when they thought they could get away with it.

The most common place to hop a train, free from the threat of the bulls, was always on what was called a blind. This was usually a place on the outskirts of town, sometimes on an upward slope that slowed the train, and not far enough out of town for it to have picked up too much speed, for otherwise it would be too hard for us nonpaying passengers to reach. Where these conditions coincided with a curve, there was often a blind spot toward the rear of the train where the driver and guard could not see what was going on, and that was the perfect spot for jumping on.

Years later, trapped behind the multiple layers of wire in prisoner-of-war camps, I was to find this early training in blind spots very handy. Sometimes prison machine-gun posts were built along the wire in such a way that there was a small blind spot between the guard posts where the searchlights or lines of sight could not reach, and these were perfect places to dig a lightning tunnel or to attempt to chop through the wire with homemade cutters.

But back in Depression America, I had no reason to appreciate this education as I raced alongside a freight train that seemed to go on forever in either direction, and did not seem to be moving all that slowly compared to me. My worldly possessions were slung in a bindle, or blanket bundle, around my neck, and I was often one of a small army of people, all trying to get on the same train at the same time. The art of "chasing a train" must now be largely forgotten. I would look for a freight door that had been left open a crack and try to prise it open enough to hurl myself on board, sprawling in the dust or the straw on the floor. At other times there were already hobos and travelers on board, and sometimes helping hands would be extended, hauling us newcomers up. This was partly an act of humanity, but it also had a certain logic. Hobos tended to share what little they had, and sooner or later each of us would be the one trying to get on, looking for a hand up from a new friend.

As I sat in the open doorway and the train picked up speed, I met other voyagers from a remarkable variety of places and backgrounds, all reduced to riding the rails and living rough in search of work. My childhood may have been precarious, and I may have worked jobs to help pay the bills since I was old enough to toddle, but at no stage in my strange, wandering boyhood had I ever gone to sleep really hungry or without a roof over my head. The seemingly endless Depression had created a vast tide of humanity that swept back and forth, breaking like waves on the outskirts of each city. The sense of injustice that I was born with started to grow keener, aimed not just at people and places on the newsreels in faraway Europe, but also at the complacent politicians at home who could regard this vast waste of human hope and potential as a price worth paying for their own cozy lives.

Looking around the straw-strewn cattle car in which I had landed, there was all too much evidence of its previous four-legged inhabitants, but now it was occupied by a small band of those united by the search for nonexistent jobs and—in the shorter term—for their next meal. They ranged from morose loners to small groups optimistically exchanging leads for work with each other.

In another corner, there was a lean man picking out a tune on a battered guitar. Hoboes respected musicians for their skill and their ability to raise the spirits of people with little hope of a job and temporarily make them forget their hunger. From their own point of view, a musician could often make enough for a meal by playing on the street corner for a few pennies and nickels. Most hoboes never found the mythical job they were searching for; they got by on a day's work here or there, often odd jobs, from pushing a broom to a little bit of gardening in return for a meal. In short, the only thing that kept them alive was small amounts of work provided by other people not too different from themselves. I never felt much of a sense of stigma as I rode the rails, partly because I was one among so many, but mostly because a quick look around me told me that wherever the blame lay for our tough, rather hopeless condition, it did not belong to these decent people, swaying in the perpetual twilight of a rolling boxcar, just trying to get by.

Most of the travelers were single men of all ages, but there were women and children, too, particularly traveling by the roads and living in the jungle camps that sprang up on the edges of most towns. Some estimates put the number of women and children riding the rails in the 1930s as high as a quarter of a million.

Over in another corner of the boxcar was a whiskery older man, who had obviously been riding the rails for some time. Indeed, he was part of a hobo tradition that stretched back to the days of the Civil War, and which grew along with the hoboes' unwilling hosts, the railroads themselves. While the old guy in the corner was no doubt tough as an old boot, I remember feeling sorry for him, since jumping on or off a moving train was not easy for a young man, and it must have become more and more of a struggle for some of the older hoboes who had been riding the rails for decades. Suddenly, in recent years their world had become full of newcomers, many of whom were like me, following in the footsteps of Jack London, unsure of the rules and still finding novelty where the old-timers only saw yet another day on the iron road. After my time at the university, it gave me a very different but equally valid education in the ways of the world.

This second education introduced me to a world that had its own unique language and symbols, now largely forgotten. Hoboes were called many things, few of them polite, but they ranged from bindle stiff, from the blanket rolls many of them carried, to bum, bumper, or boxcar jockey—and that was just the B's. Everything was a euphemism, from California blankets— newspapers used to keep warm at night—to "hitting the grit," which was being forced to jump from a train unexpectedly.

Alongside the spoken language were the symbols or glyphs that some of the old-timers would use to help fellow hoboes know where to go or what to look out for, much like present-day Internet chat icons. They were simple symbols usually hastily chalked on a gate or a wall. There were cartoons or squiggles with meanings for those who understood them, like "bone polisher [fierce dog] lives here" or "take care—cops around," but there were good ones, too, like "nice lady lives here" and "safe place to sleep."

In the boxcar, the old man jumped up, almost as if a sixth sense had told him where to get off, but in reality he probably had grown to understand the sounds of the train itself, like a second language, and he could hear it slowing down at a favorite jumping-off point. Just as it was advisable to avoid the bulls at the starting station, it was also smart to get off before the train reached its destination. Waking up in a station, a dozy hobo could still expect a night in jail for vagrancy or perhaps a beating from an overzealous bull who didn't yet know that the war with the hoboes was over and they had lost to our sheer weight of numbers.

Swinging the doors open, the old man led the charge as one by one the inhabitants of the boxcar would jump like paratroopers from the open door at a point where the train was going slowly, though sometimes it did not feel quite slow enough.

Struggling to keep up with my aged companion, we headed for the nearby hobo jungle. These encampments ranged from a huddle of ramshackle tents to small metropolises made of shacks and junk. Some sprang up and disappeared like mushrooms, while others lasted for years. They were inhabited not only by single men looking for work, but also by destitute families drifters, grifters, and shifters. Some were farmers or farmworkers pushed off their land when the banks used the Depression as an excuse to foreclose on an entire generation, to move the land from small farms to larger tracts owned by conglomerates. Others were factory workers, pushed out of work when the mills and steel works closed as the slump began to bite. A few were trade union organizers, blacklisted for trying to organize workplaces in the teeth of the Depression, when there were always ten men willing to take the job of anyone who objected to low wages or dangerous conditions. But mostly they were just ordinary young men in need of a good meal, a roof, and a job to wake up to.

Like all societies, from native tribes to prisoner-of-war camps, the hobo jungle had its own set of rules. It was usually positioned on the sunny side of the hill, where possible near an easy source of clean water. Most important, it was rarely far from roads or a "catching-out" spot on the railroad line, where a hobo in a hurry could leave town. In other cases, small groups gathered inside towns, often in derelict or burnt-out buildings, but the outlying jungle camps tended to be bigger and friendlier.

The camp rules were unwritten and enforced by collective

willpower rather than a police force. They included always leaving pots and pans clean, never stealing from other hoboes in the camp, and generally not committing crimes such as burglary that would lead to trouble for the whole camp. These were generally tough men in search of honest work, and while it would be foolish to say that there was not a certain amount of lawbreaking, it was remarkably civilized, given what these people went through daily just to survive. Crime, such as it was, tended to consist of the odd piece of food snatched from outside a store or maybe an item of clothing filched from a clothesline.

At nights the camps glowed with a collection of campfires large and small. Some families kept to themselves, but others shared what little food they had, with each person showing up expected to do the same. After eating whatever we had managed to acquire during the day, there were often discussions as the campfires died down. There was no electricity for radios, and television was just a rumor, but there were often musicians who would play the music of the fields or the streets as the darkness crept in.

Sometimes we had discussions about the world we lived in and what we would like to see happen, though most people were too busy surviving to care very much. I remember one young man asking me about the Spanish Civil War. I told him about the battles of heroic loyalists against Franco and his fascist army and said I had wanted to go to fight with the International Brigade, but that the war had ended already. He asked me who had won. I told him my guys had lost to the fascists and he looked at me like I was slightly touched. "Why would you want to go over there and fight for the losers?" Years later, when I was holed up in a prison camp and the outcome of the war looked far from certain, I often thought what a good question it was, but sometimes even the losers can win.

Thinking about it, my brief immersion in this twilight world prepared me for a lot of my wartime activities—being an unwelcome nonpaying passenger, learning how to avoid the attention of guard dogs or the authorities, sharing food and political discussions with men just as badly off as myself, and sometimes just learning to laugh in the face of everything the world could throw at me. As I dozed off that night in the hobo jungle, someone was playing an old tune on the harmonica, singing about hobo heaven, a world in which "the guard dogs all have rubber teeth and the hens lay hard-boiled eggs."

Next morning I was up early as usual. I've never been able to laze in bed, since I always have the feeling I may be missing out on something exciting. The Nazis were later to attempt to cure this by locking me in solitary confinement, but then I would spend large parts of my day hanging from the bars over my cell's one tiny window in hopes of glimpsing whatever it was I was missing. But in the Depression, most of the excitement had to be self-generated and usually related to procuring the next meal or day's work.

Among my early careers was my habit, on arrival in a new town, of signing up as a door-to-door salesman, getting my suitcase of samples, and then selling the contents at some flea market for enough food for one good meal. Some people may tut-tut at such a practice, but I suggest they try not eating for a day or two and then see if it does not seem like an excellent idea. In a strange way, it also felt like divine justice for all the hard-nosed men who had slammed doors in my quiet and polite salesman father's face.

Then there was my spell as a shop assistant at a clothing store in Kansas City. My efforts to sell men's fashions were hampered by my own wardrobe, which at the time consisted of a pair of second-hand tomato-colored lady's slacks, a purple shirt, and a large Scout knife that was useful in a hobo encampment but intimidating to the more nervous customers. Even though the store fired me, I heard later that after I was shot down over France and declared missing and presumed dead, the store bosses put up a plaque in my honor. It mournfully recorded that I was a loyal employee who had fallen fighting for freedom. I always meant to go back after the war and put them to the trouble of taking it down, but never quite got around to it.

One other job I remember was a brief spell working in a bank. When my counting skills were found lacking, they deployed me as an elevator operator, a job whose ups and downs seemed very appropriate for my career at that point. While I was working there, I bumped into someone who recognized me from my precarious days at the University of Texas. They inquired whether my employers knew I actually had a summa cum laude arts degree. "Yes," I replied, "but they've agreed to overlook it."

This was about the time of the declaration of war by England on Germany, though to most Americans it was a distant event until their own country was finally galvanized into battle by the bombing of Pearl Harbor two years later.

During my travels, I had gotten into a few rather vigorous exchanges of views and blows with some early, enthusiastic German-American Bund supporters of Hitler, who felt that we should be doing the same sort of thing to whoever took their fancy—usually to the lefties, the Jews, or the unemployed. In an extension of some of my earlier playground battles, I had become quite a useful boxer. In one such altercation a helpful bystander pointed out that if I wanted to fight so much, perhaps I should pay Hitler a personal visit.

After a year of hoboing from job to job and place to place all over the country, I arrived in early 1940, slightly ragged and fresh off a freight train, at the Hungry Man Diner in Detroit. It was a rough "one-arm joint" where you leaned on the counter with one arm and shoveled stew with the other. There you could have all the stew you could get on a plate for fifteen cents, but you were fined another dime if you left any on your plate. This was the unlikely jumping-off point for my war against Hitler. I remember some of the locals having a laugh at my expense as I set off walking over the border-spanning bridge to Windsor, Ontario, where I attempted to enlist in the Royal Canadian Air Force.

In Canada, a dour British recruiting sergeant gave me a physical exam and pronounced me too malnourished to be any use. I complained that since I wanted to join the air force it was in their interest for me to be as light as possible. Think of all the fuel they would save! Despite my seamless logic, I was sent packing. I limped my way back to the Hungry Man Diner to be scoffed at by my detractors for having won the war so quickly.

I persuaded one of the doubting locals to lend me twenty dollars, which he reluctantly did at 20 percent interest compounded monthly "just to teach me the value of money." I handed over my new riches to the short-order cook at the diner and took up residence at one of the tables. Every day for two weeks solid, like a desperate man in an eating contest, I consumed everything they could shovel into me. I even became something of a local landmark as people checked in at the diner to see my progress. The cook wanted me to stay on, since business was booming, thanks to this new tourist attraction, but two weeks to the day after my rejection, I waddled back to Canada.

As I walked across the bridge that morning, I stopped and looked down at the swirling waters, wondering where they might carry me. I was leaving a country at peace, still becalmed in the Depression and going to one at war, fighting for its survival. I was more excited than frightened. Most of my family and friends were baffled. My own government was still stalled by those who wanted to turn a blind eye to Hitler. It was not our war. It was not my fight. I had heard it all, but I kept on walking.

For a moment when I reentered the RCAF recruiting station, my thoughts became a bit more practical. Would they throw me out again, for being too thin, or too fat, like some mad version of Goldilocks and the Three Bears? This time, when I stepped on the air force scales like a prizefighter, the entire office cheered. I was in.

But there was a price to pay. I, like every American who joined up in Canada, long before America entered the war, immediately had my citizenship and passport revoked for the crime of fighting for the king of England. The fact that so many of us Americans who volunteered in World War II before the United States entered the war lost our citizenship for the privilege of getting shot at in the defense of freedom, remains to this day one of the least reported and least glorious chapters in the history of our early neutrality in the conflict. The U.S. government's attitude was simple—to fight for Britain a person had to swear allegiance to the king, and to do that you lost your American citizenship. I thought about it for a moment, my pen poised above the enlistment papers that would change my life. Then I went ahead and signed up. There are some things that are more important than bits of paper.

If I had thought it would have done any good, I would have pointed out to the president of the United States that I was not so much *for* the king of England as *against* Hitler. Maybe, I reasoned, the president would feel differently after Pilot Officer Ash returned, having sorted out the Third Reich.

My basic training in Kingston, Canada, during 1940 at last revealed something I was better at than being an elevator operator or seller of hats. It seemed I had a natural aptitude for flying. I made new friends among the Canadians and a handful of equally mad Americans who had joined up about the same time. The instructors were mostly British former RAF pilots, this being before the introduction of the Empire Training Scheme, the Canadian pilot training regimen that was later to mass-produce Allied fliers for the war effort that led up to D-day.

At first I was a little dismayed to find that the British connection even extended to the food. There at the training base, amid a sea of Canadian plenty, was a little desert island of English rationing. Luckily, one of my first friends there, Paul Burden, was from New Brunswick, where his parents ran a chicken farm, so we were never short of supplies. Just to make sure, we took the precaution of making our unofficial headquarters in the local Chinese restaurant. Each payday we turned our air force paychecks over to the proprietor, and he fed us all month and even doled out pocket money.

The reality was that there was little time to spend it. We were woken at six for a particularly grueling series of exercises and then it was straight to flying practice. We did our service training on Fairey Battles, a rather underpowered fighter-bomber that had been retired after the aerial skirmishes over France during the blitzkrieg a few months earlier. It was a sluggish beast, and I could just imagine the thoughts of the British pilots who had to face roaring Messerschmitts in them. They must have felt like they were riding a turtle.

The defeat of France in 1940, with the British troops being practically driven into the sea at Dunkirk, with hundreds of thousands rescued in a heroic evacuation operation involving thousands of tiny boats, was fresh in our minds. We had huddled around radios, listening to stories of horror and heroism, feeling very far away and unable to help. The disaster in France had opened the immediate possibility of Hitler's invading Britain, which now stood as the last bastion of opposition to fascism in the West. The only thing that had delayed the invasion, code-named Operation Sealion, was the battle for air supremacy that raged over the skies of southern England between the Luftwaffe and the RAF while I and my volunteer friends were frantically training in Canada.

The Battle of Britain was a period of the war, rather than a one-off conflict, at its most intense in the second half of 1940. Reports of the heroism and the losses in Britain made us itch to get into the fight to even the odds. A few pessimists wondered if there would be any Britain left for us to defend, but most of us burned with a desire to be out of training and into action. We studied and practiced as if our lives depended on it, which of course they did.

I remember the final seconds before my first solo flight. We had just studied the theory of flying. Thrust by a propeller creates a vacuum over a curved surface such as a wing, and that vacuum lifts the object skyward. Staring at this hulking great machine on the runway, I was utterly unconvinced that anything other than a stick of dynamite could cause it to move upward. But once I was airborne, all my doubts evaporated.

Suddenly I was soaring. I had left the ground, the Depression, and the landlocked expectations of others far below, where people looked like ants and even the huge aircraft hangars looked like toys. My destiny was in my own hands, and I felt like an eagle looking down, master of all I surveyed. I knew that my new power and liberty was a fragile thing and that I could be brought crashing down by a single mistake, like Icarus flying too close to the sun, but I also knew I was alive, that flying was a form of music, and that the song in my head was the one I had been born to sing.

The only other experience I can compare to that first flight is swimming under water, where the effects of gravity are suddenly changed and you can do all sorts of things that would be impossible on the ground. I didn't dwell on the science too much, since I figured if I did, I might plummet to earth in a burst of logic. Maybe that's why I loved flying so much—the incredulity and delight that accompanied actually being up in the air never left me, at least not until I was shot down. That certainly put a crimp in my sense of wonder.

After lunch each day there was on-the-ground training in navigation, tactics, and Morse code, which we had to comprehend at fifteen words a minute. Then it was back in the air to put the theory into practice. Some of the early training took place in a Link Trainer, a very primitive sort of flight simulator, but most of it was up in the air. As the weeks turned into months, we flew for three or four hours a day, and much to my surprise I found myself becoming a real pilot.

Paul Burden was also progressing very well. In the air we encouraged each other and discussed what we had learned when we were back on terra firma. Together, we bought an old car and used it to venture out of the camp. Paul was a big, amiable, handsome man, and the local girls definitely gravitated to the dashing man in uniform, so he was a great companion. More importantly, the car allowed us to get to his parents' farm in Fredricton, where we were treated like royalty and allowed to bring back all manner of food, including cans of chicken and fresh eggs, to the ration-hit training station.

The days were long and tough, crammed with both theory and practice, but the novelty of being fed regularly and paid to do something I loved made me strive for ever better performances in the air. I particularly took to aerobatics, even squeezing creditable loops and rolls out of the bumbling Fairey Battles. As our confidence increased, we were given altitude tests in them, taking them up with a full bomb load to 18,000 feet without oxygen, then making three perfect landings in a row.

The best thing about this experience with the lumbering Battles was that later in Britain when it came to flying sleek, responsive planes such as Spitfires, I felt like that man who runs marathons while wearing a deep-sea diving suit, then is suddenly released and allowed to run free and feels almost weightless.

We learned to read the instrument panels, then practiced air navigation over the silent vastness of rural Canada, where I remember a thousand ribbons of silver lakes winking up at me. To a young, lost pilot who has been told to fly a triangular journey of a hundred miles and end up exactly over the training airfield he started from, they looked almost identical. Somehow we all made it back.

I started to get something of a reputation when my desire to experiment led me to a phase of flying upside down for as long as possible, working out how to use the controls while inverted, like someone learning to write while looking in the mirror. I liked the sense of precision and knowing the limits of responsiveness. Perhaps that is what led me to fly under my first bridge. The feeling of dread you get when approaching a bridge flying low above a great expanse of water is only surpassed by the feeling of exhilaration when you emerge unscathed, having somehow squeezed a hurtling metal machine below a concrete span, between two arches and a few feet above a raging river. Soon under-bridge flying became a significant part of my unofficial training curriculum.

While it would be fair to say that the authorities were less than keen on my aerobatics, they recognized that soon the mad young men they were training would be facing experienced Luftwaffe pilots in sophisticated planes. We would be fighting not just to conquer our own fear, but to preserve our lives, and potentially to determine the fate of soldiers and civilians far below.

When it came to firepower, they wisely started us with camera guns that took pictures of the targets we were meant to have shot, which showed, as often as not, empty spaces and interesting clouds when we missed. But soon we were playing for real, with Browning machine guns, churning out .303 ammunition, with the wiser instructors staying well behind us as we learned.

And so, after a few more months and 150 hours in the air, the powers that be decided I was safe to unleash on Hitler and awarded me my wings. Better still, they recommended me as a fighter pilot. As I emerged with my wings, I felt ten feet tall. There would be plenty of time to ponder the dangers that came with the wings later. For this one moment I had left the Depression behind and felt a sense of elevation I could never have known in the elevator of a Texas bank, no matter how many times I went up and down.

Paul Burden also passed with flying colors, and he was asked to stay on as an instructor. It was typical of him that while I galloped off in search of adventure, he agreed to stay on, probably making a bigger contribution to the war effort by helping to train a whole new generation of pilots than either of us flying alone. Later in the war he saw active service, too, piloting a Lancaster bomber and winning a Distinguished Flying Cross before he returned to Canada.

By then it was early 1941 and still a very bleak point in the war. Hitler's armies and air force dominated both Eastern and Western Europe, and a small British island at one end and a still-neutral Russia at the other offered the only hope of a future other than fascism. Opinion in America, particularly that of the rich industrialists, was still staunchly neutral, but sympathy for the British was on the rise among working people. This was countered by business tycoons and many newspaper proprietors who were determined to keep America out of the war at all costs, either because they quite liked Hitler or they feared the derailment of their own gravy train.

Luckily, not every newspaper was against intervention. When I left for Britain, my home town papers the *Dallas Journal* and *Dallas Morning News* ran front-page stories of how a local boy was going off to sort out the Luftwaffe. When a group of Texas newspapermen visited the Canadian training field shortly after I had left for England, they crowded round Paul Burden as he told them tall tales of life in the skies in a convincing Texas drawl. When they eventually found out he was Canadian, he told them that I had left my accent with him in Canada for safekeeping, along with my half share in our ancient automobile. He claimed he was just looking after them while I was away, but I took slightly longer to get back than had I planned.

The same Texas newspapers had given me a rousing send-off. Their reporting was exciting and sympathetic, if not very accurate. They announced that while everyone in Dallas was having their dinner, I would be "winging my way across the ocean, flying a bomber," and within a week would be "spitting death at German Stukas." At the time I was rolling around belowdecks on a troop ship destined for England, hoping that neither the Atlantic seasickness nor the U-boats would end my career before the Luftwaffe even had a chance.

My journey from Canada in a 28,000-ton troop ship called the *Georgic* was a tense few days. The ship had just been converted in a Belfast shipyard from being the last luxury liner of the White Star line, which had produced that other memorable vessel the *Titanic*. Having said that, the ship felt as big and sturdy as an island, even if the original guests would not have recognized it once three thousand seasick troops had been on it for more than a week.

On deck, looking about at the vastness of the gray Atlantic, I found it hard not to think about the U-boats circling the convoys, always waiting their chance. The rules of war were harsh. If one ship in a convoy was hit, the others often had orders to steam ahead rather than lingering to rescue survivors and then themselves becoming victims of another torpedo. Our nervousness was increased by a cheery sailor who informed me that one of our main cargoes was "aviation fuel for you flyboys." He assured me that if the ship was hit, it was more likely to go up in the air in tiny pieces than down.

Despite the nervous days and the seasick nights we made it to England's shore in one piece, and I promised myself if ever I got to guard a convoy, I would look after it with every ounce of energy I had, and in the coming months I was to get a chance to repay the debt. I also had a chance to remember the words of the cheery sailor when I read just a few months later that the same ship had been bombed while on transport duty carrying nearly a thousand Italian prisoners of war and internees near Suez. Her fuel oil caught fire, then her massive ammunition magazines exploded, leaving the once mighty ship half submerged and burnt out. Amazingly, she was salvaged, returned for repairs in Belfast, and back in the war by 1944. For myself, I was just glad to be back on dry land.

3. 411 Squadron

I arrived in early 1941 in a country in flames from the Blitz and under siege from an all-conquering Nazi army just a few miles across the English Channel. After just a few days I was sent to the operational manning unit, a sort of mustering and orientation station in Hawarden, in Clwyd, North Wales. That is where I caught my first close look at a Spitfire. It was love at first sight.

Whatever my mental picture of a Spitfire, in reality it was so much smaller than I expected. There it sat, a compact, finely engineered bundle of power and grace, like a platonic idea of a perfect airplane. From the elegant curve of its wings to the in-line engine tucked away behind its elongated nose, the whole structure had style. Long noses, whether on British gentry, borzoi dogs, or Spitfires, have always seemed very aristocratic to me.

Of all the planes I flew, Spitfires were the only ones that had no discernable bad habits. While other planes were sluggish just when you needed power most, or others tightened up when you were in a spin, Spitfires always seemed to know what to do and when to do it. Even throttled back to just 40 mph, a Spitfire would simply glide downward on an elegant and even keel.

But if the plane itself seemed heroic, some of the instructor pilots I started to meet seemed more like figures of legend. This period was the immediate aftermath of what has come to be called the Battle of Britain, and the instructors were mainly outstanding pilots, such as Joe Pegge, taking a well-deserved break after a year of intense aerial combat. Still, the idea of playing nursemaid to a bunch of nervous rookies flying close formation in brand-new Spitfires may have made these veterans yearn for the simpler dangers of facing the Luftwaffe at odds of five-to-one against.

Like most rookie pilots, I was desperate to get into action, though I was to discover in the coming years and months that there were still plenty of fascists to go around. So, while at the time some of these preparations and training seemed like an obstacle on the way to doing my job, in reality they were saving my life.

As I sat in the cockpit of my Spitfire, waiting to take off on my first solo in it, under the stern eye of the instructor who was there to grade my first flight, my hands fluttered around the unfamiliar controls. In a single-seater aircraft, there is no one around to tell you what buttons to press, and which knobs and levers you should definitely leave alone. I was in awe of this complex, elegant piece of machinery, with its purring Merlin engine and such firepower—two cannons and four machine guns—waiting only for the gentlest touch on the control-column gun button. Suddenly it did not seem so small after all.

But as soon as I was airborne, all fear left me. I was too busy trying to make sure that everything went well for the watching eyes below. In a Spitfire, making everything go well meant applying the gentlest, most subtle of guidance and letting the magnificent plane do the rest. Unlike the ponderous old Fairey Battles I had trained on, which had to be pushed and pulled to do what you wanted, the Spitfire needed only the gentlest of hints.

Soon I was diving and climbing and then, probably far too soon, I tried a full roll. It worked beautifully. I landed and as I walked past the instructor, still writing notes in his clipboard, he had a little half-smile on his otherwise stern face. He looked up and gave the tiniest possible nod of approval, though whether it was for me, or out of respect for the remarkable airplane, I will never know.

We learned about shooting an aerial target when we were sent to shoot down a barrage balloon—a sort of airborne obstacle for enemy aircraft—that had escaped its moorings and was wandering about somewhere near Liverpool. I remember being very pleased when we blasted it from the skies, but as one of our battle-hardened instructors warned us, balloons are easier than enemy planes: They don't shoot back.

And the shooting was indeed in earnest, even before we reached our first posting. I had become friendly with another new pilot at the training unit and watched one day as he taxied along the runway. A workman was crossing the strip at the same time and my friend pulled up too sharply to avoid him. His plane flipped over and, full of fuel, it burst into flames. Several of us ran over and tried desperately to get him out as machine-gun bullets from his magazines started to crackle and explode all around us as the fire took hold. We could not reach him and we had to watch as he died, engulfed in flames.

From then on I understood that while the turbulence of wartime forges some of the closest possible bonds among strangers, few pilots liked getting too friendly with their fellow pilots. Behind the laughter and the camaraderie was often a reserve, not caused by any coldness, but really the opposite—knowing that any day I or any of my colleagues might simply be dead and gone, and that the others would have to keep going, that day and the next, and the next, until the war was over or we, too, were memories.

I was quickly posted to an RAF squadron in Eleven Group, which meant I would be in the thick of things immediately, but somewhere along the line my orders were changed. The plan was to build a new squadron with all the Canadian pilots, and since I was one of the very few Americans, they seemed reluctant to make me a squadron on my own. Being that I was from somewhere in the general direction of Canada and had trained there, they clearly decided I would fit in best among my New World cousins and transferred me to the newly formed 411 Squadron at Digby in Lincolnshire as part of Twelve Group.

I remember being impatient at this move, as I knew that the new squadron would take weeks to get in shape, but arriving at Digby in June 1941, I soon recognized that there was a great deal to do on the ground as well as in the air. Many of the Canadians I had met at initial training were being funneled into this new outfit, and they were a great bunch.

Our new abode was stunning—a magnificent old home called Ashby Hall, built on the edge of a tranquil lake. It was quite a culture shock for the young man from downtown Dallas who had been sharing a can of beans over an open fire in a hobo jungle encampment only a few months earlier.

My new comrades sent me out to buy phonograph records for the officers' mess in the nearest metropolis, sleepy Lincoln town, but were horrified when I came back with Bach, Mozart, Brahms, and Beethoven. That wasn't quite what they had in mind. Even my protestations that I got them some pop music fell on deaf ears when they discovered it was a selection of Strauss waltzes. My plan worked. The records were banished as I knew they would be, and I got to listen to Beethoven's Fifth again in my own room, a long way from Texas. As Spitfire engines droned in the background, I wondered where I might find myself listening to it next. As it turned out, I'm glad I did not know the answer.

Life in the air was just as exhilarating as on the ground. Flying a Spitfire is at once an intensely individual experience and yet a completely collective one. When you are in the air, it quickly becomes obvious that you are relying for your life not just on the colleagues whom you can see on either wing, but on a small army of ground crew, from those elegant young women monitoring enemy aircraft on giant plotting maps to the oil-smeared mechanics working long and hard overnight to repair the damage of the previous day's battle and to nurse the Merlin engines back to health after they had been put through the punishment of aerobatics in a dogfight.

Yet ultimately it was also the most personal of all experiences. The Spitfire cockpit is tiny, barely big enough for a young man to squeeze into. During combat, apart from a dry mouth, there would usually be no time to be afraid. That came before or after. In the air, as a pilot climbed at dawn he would sometimes get the amazing sight of two sunrises, one at 30,000 feet and a second at ground level as he landed.

In the air, as the pilot of a fast single-seater aircraft, you were the king of all you surveyed. At high altitude the air was thin, and no matter how warmly one was dressed it was still freezing. Some of what today are regarded as affectations, such as fleece-lined flying jackets and silk scarves, were just as vital to survival as the machine guns and landing gear. The scarf was silk so a pilot could crane around to check for enemy planes from all angles without wrenching his neck against leather.

As for the fleece and leather, warmth was a matter of life and death, too. If a pilot's brain slowed down for even a split second due to the altitude and cold, it could cost him his life as his reflexes to evade or to fire kicked in a second too late. The drone of the Merlin engine and the popping of your own machine guns would mix with the crackle of the radio, with pilots calling warnings or a leader calling short, sharp orders over the cockpit radio. Suddenly, the icy cold would seem very hot indeed.

The feeling as you lined up an enemy in your sights and a thumb pressed the firing button was very different from in the movies. A Spitfire has a maximum of fifteen seconds' worth of ammunition. Every single burst had to be calculated. Would you waste it on a half-lined-up shot and risk being left defenseless for the rest of the battle and the flight home? Or would you end up going home with unspent ammo and a regret that you let the enemy get away? In any case, you might have half a second to make the decision, and often even that half second of thinking time would be interrupted by an enemy pilot or flak crew on the ground, all intent on doing the same to you. There was rarely any time to feel sorry for your foes during the battle, and afterward, it was too late.

Not long after we arrived at Digby, we got news that Hitler

had launched Operation Barbarossa, his massive invasion of the Soviet Union. From then until the end of the year, news from the Eastern Front was universally bad. The Nazi blitzkrieg rolled all the way to the gates of Moscow, scooping up millions of prisoners and leaving that country scrambling to relocate its industry far to the east while leaving nothing for the invaders but scorched earth. The reality behind this for us was that if we had continued to face the entire might of the Luftwaffe over the following years, rather than only a part of it, with the rest being kept busy in the east, fewer of us new arrivals would have survived.

Most of the pilots were even younger than I. One very fine pilot whom I was to meet later in the war was a good example of the breed. Patrick "Paddy" Barthropp was an amiable, slightly wild young Irishman from an upper-class Anglo-Irish family. He had flown in the Battle of Britain period while only nineteen. Like most of us, he lived wartime life to the full, never knowing what was coming next. He had one almost miraculous escape after his plane was badly shot up in a dogfight over the Channel, when he seemed to make it home fueled by sheer willpower, defying the laws of engineering and gravity. He explained this away by saying that he had been out for a somewhat lively evening of drinking and dancing with some of the apparently infinite supply of beautiful young women drawn to a pilot's uniform and he was determined to make it home because, being Catholic, he did not want to crash before he had a chance to go to confession.

While most of us were young, I remember being deeply impressed when I met and learned from older men such as Harry Broadhurst or Victor Beamish, with whom I was to have some adventures later. It seemed remarkable to me that these "old men" of about forty were still flying and still shooting down enemy planes on a regular basis. To my young eyes it was almost as if the managing directors of some huge companies still regularly left the boardroom to go out selling door-to-door.

Harry Broadhurst with a square, pugnacious face and eyes that flashed electricity beneath bushy eyebrows, was universally known as Broady. He had started out in the RAF in the 1920s and must have quickly built up an immunity to fear of crashing. He originally failed his medical to get in, due to low blood pressure, but a kindly doctor told him to run twice around the block, then reapply. This time he was accepted.

On his way to his first day of service he came off his motorbike at high speed and spent his first month of duty in the hospital. Then, after six weeks of training, mostly on planes left over from World War I, he was sent to complete some exam at another airbase, hitching a ride in a bomber. The bomber crashed, killing the pilot, and Broady woke up three days later, back in the hospital.

From these unpromising starts, Broady became one of the most skilled prewar pilots in the RAF, and a member of an aerobatic display team. He was sent on a fact-finding mission to Germany in the 1930s, where he was grilled by an overly friendly Hermann Göring about the capabilities of the new British planes such as the Spitfire and the Hurricane. Broady could see that war was looming and gave little away while trying to learn as much as possible about the enemy air strength.

He was soon able to test his knowledge as he was put in charge of the Hornchurch Wing at the start of the Battle of Britain in 1940. He was hugely popular with his pilots, partly because he was a great pilot himself and flew alongside them and partly because he was a good leader on the ground, too, spending time talking to his men, both teaching them how to survive and listening to their grumbles. His own exploits in the air during the pivotal battle for air superiority over southern England earned him the first of two Distinguished Service Order medals. By the time I got to know him, he was something of an institution, and meeting him along with Victor Beamish gave me a sense that I would ultimately be on the winning side.

Knowing that my life would soon depend on it, I tried to learn from experienced pilots and also started to get in as much flying in my new Spitfire as possible. My practice flights took me soaring all over the south of England. One of my most enduring memories is climbing up above the clouds to see the sun bursting though and then diving down again to find myself flying above the ancient stone circle at Stonehenge as the sun gradually illuminated the stones. Still in the West Country, I added the Severn Bridge to the list of those I had enjoyed flying under while training in Canada. On my way back from these forays I became fairly proficient at navigation and always looked out for the three great gothic towers of Lincoln Cathedral, soaring above the vast, flat fenlands, as a sign that I was nearly home.

For a Texan used to wide blue skies, the variations in the cloud formations I flew through in England were amazing. One day, flying over the cathedral, I pushed through what felt like great draperies of cloud and rain, streaming in the wind, and when the celestial drapes opened, there below me was the cathedral and around me a sight you can only see from the air—a perfect, complete circle of a rainbow, with my small, sleek Spitfire flying apparently though its middle. The effect was magical.

My flying was improving with practice. In the brief lull while the squadron was being formed we got in a good deal of practice on the station Magister, or Maggie—a two-seater with dual controls often used for training or for ferrying people from one airfield to another. On one occasion I was at the controls, flying back to Digby with Robert "Buck" McNair, a great, larger-than-life friend from western Canada who had enlisted about the same time as me.

Buck had his eye on one of the rare "golden caterpillar" pins that were awarded to anyone whose life was saved by a parachute. He was also curious as to just how well our parachutes might work, so he decided to jump rather than wait for me to land. I was less than keen on the scenario, since I thought some unkind soul might take it as an unfavorable comment on my flying, so I ruddered down and started losing altitude for the landing. Meanwhile, at the controls behind me, Buck was attempting to stage a coup, hauling back so we would gain altitude for his jump. As we went up and down, wrestling for the controls, he clearly decided we were high enough, and out he jumped. Luckily, his parachute worked.

In the inevitable disciplinary inquiry that followed, there was some wild speculation that he had fallen out by accident during one of my admittedly frequent unauthorized aerobatic displays, but Buck stuck to his claim for the golden caterpillar, arguing that a landing with me at the controls represented a grave danger to passengers, so his jump should be classified as a lifesaving action.

Buck went on to a remarkable career as one of Canada's top pilots in the war and beyond, becoming a wing commander and winning the Distinguished Flying Cross. Just a few months after his valuable unofficial parachute training Buck shot down one ME-109 and then was shot down himself. As he was losing altitude with his plane belching smoke, the second ME-109 that had shot him down came down to gloat in a flyover. Buck managed to hit him, too, as he whizzed by. A few seconds later, Buck parachuted safely as his Spitfire plunged into the sea. He landed in the chilly waters near the French coast. He was lucky not to be captured and made a prisoner of war. Instead, he was saved in some style by the brave men of the Air-Sea Rescue Service and was back with the squadron almost before he had been reported lost. Along the way he not only picked up his golden caterpillar badge for a legitimate parachute jump, but also got a golden goldfish to add to his collection, a badge produced by the inappropriately named Messrs. P. B. Cow and Sons, purveyors of air-sea rescue equipment to the services.

Many of the new pilots were very young, some still in their teens. One was John Gillespie Magee, a fellow American who had enlisted in the RCAF at about the same time I did. He was with 412 Squadron, also at Digby, but was a great friend of one of our small band of 411 Squadron pilots, Jack Coleman, who had trained with us in Canada. A few months later both were dead.

As the squadrons started to shape up at Digby, Magee—a slim boy with a sparse mustache and intense eyes—flew a test flight in a newer version of the Spitfire, the Mark 5, soaring and twisting at 30,000 feet. When he came down he wrote to his parents in America, saying, "Am enclosing a verse I wrote the other day. It started at 30,000 feet, and was finished soon after I landed." On

the back of it he scribbled what was to become the most famous
aviation poem of the war: "High Flight."

Oh! I have slipped the surly bonds of earth
And danced the skies on laughter-silvered wings;
Sunward I've climbed, and joined the tumbling mirth
Of sun-split clouds—and done a hundred things
You have not dreamed of—wheeled and soared and swung
High in the sunlit silence. Hov'ring there,
I've chased the shouting wind along, and flung
My eager craft through footless halls of air.
Up, up the long, delirious, burning blue
I've topped the wind-swept heights with easy grace
Where never lark, or even eagle flew—
And, while with silent lifting mind I've trod
The high untrespassed sanctity of space,
Put out my hand, and touched the face of God.

A few months later Magee was killed in a midair collision
with an Oxford trainer out of Cranwell airfield, not far from
Digby. Both planes were in thick cloud cover and must never
have seen each other. He was buried nearby at Scopwick. His
friend Jack Coleman lasted only another few months. He was
shot down and killed while flying escort for bombers over
France.

In the early months of building the new squadron, such losses
were all too common. Bringing together so many new pilots and

new machines under the pressures of a war that was already in full swing was never going to be easy.

Another one of the small, tragic events from which all wars are built still sticks in my mind. The nice old man who served in our officer's mess would go out at first light hunting for mushrooms on the airfield perimeter "because my boys love them so much with their breakfast." One day a Spitfire scrambling in the half-light of the early morning failed to see him. It took his head off with its propeller.

Luckily, most of the accidents had less tragic consequences. Our squadron adjutant, Flying Officer Richard Whalley, whose job it was to keep us airborne, had a wry sense of humor that rings out across the years in his entries in our operations record book, a sort of military daybook. His less-than-formal observations from that period include the suggestion that our squadron motto be changed from *Inimicus Inimico*, "Hostile to the Enemy" to "Hostile to Ourselves" due to the frequency of accidents. A few weeks later he even added, "The squadron appears to be up to form—at least in the way of accidents." So frequent were the accidents that he actually wrote about it when there was a week without any, commenting simply, "Most gratifying, no prangs."

In desperation to slow down our ability to demolish both ourselves and His Majesty's property, Wing Commander Ernie McNab came up with a proposed punishment, threatening to redeploy accident-prone pilots to tow targets at gunnery schools. Since the trainee gunners were just as accident-prone as we were when shooting at moving targets, it was not a very popular option.

The accident rate, high in all of the new squadrons, was a by-product of the huge expansion the RAF was undergoing at that time, both in men and new machines, following the high casualty rate among experienced pilots in the Battle of Britain fought in the previous year. The 411 Squadron was fairly typical in managing, during our establishing period of June to October 1941, to chalk up sixteen major accidents in just 2,601 hours flying. Yet while the services are always good at identifying problems, the solutions are not always so speedy. When our new version Spitfires, the Mark 5Bs arrived, we were given all of two days to get used to them before testing them in combat.

When we were not causing problems for ourselves, the Luftwaffe was doing its best to give us new ones. I remember a group of us walking around the perimeter of an airfield on the east coast around that time. Suddenly our stroll was interrupted by the drone of enemy engines. Two ME-109s howled out of the sky, intent on shooting up the airfield. They zeroed in on us as easy targets, out in the open. We ran like ants in all directions as bullets started to chew up the airstrip. I dived for cover and made it into a bunker as the world seemed to be ending a few feet above my head. One of my colleagues was less prudent. He dashed past a sturdy dugout and into a rickety wooden shed that would not have kept out a stiff breeze, never mind enemy cannon fire. When the smoke cleared and we emerged, we found him unscathed. His first action on getting inside the flimsy hut had been to lock the door behind him, though quite what good that was meant to do we never found out. People do funny things in wartime.

On one occasion, returning from a successful September sortie over France, with nothing much more than dinner on my mind, I was surprised to see a reception committee. As I taxied to a halt, a clutch of people hurried toward the plane. It was all a bit surreal. There were important-looking officials and top brass and a photographer and a portly, balding gentleman in a tweedy suit.

As I opened the cockpit and stood up to get out, the man was helped up onto the wing. He shook my hand as flashbulbs popped and he introduced himself as Mackenzie King, the prime minister of Canada.

King was over on a morale-boosting visit to see how the first squadron of Canadian pilots in England was shaping up. I remember thinking it was odd that he should be perched on my Spitfire wing, shaking hands with an American when there were so many Canadians about, but part of the war effort was to convince the rest of the United States that they might as well join me. In reality there were several thousand Americans, mostly in the army and navy, who like me had lost their citizenship in order to fight the Nazis before the country as a whole decided it was a good idea, but in 1941 American Spitfire pilots were still something of a rarity.

One thing that my time at Digby started to teach me was just how different this conflict was from the Great War that had shaped my generation and my parents'. In that war, the men had gone off to fight their war elsewhere, while life at home continued, apparently little changed. The Great War produced a lot of great poets, but unlike young Magee they mostly wrote of despair and disillusion. In our war, everyone was at the battlefield. We pilots got recognition because our fight was plain to see in the skies above Britain and France, but there were just as many acts of heroism carried out without much fanfare and with much less recognition by the ordinary men and women who worked around us and shared the risks.

One typical unsung hero was the jolly, red-faced farmer in Lincolnshire whom I often saw enjoying a pint in one of the wonderful local pubs. But when he was not propping up the bar, the farmer was quietly carrying out his own private war with the

Luftwaffe. Each night, presumably after a full day on the farm, he would hitch up his tractor and head for a local Q-site. This was effectively a dummy airstrip, designed to lure the attackers into bombing nondescript countryside while thinking they had hit an RAF base.

Q-sites consisted of mock landing strips, up to a mile or more in length, with a V-shaped approach funnel and rigged-up runway lights. They sometimes had makeshift structures designed to look like aircraft taxiing on the ground, and as you can imagine, a Q-site was not somewhere you wanted to be during a German bombing raid. But the farmer headed straight for it on a regular basis. He rigged up his tractor with two long planks in the position of wings, with a red lamp on the left wing and a green one on the right.

Each night, as the Luftwaffe bombers came over, hunting for the local RAF base, but wary of dummy sites, the lights would go on at the imitation base, the farmer would start up his tractor engine and rumble up and down the length of the field, a finishing touch that frequently induced the enemy to drop their bombs on the site and head for home. The fact that for the farmer success meant being on a tractor with wooden wings in the middle of a bombing raid seemed simply to add to his satisfaction. Back in the pub, rubbing shoulders with the pilots, he would smile and tell us, "Got the bastards to drop three sticks on me last night." Then he would go back to sipping his beer.

Despite all the disasters, tragedies, and comedies of the time, we somehow shaped up into a real fighter squadron. Our first duties, since we were located so near the east coast, were to fly guard duty on the shipping convoys that were Britain's lifeblood, and which were under constant danger of air attack as well as the invisible menace of the U-boat sea wolves beneath the chilly surface of the North Sea. Looking down on the convoys, either nervous because they were so close to home after an incredibly perilous transatlantic journey from America, or perhaps just setting out on an even more dangerous voyage through ice floes to Murmansk with supplies for Russia, I hoped that the sight of us would give the sailors heart. At the same time, flying over British escort ships was always a bit nerve-racking, for we had to make sure they knew we were friendly aircraft and not hostile ones. There is nothing quite like the feeling of having to trust people you have never met as you fly low and close around a ship and you see the huge guns on the deck swivel around to follow your progress.

At about that time, I became tangentially involved in one of the most remarkable deceptions of the war. Several of us were sent to fly guard duty over an aircraft carrier in the English Channel, only it was not an aircraft carrier at all. In reality, it was an old tramp freighter with a huge false wooden deck, painted up to look like an aircraft carrier. It was designed to lure the enemy bombers out to attack it, and very obligingly, they did just that.

For some days the enemy planes returned, wasting ammunition and energy on a wooden dummy boat, as we and the guns on board the decoy hammered back at them. Then, on one particularly dark night, a single Stuka dive-bomber risked oblivion to swoop down over the ship. Before it veered away, it dropped a single bomb that clattered on the deck but did not explode. A bomb disposal expert inched up to examine it. It was a wooden bomb, dropped on a wooden boat, the Germans' way of saying the game was up.

Not all our coastal duty was so successful. Germany's most famous battleship, the *Scharnhorst*, was bottled up alongside a good chunk of the German fleet in the French port of Brest, together with the formidable pocket battleships *Gneisenau* and *Prinz Eugen*. Together, these ships had wreaked havoc on the shipping in the North Atlantic, sinking more than twenty vessels, and sending over 100,000 tons to the bottom—at the cost of thousands of Allied lives.

Now the tide of the sea war had changed. The enemy U-boats continued to wreak havoc, but the Royal Navy controlled at least the surface of the English Channel, and the Royal Air Force could support them from the air. The British command knew that at some point the enemy ships might make a break for it, either south into the Atlantic to attack convoys or north through the Channel to the safer German ports.

The Air Ministry started issuing edicts in April 1941, telling the Fighter, Bomber, and Coastal Commands that they should prepare to meet the foe as they left port. Coastal Command was told to keep an eye on the ships, but neither the fighters nor bombers that would be needed once the ships were on the open sea were to be kept on standby. We were ordered to go about normal operations as there would be plenty of time once the warning came that the ships were leaving port. In the meantime Bomber Command with fighter escorts would try to sink the ships in Brest harbor.

I and my colleagues started going on joint training exercises with a squadron of Beaufort bombers, flying from Manston on the English east coast. Although officially called Operation Fuller, among us mere participants the drills went by the ingenious code name of "What to do if the boats come out." The Beauforts were sophisticated torpedo bombers, and it was almost possible to feel sorry for a huge, lumbering warship like the

Scharnhorst, a floating island waiting to be sent to the bottom. Still, a few seconds' thought of the lives of the brave merchant seamen who were keeping Britain going on the U.S. convoy runs and facing the atrocious Arctic run to keep the Russian war effort supplied meant that none of us would have any hesitation about sinking the pride of the German navy.

While our drills of fighter escorts and torpedo bombers went on long before the actual German breakout, there was a war of hide-and-seek between Bomber Command and the German navy, centered on the ships at rest in Brest. Attempts to bomb them while they were under repair in the harbor started at the end of March 1941 and continued over the summer months, with up to a hundred aircraft in each raid. Most of the raids were made at night, which kept the casualty rate among the air crews relatively low, but had the drawback that it was virtually impossible to hit the targets despite repeated attempts.

Yet the raids, although failing to dent the *Scharnhorst* or its sister ships, did have the advantage of prompting the enemy fleet not to hang around in Brest waiting for one of Bomber Command's five-hundred-pound armor-piercing bombs to strike lucky. The bombing took up more than three squadrons, about a tenth of British bomber capacity, but given the incredible threat to Britain's maritime supply routes that the ships posed, the Air Ministry and Churchill himself were determined not to let them get back in the war.

All of this was bad news for the people of Brest. The Germans, in an echo of the British dummy aircraft carrier, dressed a French cruiser, the *Jeanne D'Arc,* with planks and canvas to look like the *Scharnhorst* from the air, while the real ship was disguised with a small dummy town of mocked-up buildings on parts of her deck. The result was that many of the Allied bombs fell on the town of Brest.

By December 1941 the *Scharnhorst* had been hit several times, but the damage was relatively minor, and over the months the RAF had lost more than a hundred aircraft. The Air Command was growing impatient, and the Royal Navy, even more stretched by the war against the Japanese in the Pacific, was reluctant to send larger elements of its fleet to that theater of war only to find the *Scharnhorst* causing trouble closer to home.

Air Commodore Albert Durston, the senior liaison between the air force and navy, grumbled that "we cannot continue ad infinitum to waste our bomber effort on these ships . . . or allow a large part of our bomber force to be held idle at the mere whisper of the departure of one of them." All the services then agreed on a plan—there would be one huge attack, involving more than three hundred aircraft, dropping vast amounts of explosives, with bombers going over in waves every half an hour for several hours. In the words of the Air Ministry, the objective was to leave the destroyers and battleships "as twisted masses of metal, or very seriously damaged, in the shortest amount of time."

Meanwhile, my unit and other fighters were ready to escort the Beaufort torpedo bombers should the ships try to make a run for it before they could be flattened in the harbor. Another Air Ministry letter contained the immortal phrase, "It is considered unlikely that the enemy would attempt the passage of the Straits in daylight." Unfortunately no one told the Germans, for that is exactly what they did.

At this point a friend of mine, and one of the most remarkable leaders of fighter aircraft in the war, became more involved than he expected in the bid to sink the *Scharnhorst*. Group Captain Victor Beamish was an almost legendary figure by the time I arrived in Britain in 1941. While most men of his rank quite rightly concentrated on "flying a desk," Victor's philosophy was never to ask a pilot to do something he would not do himself.

Unfortunately for the rest of us, he was a superb pilot and utterly fearless, so that did not leave much that he would not ask of his men. He made up for this by always being there, often flying alongside the formations under his command, and increasingly getting in hot water with his superiors for risking life and limb as a common fighter pilot.

Victor inspired me and other young pilots like me, and he was also a source of excellent tactical advice. He was fearless in close-quarters dogfights, but also a superb aerobatic pilot, leading the British national aerobatic squad in peacetime, before he had to leave the service due to a bout of tuberculosis. It was characteristic of Victor that he battled his way back to fitness and rejoined the RAF a few years before the start of the war.

He really came into his own during the Battle of Britain. Surrounded by fresh-faced youngsters, this square-jawed Northern Irishman, then in his late thirties, flew an astonishing 126 sorties. By the time I met him, his status was near mythical. He could be dogmatic and stubborn, but there was no man who was better able to raise the morale of tired, frightened fighter pilots, either appearing from nowhere in the sky to join a fighter sweep, or shambling around on the ground at the many airfields under his command in tatty overalls with no indication of his rank.

Most infuriating to his commanders was his habit of flying off on his own "looking for luckless Huns" in his Hawker Hurricane, painted with a large trademark letter B. He found them more often than not, as he roved over the North Sea and English Channel, and in the course of his career shot down at least eight enemy aircraft and was credited with another dozen probables. Frequently he would run into large enemy fighter formations, and more than once he was lucky to make it back from the Channel, chased by what must have felt like half the Luftwaffe, his plane, and on one occasion his posterior full of shrapnel.

It was on one such solo shopping trip over the sea, when he was busy at his favorite pastime of shooting up E-boats along with Robert Finlay-Boyd, a small, pugnacious Scot who was wing leader at Kenley, that Victor looked down through a break in the cloud on a rather remarkable sight. The German ships were indeed coming out. In fact, in broad daylight at ten in the morning, the ships were happily steaming up the middle of the English Channel in a little armada, flags waving, with a flotilla of smaller support ships and a swarm of German fighters giving them cover. For some reason the early warning system had failed.

Visibility was good at that time of the day, with some cloud cover at about 3,000 feet, and the two pilots nosed down to get an amazing view—the *Scharnhorst, Gneisenau,* and *Prinz Eugen* were surrounded by destroyers, minesweepers, and E-boats in a grand naval formation, sailing gracefully in the general direction of Germany.

After the war it emerged that most of the German navy commanders had not been at all keen on heading up the Channel at any time of day or night, but Hitler, no doubt in consultation with one of his court astrologers, had decided that the war would be won or lost in Norway, and he wanted his ships where they could do the most good, fearlessly defending the fjords. The German fleet commander, Otto Ciliax, knew that the journey had to be made and came up with the plan to use surprise, leaving at night but sailing in broad daylight with the support of 250 planes. So while we were busy practicing for Operation Fuller, the German navy was busy sailing off in Operation Cerberus.

Victor Beamish and Finlay-Boyd stared saucer-eyed at the armada below and went down for an even closer look. Suddenly the sky erupted in a wall of blue and red antiaircraft fire. The heavily armed ships which had been expecting a full-scale battle were so far faced by just two British planes. The fire was so intense partly because the ships had added to their already formidable arsenal by placing 20mm quadruple-mounted guns from the local coastal defense batteries aboard the ships as an extra layer of antiaircraft defense.

Beamish, never being a man greatly dismayed by long odds, peeled down almost to sea level, and both planes attacked an E-boat, which they left listing and engulfed in smoke. By this time their presence had been noted by a dozen ME-109s flying cover above the flotilla, and the German planes started to peel down to take on the raiders.

Beamish realized that he had to get back with the news. All pilots were under strict orders not to use their radios for highly confidential messages, so they made a dash for home. Luckily for them, the enemy planes were slowed down in their pursuit by the wall of flak from their own ships, and once Beamish and Finlay-Boyd had outturned them, the German pilots decided to stay with the convoy rather than engage in a probably fruitless chase, which would end over Britain, with them low on fuel and having to worry about British flak instead of their own.

Beamish landed at Kenley aerodrome and charged to the nearest phone. He told me later that the first response from baffled officialdom was something like "No, no, old boy, the exercise is later on, get off the line." They assumed he was still playing the popular game of "What to do if the boats come out." Gradually he convinced the person on the other end of the phone that he was serious and was passed up the chain of command. They still seemed reluctant to believe him. Was he sure? Might it not just have been a smaller ship that looked bigger at the time? Victor hit the roof. "Now see here!" he bellowed. "I know a bloody battleship when I see one!"

The astonishment in officialdom may simply have been based on the certainty that a daytime escape by such a flotilla up the Channel was virtual suicide, but it may also have been based on well-intentioned secret intelligence reports from in and around Brest. A brilliant German deception, intended to show that the ships would eventually be heading south, included oil drums marked "For Use in the Tropics" being loaded at the Brest docks, along with white hot-weather uniforms. The German admiralty even sent bogus invitations for an onshore party to all their key naval officers, dated for February 12—the day the fleet sailed north. Some or all of this may have got back to the British, as was intended, and reinforced their faith that the ships would probably sail south, and even then only under the cover of darkness.

In reality, the *Scharnhorst*'s gamble, though risky, was well calculated. The Germans knew that a large part of the British fleet was anchored off Iceland and that other elements, including several ships armed with torpedoes, were on exercise in the far North Sea, unable to be recalled in time. Most of all, they knew that if they stayed in Brest they were sure to be sunk. Both sides were playing for high stakes. When Churchill heard that the ships had made their daytime break, he was enraged and ordered,

"At all costs the ships must be intercepted and made to pay dearly for their audacity."

My own squadron, with no advance warning, was only at an hour's readiness when we were ordered to scramble, with me leading eight planes because the squadron leader and other more senior pilots could not be recalled in time. Our few planes headed for Manston, joining up with a greater number from 72 Squadron. I assumed we would rendezvous with the Beauforts as we had on previous drills—sophisticated torpedo-carriers that we would escort to the *Scharnhorst*. What happened exactly is still unknown, but one theory is that some Beauforts had just returned from an exercise and had been disarmed while others were away on another exercise. The Beauforts were also normally stationed at Britain's extremities in Scotland, Cornwall, and Portsmouth, and the plan relied on there being enough warning notice to get them in the right place for a concerted attack.

Whatever the reality, those of us in this confused group of Spitfires from several squadrons found ourselves escorting just six Fairey Swordfish aircraft from Manston. The Swordfish was no doubt a mighty weapon of naval warfare in its time. This was not its time. The biplanes, their two wings held together by not much more than struts and string, looked like they had just flown in from a previous war. Their top speed was under a hundred miles an hour, and that was downhill.

The half-dozen Swordfish were led by Lieutenant Commander Eugene Esmonde, already a hero for his part in torpedoing the *Bismarck*. He must have known that the task was hopeless, but he and the six planes under his command pressed on as ordered. On the way out over the Channel, our biggest problem as a fighter escort was flying slowly enough for the Swordfish to keep up. The weather, from a sunnier start, was turning vile, with cloud cover down to a few hundred feet, and more than a hundred German fighters, far above, were waiting for us to show up. We still looked in vain for the Beauforts, some of whom were looking in vain for Spitfires somewhere else.

The Swordfish were piloted by incredibly brave men, and despite the fact that most of the planned attack force, most of their fighter cover, and virtually all the logic had been left behind in the garble of miscommunication and surprise, the Swordfish did what they had come for and attacked anyway, like tiny, fearless mosquitoes hurtling toward an elephant.

The Spitfires guarded them as best we could, but the German aircraft were keeping us busy from above, and the waves of anti-aircraft fire blazing up from below added to the sense of being trapped between a hammer and an anvil. Each of us was twisting and turning, trying to stay out of the thick of the red and green flak surging skyward, while also engaging with the ME-109s, which were out in incredible force and with the advantage of altitude. As best we could we sheltered the Swordfish from annihilation by fighters from above, though the main thing keeping many of the German planes from coming down to engage was fear of their own ships' flak rather than fear of us and a handful of Swordfish. Through all this, Commander Esmonde led his own crew and those of his followers into low-level torpedo runs one at a time on an ironclad armada that was steaming ahead at 27 knots.

I learned later that the German captain Kurt Caesar Hoffman on the bridge of the *Scharnhorst* followed their progress, then put down his binoculars, shook his head and said, "Poor fellows. They are so very slow. It is nothing but suicide." A terrible wall of antiaircraft fire filled the sky. One by one the Swordfish went down, Esmonde first. Sometimes they managed to get an ineffectual torpedo off before they crashed in flames. Sublieutenant Brian Rose in another Swordfish managed to fire off a torpedo despite being shot in the back, while crashing into the water and with his gunner already dead behind him. Of the six crews, all were shot down. A few crew members, including Rose, survived and were picked up by small British boats, but most were dead even before they hit the icy water. It was heroic and tragic at the same time. Even our foes were impressed yet horrified. Fleet Commander Ciliax described the action later as "a mothball attack by a handful of ancient planes, piloted by men whose bravery surpassed any other action by either side that day."

Eventually, after we had run out of Swordfish, but there still seemed to be no shortage of Germans both above and below, we unhappy few of the fighter escort went home, had a few pints, and tried to work out what it was all about. The German fleet made it to their home waters, though their days of terrorizing the shipping lanes were over. The *Scharnhorst* was damaged by two sea mines, and the ships were to play little active part in the rest of the war.

Back on land, I attended some of the military postmortems on the fiasco, with a litany of reasons being put forward, from faulty equipment to some messages being sent in Morse for people listening for voices. As I sat at a highly polished table in Whitehall for the postmortem, the most junior foreigner among all those senior officers, with wide white hat bands and gold scrambled-egg uniform decoration much in evidence, I was dismayed that the best they seemed to come up with was a rather fatalistic "You win some, you lose some." But that was the real war—heroism and stupidity, tragedy and farce, usually side by side.

Victor Beamish, who also gave evidence at the inquiry, was as enraged as the rest of us, and a few pen pushers even quietly tried to blame him for not sending a radio message back instead of maintaining radio silence and bringing it back in person some twenty minutes later. The reality was that without Beamish being on one of his freelance hunting trips the first Winston Churchill might have heard of the German fleet leaving Brest would have been the news of their safe arrival in German waters, which probably would have made him swallow his cigar. The inquiry was as feeble a whitewash as most modern government inquiries, where senior officers and politicians play Pass the Buck with blame.

In those dangerous days there was little time to dwell on the past, and soon we were back in action. Victor certainly did not have the time or character to brood on political parlor games.

A few days later, heavy snowfall clogged many of the runways on the southeastern air bases, including Kenley. Beamish not only ordered them to be cleared and ready for action by every man capable of holding a shovel, he turned up himself, rounded up a few more "volunteers" from the station kitchen staff, and joined the surge toward the NCO who was giving out brooms and shovels. In his haste to get going, he charged to the front of the line. He was as usual wearing his battered old flying overalls, with no trace of rank or insignia. The NCO failed to recognize him and barked "Oi, you! Get to the back of the queue!" Victor Beamish, a man who would tell it like it was to anyone up to and including Churchill, and who would calmly face odds of twenty to one in the skies, smiled and meekly went to the back of the line before picking up a shovel and helping to clear the runways. Less than a year later he was killed in action, plunging into the same icy waters over which he had soared like an eagle.

4. London's Burning

Toward the end of 1941, 411 Squadron had relocated south to Hornchurch in Essex and was starting to take the air war to the enemy. Tactics had changed, partly due to the success of Douglas Bader's theories about massive force strategically applied in the form of wings of dozens or even hundreds of fighters, as well as his observations about the importance of altitude supremacy. Essentially, if you hit them hard enough and from high enough, you tended to win.

Hornchurch, just nine miles from Central London, was a long-established fighter base, and arriving there gave me the feeling that I was joining part of a well-oiled machine that had been running for a while. The first time I tiptoed into the plotting room and watched the elegant ballet of female WAAFs (Women's Auxiliary Air Force) listening to positions from radar and radio, then plotting movements on a huge map, I felt that it was not just a few brave or foolish souls throwing themselves around in the air, but a real war effort.

But Hornchurch had three other appealing aspects to me—location, location, and location. From the outskirts of London, it took about the same amount of time—under an hour—to be either in the air war over France or listening to a concert at Piccadilly in the heart of that remarkable, vibrant city. It is hard to overstate just what an amazing time it was to be a young American in London, never mind a young American Spitfire pilot.

The Dallas of my youth had not been exactly a haven for good music or theatre, and on days when the weather closed in on Hornchurch, making operations impossible, I would hurry into London on the tube train, often passing the devastation of previous blitz attacks. By lunchtime I would be sitting in the National Gallery, coffee and sandwich in hand, listening to the lunchtime classical music recital by a chamber orchestra. The music seemed to sound all the better for the fact that there was a huge force not very far away on the French coast determined to stamp out everything beautiful and good. I remember being in love with the girl who played the cello. I never actually spoke to her, but one day, before hurrying back to Hornchurch to resume operations, I bought her a huge bouquet of flowers.

As I explored London in the midst of wartime turmoil and destruction, I seemed to see ghosts from much older times. It was Shakespeare's London of narrow alleys with ancient names, or Dickens's London with the fog rolling in over the Thames, wrapping gray water and silent ships in its embrace.

Walking the streets of London in pilot's uniform, I soon realized that I was benefiting from the affection felt by the population for the flyboys who had fought for the previous eighteen months to save the country from invasion, and more recently to reduce the threat posed by the nightly bombing raids on cities such as London and Coventry. But being a restless young man, I aspired for even more. Looking around me, I could not help but notice how well the Londoners took to volunteers from overseas, whose presence seemed to affirm Britain's role as the center of opposition to Hitler, and perhaps in some odd wishful way, to promise ultimate victory. Many of the overseas volunteers had shoulder flashes on their uniforms proclaiming Free France or Free Norway. I rustled up my own patch and sewed it on my sleeve. It read: Free USA.

Whether it was the uniform, the label, or the accent, 1941 in London represented a very pleasant war for me. If I went to the cinema and bought a ticket for the cheap seats for the princely sum of one shilling and threepence, I was immediately herded to the best, more expensive seats, the "two-and-nines," by some patriotic usherette. Londoners loved their fighter pilots, wherever they were from. They knew, without ever saying so, that for some of the young men enjoying themselves in London that night, depending on their fortunes in the air war the next morning, this might be their last visit.

Probably in an attempt to curtail the worst excesses of marauding amorous pilots, the Powers That Be attempted to regulate our social life by staging tea dances at Grosvenor House, where well brought up young ladies would risk life and limb dancing with foreign pilots. In order to get on the social register, we pilots had to turn up at an imposing house near Cadogen Square for a sort of upper-class interview. I think we were given points for polite chitchat and not slurping our tea. The winners were invited to dances or to weekends in stately country mansions that looked like the setting for Agatha Christie murders. I seem to remember the person in charge of such things was called Lady Frances Haggard—probably even more haggard because of the behavior of some of her adopted pilots.

After my teatime interview, I was curious to know how I had scored. I got to know one of the girls who worked there and persuaded her—probably at the risk of a firing squad for supplying information to The Enemy—to retrieve my notes from their files. The report read "Nice American manners . . . can go most places." I felt like I had been awarded a medal.

At about the same time, I got to know Sir Walter Elliot, a former government minister and adviser to the royal family, who was now devoting his time as a sort of PR man, particularly attempting to encourage America as a whole to join the war effort, rather than just sending me as a delegate. One day, when I was looking spectacularly disheveled after some particularly good party the night before, he dragged me off to a reception somewhere in the center of town, where I found myself slightly sheepishly being introduced to Queen Elizabeth, the present queen's mother, by this latter-day Sir Walter as "a somewhat disreputable friend from the other side of the Atlantic." Her ladies in waiting stared in horror at the unkempt colonial, but if Her Majesty shared their doubts, she was good enough to keep them to herself. She simply smiled and welcomed me to London, probably in hopes that a few million more just like me would be persuaded to join in. As we chatted about her little daughters, Princesses Elizabeth and Margaret, and about what a wonderful city London was, despite the wail of air raid sirens in the background, I tried to remember not to bring up the fact that my countrymen had kicked King George III out of the colonies.

My only other experiences of the Royal Family had not gone very well. One was lining up in the rain on the most miserable day imaginable in Lincolnshire when her husband, King George VI himself, came out to inspect the new squadron. We had waited in the rain for the Royal arrival, and if we had ever looked like an impressive body of fighting men, several hours under an almost biblical deluge had reduced us to a soggy chorus line, standing at attention, but shoulders hunched in a vain attempt to stop more rain trickling down the inside of our shirt collars.

Royalty, then as now, has developed a skillful line of small talk about the weather, but when the king reached me, he stopped. He had a craggy, honest face and had clearly been told there was a stray American or two among all these loyal Canadians. He seemed genuinely interested to find out what had made this strange import volunteer. He asked me why I had come over all the way from Texas. As rain trickled off the end of my nose and the Lincolnshire dampness soaked into my uniform, I told him I had been attracted by the weather. He smiled and moved along swiftly.

Despite the fact that I've always sided with the rebels against the royalists, I must admit that every time I bumped into a Royal during the war, they were doing their best to be useful. At a time when the very country was under threat, they acted like a sort of social glue. When they refused to leave London after Buckingham Palace was bombed in the blitz, they also went up in the estimation of many Londoners. One of the very few good things about wars is that they force everyone to reexamine their own ideas and attitudes about what is important, and that applies whether you are a king with a bombed-out palace or an American in a Spitfire with a jammed machine gun.

By now I was on a roll in terms of dealing with royalty. A few months later, when the Duchess of Kent visited a fighter station I happened to be at, some bright PR man decided the resultant photo opportunity would look more heroic if the duchess was in the foreground, waving off some valiant Spitfire pilots who were about to take off on the runway behind her. My plane was closest to her, and as I took off across wind on our simulated scramble the slipstream from my plane blew her skirt over her head, rather like that later famous picture of Marilyn Monroe. After that, I was not asked to participate in too many photo opportunities with royalty.

Yet whether king or commoner, in the services or civilian, it was a dangerous, exciting time to be around London. I remember sitting on a park bench, late one night in St. James's Park, stuck during the blitz, watching as the bombs fell and the arc lights searched the sky and fires from burning buildings glowed on the skyline all around me. The rumble of exploding bombs was counterpointed by the chatter of ack-ack guns, like a vast demented symphony and firework display all rolled into one, and I had a free ringside seat in the park. Meanwhile, the theaters played on and the concerts continued. In the course of the blitz there were some 100,000 civilians killed or wounded and more than 130,000 houses destroyed, yet the more the enemy bombed, the more determined the Londoners seemed to resist.

This was particularly impressive to a young American. In general Americans are demonstrative people, not known for their stoicism. I remembered the reaction about four years earlier in America to the broadcast of *The War of the Worlds*, Orson Welles's radio drama about the Martians invading Earth. The response of many listeners who thought it was all real was to drive off in all directions in a panic, crashing into each other, taking up arms and generally causing mayhem. In London, in the middle of an air raid, I watched as the locals calmly lined up to get into a shelter: "After you," "No, please—after you." It would have given Hitler a migraine to see it.

Unlike World War I, this was a battle that involved everyone in the country. People knew what they were fighting for, and they did so in whatever way they could. Despite that difference, one of my Hornchurch colleagues, Hankin, an intelligence officer and veteran of the Royal Flying Corps from the Great War, used to get his world wars mixed up, particularly after he had too much to drink. He would drag a group of us around the back streets of London, often in the middle of a blackout or blitz, looking for some wonderful little bar that had usually disappeared from the real world twenty years earlier but still existed inside his fuddled head.

When, at the end of such evenings, we would weave our way back to the tube station to catch the last underground train back to Hornchurch, the Londoners would already be settling down with blankets on the platforms, which were being used as ready-made air-raid shelters. Sometimes they would call to us as we staggered onto the train, "Give 'em hell, boys." With their homes under threat or in ruins and their capital city under nightly attack, the thoughts of us taking the war to the fascists seemed to cheer them up. Having said that, the sight of a handful of merry, weaving pilots propping each other up as they barely managed to catch the last train, may not have inspired them with much confidence. I and my fellow pilots lost count of the times we fell into a hazy slumber on that last train of the night and woke up at the terminus in Uxbridge, for a long late-night walk or hitchhike back to the base.

After we got back to our quarters at Hornchurch there would often be further festivities in the officers' mess, usually into the wee small hours. For those like me, not always used to getting enough to eat, it was heaven. Spitfire pilots, even in the midst of severe rationing, were fed like prize geese, in order to ensure that we could function under the pressures of aerial combat, where a fast mind and quick reflexes at high altitude made the difference between a fighter ace and a dead pilot. The rest of the population, faced with endless rationing of even the most basic foods, did not seem to begrudge us fighter pilots the extra bacon and eggs. The person in charge of catering at Hornchurch was no less a figure in peacetime than the chef of the Dorchester Hotel. As I crammed in some great meal before or after a sortie, I would sometimes smile at the thought of my having to eat my way into the war in Detroit because I was too light. At this rate, I might end up too heavy to get out again.

But combat was always good for burning off calories, or if that failed, an average night in the officers' mess would often do the same. One of the most impressively wild parties I have ever been to must have taken place around that time. Someone fairly high up the RAF food chain decided it would be much more efficient to administer all the air force station mess funds centrally. Previously, each location had operated its own fund, and some of these had built up quite impressive surpluses. All of us recognized that it was a worthy cause, but we felt we should at least see all that cash off by using a little of the surplus to throw it a farewell party or two. The best one was at Biggin Hill, where there were pilots from all twelve group stations who arrived by air and parked their Spitfires and Hurricanes like stylish limos outside the Oscars. It was quite a night, and as I watched the wobbly takeoffs and several dozen pilots weaving around in the sky the next morning, I remembered sitting by that riverbank in Texas watching a bunch of drunken Texas robins doing much the same. If Hitler had chosen that exact moment for his big offensive, we would have been in some difficulty.

Such parties usually resulted in mayhem and destruction of His Majesty's property, but few fatalities. I have slightly hazy memories of a fine party at our satellite aerodrome in Southend at which I was riding a motorbike around inside the house that was serving as our mess—and it certainly was a mess. I had a lovely young WAAF officer riding on the pillion as we raced from room to room before finally roaring out the front door and taking off down some steps. I can't remember landing, but I found out that she got engaged to one of the Czech pilots a week later.

Many of us were very keen on motorbikes and sports cars at the time, particularly if they were filled with high octane aviation fuel, which made them go like rockets. The aviation fuel was dyed bright green to prevent such wicked misuse, but our youthful wartime perspective on life and death meant that we were not likely to be overly bothered by such regulations. Some of our cars and bikes had dummy fuel tanks with just enough of the legal fuel to pass the spot checks by the stern men from the Special Investigations Branch, who sometimes paid us unexpected visits waving their dipsticks menacingly.

When not attempting to break speed records, we were avid players of demented communal games, usually resembling something between a team sport and a riot. Near the heart of virtually every such venture was a superb flier called Wilfred Duncan-Smith, known to one and all as Drunken Duncan. When he was not leading the inebriated festivities, he was one of the most skilled and deadly fighter pilots I ever met. He taught me tactics for surviving and winning a dogfight that were not to be found in any training manual and almost certainly saved my life. But when he was in party mood, he was just as unstoppable.

One of his performances that was in greatest demand was his impersonation of a Heinkel 111 bomber on a daring daylight raid over London. With no props but a few chairs and a very bad Hitler impression, he would launch his bombing raid, using anything that was handy as projectiles, and only stop when the rest of us shot him down and sent him crashing to the floor.

Other games were based on the losers buying the winners drinks, which inevitably led to more games in which the winners had to reciprocate until no one could remember whether they had won or lost. "Prisoners" was a favorite game, with no discernable rules, other than the objective to capture as many of the other team as possible and sit on them at your side of the room until eventually everyone was on the same side of the room, either being sat on or perched on top of a heap of prisoners. While it was funny at the time, my later experiences in POW camps made me realize what it was like to be sat on for several years in a row.

Best of all was the game Shipwreck. Anything that was floor space was regarded as seawater, to be avoided at all costs. Survivors would clamber on furniture rafts or use curtains and light fittings as Tarzan ropes to swing from one island to the next, knocking their foes into the deep blue sea of the wooden floor. More than sixty years later, I was reminded of Drunken Duncan's attempts to hold together his raft of tables and chairs, drifting perilously apart as he valiantly tried to repel boarders until he finally capsized to the floor, when I watched his offspring on television. His son Iain Duncan-Smith, erstwhile leader of Britain's Conservative Party, had the same look on his face when he was heroically trying to hold that unruly bunch together. He, too, ended up in the soup.

When we could take no more, we would crash into bed for a few hours' sleep before the air war began again in earnest, often at dawn. I had started out being billeted in the officers' mess, which was convenient in that there was not very far to stagger to bed after our celebrations, but not a great place to get any privacy or sleep. Eventually I managed to get a room all to myself in the married quarters, with my own bath. I used to lie in a bubble-filled tub listening to wonderful classical music on a battered old wind-up phonograph, thinking it was not such a bad war after all.

For Intelligence Officer Hankin, still feeling the effects of his night on the town, the line between work and play, and between waking and sleeping, would sometimes become blurred in much the same way as he got his wars mixed up. He shared a room with a pilot who, like most of us, would sometimes have nightmares in which the moments of tension and fear from previous dogfights would resurface. As the young pilot called out in his sleep, deep in a dream battle, Hankin would blearily roll out of bed, grope for paper and pencil, and start to make out a combat report in the dark. "Not so fast, old lad, let me get it down," he would mumble, before shambling back to bed. The next morning, on his bedside table, there would be a garbled, barely decipherable combat report of a nightmare dogfight that neither of them could quite remember.

5. Fierce, Fiery Warriors

Somehow, the next morning, we would be up early and in our cockpits, taking off with first light in one of the great fighter-formation sweeps that were then becoming a favorite tactic. As the war progressed, these great sweeps, known as Circuses, did have one drawback. Sometimes, when flying one of the huge sweeps over enemy-held territory, we would have half a dozen bombers flying out front as bait, then scores of fighters stepped all the way up to 30,000 feet. The Luftwaffe decided to avoid such confrontations and fight on their own terms, including low-level hit-and-run raids by small groups of FW-190s, which at the time were outpacing even the current Spitfire Mark 5s. In fact a captured 190 helped in the development of the more powerful Spitfire Mark 9s, the first of which were based at Hornchurch.

Returning from one of many eventless Circus sorties, I remember thinking that if I were a German pilot and I knew that
the equivalent of a flying sledgehammer was coaxing me out to
play, the invitation would be one I could definitely decline. In
fact, it would not be a prospect that would even lure me out of a
burning hangar, not even with the prospect of half a dozen juicy
bombers beckoning like bait on a celestial hook. On one such
sweep I remember a group of German planes, apparently as
oblivious of us as we had been of them, coming out of the sun
and flying straight though our formation. Both sides were intent
on going somewhere else. I found myself and the pilot of a ME-
109F passing so close to each other that I could see the pilot
clearly. I gave him a good hard glare, no doubt with devastating
effect. Perhaps at this stage in the war I was not aggressive
enough, but I struggled to equate some of the enemy pilots with
the monstrous actions being inflicted on the people of Europe,
even though the two were inextricably linked.

During that first year of combat flying, I had a few close
shaves. I had helped improve the aim of several enemy ack-ack
crews along the French coast when I was on my way home from
beating up targets in northern France, or shooting up flak ships.
On more than one occasion I had come back with a neat line of
holes made by Bofors guns, which usually ended somewhere near
the cockpit. Each time I thought about it, I reached out for a
piece of wood to touch for continued good luck.

Perhaps that's why, like most of my colleagues, I became a bit
superstitious. I always believed in the scientific efficacy of knocking on wood, but the cockpit of my beloved Spit, though brilliantly designed, was a bit short on mahogany. I solved this small
design oversight by fixing a little wooden matchbox under the re-

flector sight of my gun. As the war progressed I found that I only had to think a half-optimistic thought of the "I'm still here" variety and I would be reaching for my matchbox, like an additional instrument on my dashboard.

For much the same reason, I had an apple painted on the nose of my Spitfire, and when asked why, my answer would depend on what mood I was in. Sometimes I blathered about the Bible and the Garden of Eden apple that brought on the Fall of Man. If I was in a classical mood, I rambled about Homer and the golden apple that Paris gave to the wrong girl in the world's first beauty contest, leading to the Fall of Troy. But mostly I stuck with a third explanation, the apple that struck Newton on the head, making him realize a few things about gravity and the eternal truth of "what goes up must come down," though not necessarily all in one piece.

To save me from such thoughts, I looked to the older, more experienced pilots such as Duncan-Smith or Victor Beamish. They gave off an aura of affable but deadly capability. Added to that, some of the newer recruits such as Buck McNair were as ambitious and competitive as they were talented.

Another great comfort factor was our commanding officer at the time, Stan Turner, a Canadian who had flown with Bader's squadron. When we were on the way home from some tough sortie, but at least were heading in the right direction for survival, he had the endearing habit of lighting up his pipe. The rest of us would glance over at his cockpit as it filled with pipe smoke and imagine that somewhere in there he was warming his hands on an open coal fire and probably wearing carpet slippers. Little things like that were incredibly important to us. In a world turned upside down, anything that had even the vaguest whiff of stability and security was something to be cherished. The next day always brought more danger, or sometimes unexpected news.

Which brings me to one otherwise uneventful scramble from Hornchurch in December of that year. One of my colleagues came haring out of the hangars and ran over to the plane where I was preparing with others for takeoff. He ran alongside and shouted the news. With all the noise and commotion it took a few seconds to sink in. The Japanese had bombed Pearl Harbor and the United States was at war with all the Axis forces.

I reached out and patted the lucky matchbox before I took off. My mind was full of emotions, some of which were also at war with each other. My main feeling was a shiver of relief. At last the huge productive power of America would be turned on Hitler. The massive population of the United States, many of whom had hated the policy of neutrality when they could see the suffering in Europe, would now be employed working to build a war machine that would sweep the fascists back all the way to Berlin. Britain in the West and Russia in the East were no longer alone.

Yet a tiny part of me also marked the end of a very special time. I felt like I was no longer going to be the only kid on the block with a Spitfire. Soon the United States would be turning out phalanxes of new pilots in new fighters and new bombers. I reached out and rubbed the homemade patch on my shoulder: Free USA. Maybe I should go into mass production? But if a tiny part of me mourned the passing of my status as a rare creature, like a Texas robin who had thrown in his lot with a flock of English sparrows, most of me rejoiced. The Yanks were coming.

While that huge juggernaut of the American economy finally snapped itself out of the Depression and started picking up speed, like an express train getting up steam, life for me and my fellow fliers in 411 Squadron went on as before, though my contacts with the enemy seemed to become ever more frequent and ever more fierce.

One such day in January 1942 started much like the rest. A gentle but insistent prodding woke me from what seemed like about five minutes of sleep. There had been one of the frequent parties the night before, and the thought of getting up before the sun held little appeal. The prodding continued. As on every morning, it was an orderly bringing me a cup of coffee. Having spent so much of my life fending for myself, I was always quietly impressed at how well the RAF looked after me, but there always came a point that the service felt it was time for me to pay back all the cups of coffee and concerts, and it was usually about this time in the morning.

I wriggled into my gear and walked into the icy morning toward the dispersal hut where we waited for orders. Already the roar of Spitfire engines being tested or warmed up gave the day a sense of anticipation. The first sortie of the day was pretty routine. We roared off over the English Channel to guard convoys, and one of our group spotted a JU-88 heading for home at 5,000 feet, but we lost it in the clouds and returned to base. Our second sortie of the day was more lively. Four of us took off again from Hornchurch at about three in the afternoon. We made a quick stop at Manston and set off again with full tanks, flying fast and low across the Channel. The sea looked a cold slate gray, but there was always a rush of exhilaration when France loomed up in front of us and we crossed the coast near Dunkirk.

It was only a year and a half since the waters below had been filled with dead or desperate British troops in the chaotic evacuation that marked Germany's triumph in mainland Europe. Then the sea was covered with small boats. Anything that could float came to help with the evacuation of more than a hundred thousand men. The rescuers came in fishing boats and coal barges, in lifeboats from liners, and in brightly painted holiday yachts.

My friend Douglas Bader had been in the skies over Dunkirk that day and once described the scene. Planes milled about, both British and German, with no apparent order or plan on either side. He said that the scene at sea level during the evacuation looked like a coastal road in England on a bank holiday. There were so many boats that it seemed that a person could walk from Britain to France without getting his feet wet. Oil tanks in Dunkirk harbor had been set ablaze, and the British pilots were able to follow the smoke, which rose in a huge funnel, straight up in a windless sky, all the way from the English coast, like a pillar at the end of a long, floating arrow made up of tiny boats. Soon, every British plane was engaged in desperate actions trying to fight off vastly superior numbers of German aircraft that were bombing the rescue ships and strafing the men huddled on the chaotic beaches below.

Another of my friends from later prison camp days, Bob Stanford Tuck, had flown back and forth over the heads of the hapless British soldiers below, trying to protect them from air attack. He shot down five enemy planes in one day.

But on this day, there were no heroes, nor any signs of life below. The sea was flat, gray, and empty as we roared low across the coast. This was a Rhubarb sortie, in which we were to fly low in small numbers, identify military or economic targets of opportunity, move in fast, shoot them up, and get home hopefully unscathed. Our first target loomed below, a group of barges on a canal, loaded with supplies. It was like being back in Canada, flying low above the rivers with my own plane's shadow racing along the ground beside me. I was right behind Flight Lieutenant Ken Boomer, and we both flew directly over the barges at virtually zero height, raking them with fire as the men on board dived for the safety of the water.

Making our way back to the coast we came across a beach swarming with German troops laying barbed wire and sea defenses to repel any far-off thoughts of an Allied invasion. Boomer roared down and quite correctly strafed them. Part of me felt sorry for the poor antlike creatures running and diving for cover that was not there, maybe because I had been thinking of the other floundering and dying British soldiers who had lost their lives on the same beaches around Dunkirk two years earlier. But another part of me knew that this was what the war was about; if these men were allowed to continue with their barbed wire and tank traps, there would soon be young American and British bodies entangled on that same wire if ever we got as far as an invasion or D-day.

Suddenly, the air around us exploded like the middle of a firework display. We were being pounded by a German antiaircraft ship that was moored just offshore. A line of flak fragments thudded into the root of my port wing, but it held fast. I tried to remember everything I had been taught, and one lesson from Wilford Duncan-Smith definitely saved my life on several occasions. As he weaved about during one of our endless drunken team party games back at the officers' mess, he had stared at me wisely and said, "Never stay on the same vector longer than you have to!" So saying, he swayed off on another vector himself.

As the flak explosions crackled around me, I took Duncan-Smith's previous advice and peeled off, diving down almost to sea level before changing direction again and vectoring on to the flak ship. It was still blazing away at me, but I was changing direction and moving fast, coming up at it from the stern. I started firing the cannons just as I reached the ship, and I could see the results thudding home in impressive fiery lines that led directly to the wheelhouse. I sustained the fire as long as I could and then peeled away, changing direction again as I gained altitude. Looking down, I could see smoke coming from the wheelhouse of the flak ship. Our ammunition and fuel were getting low, so we headed for home.

The sense of relief at getting back home after a successful mission was almost palpable, and I was always anxious to get out of the plane and back into normal life for a few hours at least, to a world of good food, a wild social life, and some quiet evenings listening to Mozart while reading a cowboy novel.

Despite the illusions of normality, one by one, I saw friends and comrades who I had flown with since the formation of the squadron take off and never return. Jack Coleman and Sergeant Donald Court set off on a fairly routine mission flying top cover for a formation of Hurri-bombers, Hurricanes specially converted for dive-bombing techniques learned from the Stukas. They were jumped by a large formation of enemy aircraft, and both were shot down and killed over the sea.

A week later two of my closest friends of the time, Gordie Chamberlain and Tom Holden, were protecting a convoy not far from Calais when they were attacked by five ME-109s. Both were killed in the dogfight that followed. I came to understand what I had started to learn when my fellow trainee burned to death in front of my eyes some months earlier. The death of my closest comrades resulted in my building some of the same reserve I had originally found so strange among the veteran pilots I most admired. Like Duncan-Smith, they would be the soul of the party and ready for anything, but they had to keep something in reserve for themselves and the lonely battles ahead.

On one dusk patrol off the east coast, my wingman and I were vectored onto a couple of JU-88s, which were headed back out to sea after pulverizing some unfortunate factory or street. By this point in the war, such daylight raids were increasingly rare, with the Luftwaffe sticking more to nighttime operations. We zeroed in on the 88s and I was still shooting holes in mine when it disappeared into a cloud. That is where the plotting charts stopped, and it was assumed to have been shot down—my first victory, though like most things in life, not quite the way I had imagined it.

On another occasion, I was flying over occupied Holland with Peter "Cowboy" Blatchford when we ran into a wartime moral conundrum. We found ourselves peering down at a Luftwaffe formation flying below us and were about to scream down on them when we noticed that they were light trainer aircraft with no armaments. Now, if I had been back in London, catching the last tube to Hornchurch and had conducted a poll among the Londoners huddled under blankets along the platforms, their homes in danger or already flattened, there would have been little doubt of the outcome: Every German trainer aircraft and every trainee enemy pilot blasted out of the sky was one less to cause destruction later. But for me, looking down on a bunch of kids who could not fire back, it did not seem so clear-cut at the time.

We were still pondering this moral maze like a couple of medieval theologians when we ourselves were jumped by six ME-109s who had been flying even higher than we were, keeping an eye on the trainees below. We made a desperate bid to get back to

England, with all six of the enemy constantly trying to blow us out of the sky. We survived because we watched each other's tails, and when things got really hairy we turned back into them and gave them a taste of their own medicine before returning to our long retreat. They finally gave up on us about halfway across the Channel, no doubt reluctant to continue this adult version of kids in a fight getting their big brother to fight your big brother.

And if anyone was going to be watching your tail, Cowboy Blatchford from Edmonton in the Canadian West was a great choice. Cowboy and I had earlier tried to introduce some songs of the Old West to our reluctant Anglo-Saxon colleagues. Our rendition of the cowboy classic "Blood on the Saddle" became something of a milestone in tuneless musical history, and an unofficial anthem for our section. Cowboy, a great friend of our commander, Harry Broadhurst, was the first Canadian to shoot down an enemy plane during the war, in the chaos of 1939 over France. Later, he led an attack that accounted for eight destroyed and five damaged enemy aircraft in a single action. Badly shot up and out of ammunition, Cowboy had turned back into the enemy and started attempting to ram them, chopping bits out of his foes with his propeller, an action that won him a DFC. Cowboy was killed in action in 1943, but I was proud to be flying beside him that day, a year earlier.

And so I reached a day toward the end of March 1942, heading home for Hornchurch from a sweep which had taken us all the way to Comines in Belgium. We were on our way back and I was glancing over to Stan Turner's plane, on my wing, to see if the CO had lit his pipe yet. He hadn't. A garbled crackle over the radio from someone in the squadron called urgently for my section to break formation. I did a tight 180-degree turn, thanking my lucky stars that I had done so much aerobatic flying in my training just for the hell of it.

I was just in time to see a Focke-Wulf 190 banked over on one side as it pulled away to the right some distance below me. If I simply pushed the nose of my Spitfire down in hot pursuit, the fuel injection system that we were using at the time would have caused my engine to cough and splutter, and I would have lost a lot of speed. Instead, I did a whooshing three-quarters roll to my left, losing a great deal of height by doing so.

Much to my delight, and no doubt to the luckless Luftwaffe pilot's dismay, I came out directly behind him at the same height, level, at a range of just two hundred yards. I pressed the gun trigger, and as I closed in, I could see I was hitting home. Bright cannon shells crackled and exploded in a deadly line along one of his wing roots. Bits of the Focke-Wulf's engine cowling disintegrated into the air, and then the whole thing went down in a cloud of smoke.

Jubilant, I pulled up and looked for my formation. By now they were specks in the distance. To my left another straggler Spitfire, probably from my own section, was also trying to catch up, but he was in big trouble. An ME-109 was right on his tail. I shouted a warning over the radio and pushed the throttle through the gate as I changed course and headed for the 109.

I was closing in on his beam and started firing while I worked my way around to quarter, then fine quarter, all the time reducing my angle of deflection until I was just a hundred yards dead astern before I opened up. I could see my cannon fire hitting home along his fuselage and was glad to give the pilot something to think about other than shooting down my colleague. I held steady, sustaining the cannon fire to make sure he was going down, but suddenly there was a juddering thump. My guns stopped working.

I knew I had probably been hit and jerked around in a left-hand turn with lots of bottom rudder to try to get away from whoever was onto me. The engine began to stammer, and I realized I was in even bigger trouble than I had thought. The engine was still ticking over, but my revs were dropping fast, so my speed was falling. Worse still, a quick glance around showed that several enemy planes were closing on me from two directions.

By this time I was down to about 10,000 feet, with virtually no pull on the prop at all. If I slowed down much more, I would be standing still, which is never a good idea when you are in a large, heavy object a long way above the ground. Half a dozen enemy planes, mostly 190s, were now circling, taking turns trying to finish me off. I pummeled my dead gun in rage.

Every attack they made against me, I turned in to face head-on and flew straight at them. This made me harder to hit as a smaller profile, and an object to avoid flying into. But it also meant that I had to stare straight at the smoke coming from their guns, their lead heading straight at me. Some of their cannon fire hit home into the structure of my beloved Spitfire, which had carried me through so many scrapes and up to now had never let me down.

As a Focke-Wulf screamed straight at me, guns blazing, out of force of habit, or blind optimism, I kept pushing my silent firing button in reply. I even heard my own voice, loud and surreal in the cockpit, shouting "Bang! Bang!" as I narrowly avoided colliding with one of my tormentors.

It looked like my career as a pilot, and as a member of the human race, was just about to end.

6. The Day of Reckoning

I had cut my engine, since it was clearly full of holes and not doing much good. I knew that there are few worse ways to go than being trapped in a cockpit on fire, and I really had only one choice—pick a spot to crash-land or bail out. While the journey down on a parachute would no doubt have been much more scenic and leisurely, I knew that it would give the Wehrmacht plenty of time to have a reception committee waiting to catch me on the ground, or perhaps even provide the Focke-Wulf 190s with target practice on the way down. Landing under my own steam seemed to offer a better chance of getting away.

While I was pondering my decision, the German fighters continued to take turns finishing me off, but my lack of horsepower and rapidly lowering altitude started to work in my favor. The high-powered enemy planes would whiz by, guns blazing, while I drifted ponderously down. I was going so slowly that they all tended to overshoot. Perhaps, I thought, this was the secret of modern aerial warfare—no engine, no guns. My thoughts were interrupted by the rapidly approaching ground, and rather than finish my new theory of warfare with "no pilot," I picked a nice flat field next to what looked like an old gothic church on the edge of a picturesque French village.

Coming in to land, I realized that I was coming in a bit too high, and a bit too fast, without flaps. It dawned on me that I was likely to skid right across the field, straight into the church wall. I knew that demolishing the ancient church was not likely to make a good impression on the locals, and that the church was not likely to make a good impression on me, so I decided to stop at all costs.

As I reached the ground, I dug a wingtip into it. Almost instantly my plane turned into a cartwheel, careering over the ground. Flashes of grass and sky alternated as my plane started to disintegrate. One wing was practically ripped off, and a shuddering crunch close behind me told me my fuselage was probably gone, too. I finally came to a stop, not far from the church, which was miraculously intact. I did notice that it seemed to be upside down, but as my head cleared, I realized that I was hanging upside down in the remains of the cockpit. The straps had held me in place. I wriggled from the remains, anxious to get out before something blew up, then stood at a little distance from the wreckage. Even though my mind was racing, the events around me seemed to unfolding in slow motion. Gradually my hearing and sight came back to normal. I ached from bruises caused by the crash landing, but remarkably, apart from a few scratches, there was nothing broken, and I was all in one piece.

The same could not be said of my beloved Spit, which had taken me through so much over the previous months. The fuselage had neatly broken in two just behind my seat. The wings seemed to be going in different directions, and just about anything else that could be broken was in ruins. Standing for a moment beside the remains of the plane, as if at the funeral of an old friend, I thought of all the lessons I'd been given in England, and in training in Canada, on the importance of not allowing your machine to fall intact into enemy hands. Looking at the wreckage, I wondered if my instructors might give me a medal for Outstanding Destruction.

But the medal would have to wait. One of the German planes dipped low to see if I had survived and presumably to radio my position to ground forces to pick me up. I dived for cover, and as soon as the coast was clear hurried into the village, which was little more than one street. If I was expecting a brass band reception, I was disappointed. The village appeared as deserted as a Texas ghost town. Every door was closed, windows shuttered or empty. Not even a dog barked. Then there was a creak as one door opened and a little girl of maybe ten years peered out.

She took a few steps toward me. I took a few steps back, not wanting to get such a young child in serious trouble for trying to help a foreign airman. But she kept coming, as if odd Americans fell from the sky into her village every day. She held out her hand. I took it and she led me back to her house. I was hauled through the open door and it was shut tight behind me.

I found myself looking at an attractive woman, probably in her late twenties, with a kind, sad face. She smiled and ushered me upstairs.

I deployed the only French I could think of, which was an unconvincing "bon jour," and then started explaining in English that I was an American with the Canadians fighting for the British. She told me—in the universal language of those in a hurry dealing with possible idiots—to shut up and tugged at my clothing. Baffled, and probably still a bit shaken from my landing, I was a bit slow on the uptake. She went to a cupboard and took out some men's clothes.

I took off my flying jacket and struggled out of my flying boots. I was about to take off my trousers when I turned to see that both mother and daughter had formed an impromptu audience for my striptease. I hesitated, a bit shy, but the mother pointed out the window urgently. The soldiers were on their way. I dropped my trousers and pulled on the new ones. The little girl applauded. The new trousers were a bit short but serviceable, and I pulled on a black jacket that looked like it might fit, provided I didn't try to do up the buttons. I completed my transformation into a French peasant with a pair of clogs. I was offered boots, but like some inexperienced actor I went for overkill with the clogs—a decision I started to regret almost as soon as I teetered and clopped my way back downstairs.

There was no time for a proper thank-you, a proper hello or goodbye. This kind, brave woman and her young daughter escorted me to the back door of their house. I kissed the little girl and hugged her mother, knowing that the soldiers were likely to be coming through the front door as I was hurtling out the back.

In the coming weeks and months I was to become aware of the heroism of ordinary people who risked everything for a stranger. When I left America, I was fighting for some abstract notions, against bullying and for democracy. Now I knew that I was fighting for real people like this woman, and it made me determined to evade capture, get back to England, and climb again into the first Spitfire cockpit I could find to continue the war.

Much later, I found out a little about the first person in France to come to my aid. Her name was Pauline Cam, a widow who survived by doing odd jobs around the village. When she heard my crash landing she sent her daughter out looking for me and got the clothes ready to transform me from pilot to local. The clothes belonged to her husband, who had been killed by the advancing Germans in the opening days of the war. The fact that his old clothes were being used to open a new front against the enemy seemed to give her some comfort, though I wonder if, as she watched a fleeing stranger disappear into the countryside, dressed in the clothes of the man she had loved, she was getting one last glimpse of her husband, not just an American on the run.

But my immediate concerns were more pressing. As I clopped my way out of the village I guessed that the enemy had by now reached my crash site and would be tearing the surrounding fields and houses apart looking for the missing pilot. I found myself running along the side of a little canal or river, and having watched too many movies about prisoners escaping from chain gangs in the 1930s, I remembered that in virtually every one the escapee would throw the pursuing bloodhounds off the scent by wading down the middle of a river.

I plunged in. It was not wide, but it got deeper and deeper. Soon I was up to my waist, then my chest. I sniffed. Something smelled truly terrible. The noise of the countryside and the thought of my pursuers being just steps away propelled me on as it gradually dawned on me that the canal was actually some kind of open sewer. A particularly loud noise, perhaps a pursuer's boot snapping on a twig, caused me to submerge completely into the foul-smelling murk. I stayed under as long as I could, and when I surfaced, gagging and retching, the coast was clear.

I stayed away from towns and building where I could to avoid detection, and since my dip in the sewer the locals were probably very grateful. That night I found a secluded copse of trees and made camp as best I could. I thought of the hobo jungle camps I had used in the Depression, but they at least had the advantage of people and life and a fire to warm oneself. Clearly a fire was out of the question, since it would attract unwelcome attention, but I turned my focus to my little escape kit in a tin, examining its contents in detail for the first time.

The little box contained a map of the Pas de Calais, some French money, a steel file, a tiny compass, and some Horlicks energy tablets. I treated myself to one of the tablets and curled up in a nest of leaves, exhausted.

I woke cold and early as the first rays of sunlight slanted through the trees. For the first time I felt the full impact of the crash landing and was very stiff until the sun warmed me up. I pored over my little escape map and picked what looked like a sparsely populated area as my objective and kept walking, occasionally allowing myself another of my dwindling supply of Horlicks tablets to stave off the worst of the hunger pangs.

Setting off in the general direction of nowhere, I was soon forced to come into contact with another human being. I found my way blocked by a wider river and, having wandered about looking for a bridge, found that the only way across was via a small ferryboat. I handed over some of the French money from my escape kit. The ferryman took it silently, handed me my change, and rowed me across. We never said a word, and if he had his suspicions about the silent stranger in the badly fitting clothes who smelled like he had recently been swimming in a sewer, he kept them to himself.

Later that same day, I was walking along a deserted road when I heard the rumble of a heavy vehicle—an army truck. Looking around desperately for some cover, I saw a large haystack in a field that sloped off to one side of the road. I took a running leap from the road and dived into the welcoming hay. Unfortunately it turned out that the hay was just a few wisps used to cover the exterior of an impressively large manure heap, but I had no choice but to burrow into the dunghill and wait for the vehicle to pass. By the time I slithered out of the bogus haystack I smelled so bad that I figured if they caught me they would probably have thrown me back again.

The same pattern of fairly aimless wanderings lasted for about three days, and perhaps given an endless supply of Horlicks tablets and a lot of luck, I could have spent the rest of the war shuffling around the byways of the Pas de Calais. As it was, I wanted to get back into the war and above all to avoid spending the next several years locked up in some German prison camp. Given my precarious existence in the Hungry Thirties, I was used to not always having enough to eat, but as night fell for a third time since I had crashed, I knew I had to make contact with some locals and take my chances that they were on the right side.

At about the same time as I came to that conclusion, I found myself on the outskirts of a village called Quercamps, some fifteen miles southeast of Calais, and instead of skirting around it, I walked down the deserted main street. I could hear music seeping out of a very closed and shuttered tavern. Several voices were raised, singing French songs from the trenches of the Great War. Whatever they were singing, it sounded unlikely that there would be many fascists joining in the chorus, so I rapped hard on the closed shutters. There was immediate silence.

Eventually someone shuffled to the door and opened it a crack. Suspicious faces peered out from behind the owner of the establishment. This was Monsieur Boulanger, an elderly man who smiled a lot but said very little. I attempted to explain to him and his friends in pretty terrible French that I was a downed Allied pilot.

Boulanger listened and conferred with his friends. His left hand had been smashed shapeless in the carnage of the Great War, and I could see him staring thoughtfully at this bundle of fresh trouble that had just turned up uninvited on his doorstep. He seemed to reach a decision. Boulanger swung the door open wide and welcomed me in anyway. Some of the patrons, delighted to see evidence of resistance to the occupying forces, even in the form of one bedraggled and shot-down pilot, moved to embrace me, but a combination of my dip in the sewer, a roll in a dung heap, and three nights sleeping rough had obviously lessened my appeal. They satisfied themselves with a few friendly pats on the back.

I was ushered into the kitchen at the back of the restaurant where Madame Boulanger, a quiet but reliable and kindly woman, rustled me up one of the few truly great meals of my life. I can see it to this day—an enormous plate of greens and eggs with a mountain of fresh bread. When I had finished devouring the feast, I leaned back and drank hot, sweet coffee as I tried to communicate with these brave, remarkable people who had put their lives and the lives of their family at risk by opening their door to a stranger.

The Boulangers had two children, a charming sixteen-year-old daughter called Marthe and her amiable young brother Julien. It seemed that Monsieur Boulanger had been through a lot in the Great War, and his wife had her hands full looking after the family and cooking for the restaurant, so somehow it fell to Marthe to look after this strange stray who had fallen from the sky, to change their lives.

They made me up a bed in the cellar below the restaurant and fixed me a much-needed bath. That night, I slept the most profound sleep, floating in a sea of exhaustion, surrounded by new friends and feeling safe for the first time in days.

Days passed as I regained my strength, sleeping and hiding during the day in the basement and sometimes emerging into the restaurant when the coast was clear. Marthe took charge with a quiet maturity far beyond her years. Most of the time things were uneventful, but sometimes a German staff car would roll into the village, heading for its only restaurant and tiny bar, which doubled as my hideout.

Then I clattered my way into the dark cellar, home of old furniture and food supplies. I was usually accompanied by the children, Marthe calm and determined, young Julien frightened but brave enough to want to defend me with whatever stick or toy he had to hand. As we huddled in the basement listening to the sound of jackboots clomping their way above our heads as they made a beeline for the best table, we would smile at each other to keep our morale up and wait.

Above our heads, a simple drama would act itself out each time they visited. Mrs. Boulanger would pretend to concentrate on the cooking and stay out of sight in the back kitchen. Other French diners would stare pointedly down into their soup, trying not to be noticed. Only Monsieur Boulanger would serve the enemy, a towel over his sleeve covering the smashed hand given to him in a previous conflict with the same foe. He would serve them with the same enigmatic neutral expression that he reserved for all his face-to-face encounters with the enemy, polite enough not to raise hackles, but reserved enough not to prompt further conversation. When the unwelcome guests had dined on the best Mrs. Boulanger could muster, they would leave satisfied. After a few minutes of silence to make sure they were out of the village, we would be welcomed back to the light and noise from the twilight tension of the basement.

The village grapevine seemed to work particularly well, so we usually had notice when a particularly dangerous visit by the occupiers was coming up. In the meantime, I passed the time talking to Marthe, who was full of hope for life after the war and determined to do her part to make it happen. She would ask me about the bright lights of London and the strange wide-open world of the American West that she dreamed of seeing for herself someday, and I promised her a welcome there equal to the one she and her family had given me. As days turned to weeks, we became good friends.

Then one night I was awakened by a vigorous shaking. Marthe and Julien were standing beside my bed, wide-eyed with worry and excitement. Marthe urged me to get dressed and get my things together urgently. The Germans were on their way to search the village and my cellar hideout was the first place they would look.

Marthe led me across dark fields, with Julien tailing along behind. Julien was excited, but clearly delighted to be out on a nighttime adventure, and he so worshipped his big sister that he was determined to come along to see that no harm came to her or his adopted pilot.

I had no idea where we were going as we hurried through the moonlight, but we soon came to a very imposing house outside the village. It was owned by the local mill owner, Emile Rocourt. Emile was an impressive middle-aged man who greeted me with amiable formality before greeting Marthe like a long-lost daughter. Indeed, his own daughter was about the same age as Marthe, and they turned out to be best friends.

Emile was a local politician and something of a local dignitary. As far as the Nazis were concerned he was an obedient local bigwig, but after the war he was decorated for his active role in the Resistance, with assisting me being one of numerous actions conducted under the noses of the unsuspecting occupiers.

While the enemy troops inspected and searched in the village that morning, I was hidden in the mill itself and looked after by the Rocourt family, who were considered too important to bother with such inconveniences.

When the visit was over and the searchers were gone, I returned to my life in the restaurant cellar, gradually improving my terrible French with the help of Marthe. For some weeks this pattern continued, with me being shuttled to the Rocourt mill when my restaurant roost became too perilous. But the strain of playing against longer odds as time went by was starting to show, and I was anxious to get back in the war rather than sit it out while endangering a lot of decent, brave French people. Marthe, as always, took charge. She went away one day and contacted the Resistance—an act which would change her own life as much as mine.

Some weeks later she told me it was time for another retreat to the Rocourt mill. The trip was routine, and we were shadowed by young Julien, brandishing a stick he had picked up on the way, to defend us from any enemies we might come across on the road. But this was no ordinary trip. At the big house Emile Rocourt told me they were expecting a visitor from the Resistance, responding to Marthe's approach for help.

Moments later another man arrived. He had tough, Gallic good looks and a wiry build that hinted at an ability to take care of himself in trouble. He was introduced only as Monsieur Jean. He nodded to Rocourt and then turned his piercing eyes on me, sizing me up. After what seemed like an age, he clearly decided I was worth helping.

He was going to arrange for me to go to a safe house in Lille, then on to Paris, where I would wait for the underground railroad to take me through France to Spain. From there I could make my way back to England and the air war. I asked him when he thought I might be going. He replied, "Half an hour."

There was some debate between those assembled about whether I would need papers for the short train ride to Lille. Rocourt suggested that I was about the same age and build as his daughter's fiancé. Perhaps he might be persuaded to part with his identity for the journey. Rocourt's daughter bravely did not say a word, but I could see the tears welling up in her eyes. If her fiancé was asked, he would want to help of course, but if I was caught with his papers, he would quickly be arrested and probably shot. I was clearly uncomfortable about this arrangement. Luckily, Monsieur Jean intervened. Papers would not be necessary for such a short journey. We would take our chances.

Decisions made, we were invited to sit down for a hasty meal before we left. Suddenly my time at Quercamps was over. I had just minutes to say farewells and thanks that could have taken a lifetime. Surrounded by young friends and by men who were risking their lives for a stranger, I had a chance to practice my faltering French. I took Marthe's hand at the dinner table and said thank you to her and to all of them. I promised I would move heaven and earth to get back to England, and that the next time we met their country would be free.

Then we were away, being waved off by Rocourt, his daughter, Marthe, and Julien, still brandishing his stick. After the war I discovered that Marthe's first contact with the Resistance, to help me on my way, was the start of a new life for her. At only sixteen, she became an active and leading member of the local Resistance. For a year and a half she harried the invaders in every way possible until eventually she was captured. After that she was interrogated, beaten, starved, and systematically brutalized as only the Nazis knew how. Eventually she was deported to Ravensbrück concentration camp, where she spent the rest of the war in terrible conditions, but she survived with the same quiet determination that had made me admire her so much.

When she was liberated from the camp at the end of the war, her health was shattered. I was able to visit her a few years later, in a free France as we had planned. She sat up in bed to greet me, but she was very weak and was not thought likely to survive for long. We sat together, both in conversation and in silence, remembering. My return visit in peacetime was reported in some of the local newspapers, and I hope it in some way contributed to some belated interest from the French authorities in this brave young woman. Shortly after my visit, General Charles de Gaulle himself came to her bedside in Quercamps and pinned France's

greatest medal, the Légion d'Honneur, on her himself. Marthe
died young, a few years later.

Fortunately for me, such events, both dark and heroic, were
all hidden in the future. As I hung swaying from a passenger strap
while standing on a crowded local train to Lille, rubbing elbows
with German soldiers and curious, staring locals, I was beginning
to wonder if not having a single identity paper was such a small
thing after all. But Monsieur Jean was a professional. He rode
alongside me, showing just the right amount of boredom and dif-
fidence to fade into the background, and very soon I was breathing a long sigh of relief as we made our way through quiet streets
in Lille to the house of a widow who would shelter me.

It struck me that this was the second time since I had crash-
landed that I was helped by a woman suffering the loss of her
husband in the war, and I wondered how many other brave
women there were out there, fighting back in whatever way they
could and longing for the end of the war, even though they knew
that their own loved ones would never come marching home.

I stayed there for a week or so, being kept company by some
neighbors of my host—a young man who played the guitar and
his sister Juliet. It seemed like a little oasis in the war, sitting in an
apartment with a young man who knew all the latest songs and
could strum tunes like "J'attendrais," while I would take the guitar and teach him and his sister some songs in return, including a
few cowboy tunes I had learned in Texas and New Mexico, like
"Blood on the Saddle." But in wartime France, the illusion of
peace was always fragile. I found out from Juliet that her amiable,
guitar-playing brother was on a Nazi death list—a rota of people
who would be picked up and shot in retaliation for any action by
the Resistance. His crime had been to laugh out loud at a German

propaganda newsreel in the cinema, and some fascist sympathizer had squealed on him.

I was horrified. How could he just sit there and wait for his fate? He must come with me to Paris. Maybe we could escape together to Spain and he could resist the fascists in some way from there or from Britain. At first his sister seemed to feel this offered a real glimmer of hope, but when I raised the idea with her brother, he just smiled. He explained to me that if he ran away, they would just put Juliet's name on the list, and if she ran, they would put his mother on the list—or someone else's sister or mother.

I was still struggling with the enormity of this when Monsieur Jean reappeared. I barely had time for a new set of farewells before heading with him on the local train to Paris. This time we had passable identification papers, forged by Monsieur Jean's Resistance contacts. On the journey, I had time to think about the different sorts of bravery that this war was bringing out. Perhaps it took a certain amount of guts to climb into a Spitfire cockpit and head for the skies over France, but in reality the quiet heroism of a young man who refused to be silenced in a cinema, then who refused to place his family in danger by running away, was just as great.

Few experiences can be quite as exhilarating as a first visit to Paris, particularly if the year is 1942 and you happen to be an Allied pilot on the run. Monsieur Jean and I walked from the Gare du Nord into the very heart of occupied Paris. Suddenly, as well as being surrounded by civilians, enemy soldiers, and policemen, who were ignoring me and going about their business, I was also surrounded by buildings and history that had fascinated me since childhood. I walked along saucer-eyed as we strolled the Boulevard de Sébastopol, past landmarks like the Rue de Rivoli and the bustling River Seine. There in the distance was the Eiffel Tower, and right ahead of me, rising in all its magnificence, was the medieval splendor of Notre Dame Cathedral.

Monsieur Jean was walking at a purposeful pace, not too fast so as not to attract attention, but not dawdling so as to get to safety as speedily and uneventfully as possible. I stopped. He stopped. I explained to him quietly that I had to go in to the cathedral. He looked at me like I had just confirmed some vague suspicion he held about my sanity. I stood my ground. I needed to go in. How many Americans ever get the chance to see the inside of that magnificent building, let alone visit it in the middle of a war? He shrugged and let me go in.

For one brief moment, engulfed by all that medieval magnificence, the soaring stone columns and breathtaking arches, my thoughts soared heavenward, along with the whispered prayers of a few old ladies in the pews. There, on the run in an occupied city, I felt free, and once again remembered that there were things truly worth fighting for. When I emerged to rejoin a slightly impatient Monsieur Jean, I was holding something in my hand. He looked amused as he studied my purchase—a postcard of the cathedral. I hastily wrote a note to the teacher in Texas who had tried to drum some French into me some years earlier, with little success. On the card, I pointed out that I had recently gone to considerable lengths to brush up on my French by taking lessons from the natives. Monsieur Jean pocketed my card and promised to get it out of the country. We set off again and arrived safely at a beautiful apartment building, full of Parisian style and charm, near the Porte Dorée, just a stone's throw from the entrance to the Bois de Vincennes.

On the doorstep of an apartment, as the door opened, I turned to see Monsieur Jean already leaving. For once it was my turn to watch someone else hurry off. In all my dealings with him, I never found out anything about his life or his family, and he never asked anything about me or my life before the war. He was a man who knew the price one paid for such information if captured by the enemy, and he focused all his considerable talents on moving downed pilots from France back to Britain, where they could once again go about the task of helping to liberate his country. I never saw him again, nor found out his real name, but I recognized in his rapidly disappearing wiry frame the sort of determination that would win this war, no matter how long it took or how much it cost.

Turning back to the doorway, I was greeted by a beautiful French woman, Giselle, and her husband Josef, who ushered me in to their apartment. Josef explained that he, too, had been a pilot before the fall of France. These days, both he and Giselle worked at small jobs to pay the bills, while helping the war effort in any way they could. They showed me to a small, simply furnished spare bedroom. That room was to become my home for several months.

What had presumably started as a hideout for a few days, similar to my stay in Lille, rapidly became a long-term residence in the heart of Paris. At about this point in the war the underground railroad had been severely damaged by Nazi success at arresting and torturing some key figures in the escape apparatus. My next stop was due to be Angoulême in the south, but the escape route was at a standstill. Previous routes were unsafe, and all along a line from northern France to the Spanish border there were stranded Allied airmen being hidden in French homes, from lofty chateaux to the most lowly cottages, waiting for the routes to re-open and the bottleneck to end.

It may seem strange to someone reading about those times so many years later, but the prevailing atmosphere was not justifiable fear of being caught. These were times when life was lived very much in the present, since no one knew quite what the next day would bring, or even if there would be a next day. That led to some decisions which, with the clarity of hindsight, were not the brightest.

With days passing and me obviously feeling cooped up in the tiny room, Josef and Giselle suggested a few outings to avoid my getting cabin fever. So began a series of excursions that made me one of the only Americans on vacation in Paris in 1942.

One of my favorite outings was to the local swimming pool near Denfert-Rochereau. I have always loved swimming, and the physical exertion freed me from the cramped feeling that comes with spending too long in one small space. Still damp from the trip to the baths, it was a strange experience to find myself shar-ing a Metro strap with some SS officer on the way home.

On other days, we would go to the zoo, where I would stare at the animals behind bars and commiserate with them, hoping to avoid a similar fate myself. We also went together to the movies, and it was hard not to feel like part of a more interesting movie in real life than whatever was flickering across the screen, usually accompanied by hectoring newsreels of German victories. One of my more practical outings was to a safe dentist, a charming, dignified Jewish woman who treated me in secret for a tooth ab-scess that was causing me a great deal of pain. She was already on a list to be deported, and even if we did not at that stage know the full extent of the horror ahead, we were wise enough about the Nazis to know that they had no good intentions. Yet despite the threat of imminent deportation, she continued to help people, including risking making her own terrible situation even worse by helping me.

The general theory of my somewhat freewheeling Parisian existence seemed to be that it was safe to "hide in plain sight," and it seemed to work quite well, provided I did not open my mouth. But from there it was a simple step for my hosts to suggest that I could let myself in and out during the day for some welcome exercise. I became a regular walker in the Bois, sometimes sitting on a bench with a sandwich, watching the German troops practicing their drills in the open space.

I have had many years to ponder the foolishness of not hiding all day every day in some cupboard, being fed by a straw through the keyhole, but the truth is no one can ever know what brings about success or failure in such a strange world of escapes and captures. It may have been that someone saw the comings and goings of a stranger, or it may have been that some unfortunate person at some point in the long and winding escape route was tortured beyond endurance. It may simply have been a random raid based on vague suspicions. Whatever happened, the reality remained the same, as simple and stark as the reality of the war itself. One night in early June 1942, about two months after I arrived in Paris, the front door of the apartment was kicked in, cracking and splintering under the weight of many jackboots. All three of us were dragged from our beds and forced to dress hastily at gunpoint, then held in the living room while a group of German soldiers ransacked the apartment and demanded our papers.

Knowing that the game was up, I tried talking to the one who seemed to be in charge, attempting to explain that I had just arrived and that these people did not know who I really was. They had just taken me in off the streets and should not be blamed for harboring me.

I had only got halfway through my admittedly threadbare excuses when I was cut short by a rifle butt in the face. We were dragged into waiting vehicles and taken straight to one of the most feared buildings in the world—Gestapo headquarters in Paris, near the Opera. Josef and Giselle were dragged off in one direction, I in another. I never saw either of them again.

After a short spell in a basement cell, I was taken by two guards up to an office. There, behind a large and highly polished desk, sat a gray-haired man in well-tailored civilian clothes, with a face that I hated on sight. He motioned politely for me to take a small seat positioned in front of the large desk while the guards hovered by the wall behind me. I sat down and immediately began gabbling my series of excuses about my hosts that had previously been curtailed by the rifle butt. My French must have still been pretty terrible, since the gray-haired man stopped me in full flood with a terse request: "Speak English."

I started again from the beginning in English, but if anything my story sounded even lamer. Once again my interrogator cut me short. He told me to stop worrying about my former hosts and start worrying about myself. I responded that I was a prisoner of war and expected to be treated as one. The man leaned over toward me, confidentially. There is only one way I will believe you are a prisoner of war, he told me. He produced a pen and paper. I had a sinking feeling about where this little civilized chat was leading. "You can prove you are really a pilot by giving me the names of every person who helped you since you crash-landed. Then we can check your story."

I gave him the date and location of my crash, but he just sneered. Knowing the location of a downed plane did not prove I was the pilot. I was captured in Paris in civilian clothes. It was my turn to sneer. I pointed out that with my terrible French and no German I would not make much of a spy. He countered that I probably spoke such bad French to make my pilot story more plausible. He was beginning to get impatient. He wanted the names of every person who had helped me from my crash to my capture.

For once I was able to use the truth. Ever since I was a boy I've had a terrible memory for names. I leaned over as he had done, about to divulge a secret. "To tell you the truth, I'm terrible with names," I confided. This did not seem to have the desired effect. He turned purple and hissed at me, "You do not seem to be taking yourself seriously enough. Perhaps we can help you." With that, he tidied his desk and left the room.

He had hardly closed the door when one of the guards hauled me to my feet and grabbed my arms behind my back. The other hit me a vicious punch in the face. I turned my head away and the next blow crashed into my stomach. I tried to clench my muscles, but a third crashing blow to my solar plexus left me gasping for breath as he returned to beating me around the face.

He stopped for a second, as if some shred of humanity might have been rekindled somewhere inside him, but in reality he only stopped long enough to fastidiously take a handkerchief from his pocket, wrap it carefully around his knuckles and then start over, landing blow after vicious blow on my cheeks, jaw, neck, and eyes.

As I came close to passing out, they shoved me back in the chair, where I cradled my head in my arms. One of the guards yanked my head up by the hair. As it rose, I saw that the sleeves of my shirt were covered in blood. He jerked my head back until I was once again staring at the gray-haired Gestapo man, who had reentered the room as silently as he had left.

He waved a piece of paper at me. One of my eyes was so swollen that it was practically shut, and the other was swimming with blood. I struggled to focus.

"It's in German. I told you, I don't speak German."

He seemed delighted to translate it for me. It was an order from the Kommandantur. It said that if the prisoner calling himself Bill Ash failed to provide satisfactory proof of identity, he was to be shot as a spy on June 4, 1942. Just as I've never been great with names, I am not much better with dates. I asked him to help me out again. He leaned over and whispered, "June third," with obvious enjoyment.

He could see I was rattled, but my brain was by now racing for any shred of information that might stop them from shooting me without leading them to shoot someone who deserved it less. I couldn't think of a thing.

The Gestapo man pressed his advantage, inquiring innocently if I happened to come across a Monsieur Jean in my travels. I thought for a bit, but said I didn't think I had had the pleasure. My interrogator began to get irritated once more. He shouted that they knew I had been helped by a Monsieur Jean and that if I wanted to avoid being shot, I should start giving details of when and where I had met him. I brightened and he leaned forward eagerly.

"Does he have a very bushy black beard?" I inquired. Something in my delivery must have seemed less than totally sincere. He shut my file and stood up.

"That's it. You have not cooperated. Events will have to take their course."

I was dragged out of his office by the two goons, feeling slightly cheated that I was going to be shot without at least a little more haggling. They brought me back to my basement cell and shoved me in, clanging the door locked behind me. I lay on the floor, trying to assess my injuries, feeling loose teeth. Part of me tried to convince the other part that they were bluffing. But why should they, I retorted to my bloody and confused self. If they recognized that a prisoner was unlikely to cooperate, perhaps the Gestapo method was not to waste time beating them or feeding them. That got me to wondering if I would at least get a decent lunch to celebrate my last day on the planet. But there was no lunch. No dinner. No anything.

I settled down on a rough prison cot for a long, dark night, to await my execution. My thoughts turned to the cocky young Texan who had told a local paper just after he qualified as a pilot that he was going to bash the Hun for democracy, then come back and write a book about it. Now I thought that, like Dostoyevsky, I had the useful experience of knowing what it was like to be sentenced to death. Unfortunately, this led on to the thought that I would not be able to make much use of this information once I was dead.

Most of the rest of the night passed with a jumble of thoughts and emotions. I tried to steel myself so that I would at least not give the Nazis the satisfaction of seeing how frightened I was. One of my strongest thoughts was that I had organized my war rather badly. I had started off with a dislike of bullies and a desire for adventure, but my feelings about fascists were abstract at best.

It took actually meeting some of them and seeing their handi-work firsthand throughout Europe to know I had done the right thing in joining up. Even if I had known it would end like this, I would still have joined, and I would have been less squeamish in some of my earlier dogfights. It was simultaneously the longest and the shortest night of my life.

As morning approached, I heard the clatter of a food trolley in the corridor outside with the clank of plates and the slosh of breakfast slops, but my door remained stubbornly closed. No food, but no execution either. So much for fascists making the trains run on time, I thought. The two parts of my addled brain debated my situation. One side grew hopeful that they would not shoot me after all, but the other just laughed and told the opti-mistic side not to get my hopes up.

At lunchtime the door clanged open. This was it. The pes-simistic part of me was busy telling the optimistic half that it had told me so, when I was handed a hunk of black bread and a cup of sauerkraut soup and made my first acquaintance with Reich tea, which looked like boiled confetti but tasted much worse. For me, it was a victory feast. The optimist finally bubbled to the surface, reasoning that they would not waste good food, or even bad food, on me if they were about to shoot me. The door clanged open again and I was led out by two guards who seemed intent on con-tradicting my theory.

Yet instead of leading me to some execution yard, they took me upstairs to the office of my interrogator. I felt it too rude to inquire if he had possibly forgotten something, and since he did not immediately bring up the fact that I was alive contrary to reg-ulations, I felt it was not my place to remind him.

He was like a different man. He ushered me back to my chair

and started a cosy chat in impeccable English. He told me how well he knew London and what a fine city he thought it was. I agreed politely.

"How is Scott's Restaurant these days?" he inquired, adding, "They always made excellent steaks." For a moment I thought it might be some kind of code, but I realized this was what passed for polite chitchat in Nazi interrogations. Since I could not enlighten him about the steaks at Scott's I let him know about a very good Lyons Corner House in Piccadilly Circus where you could get all the salad you could eat for a few shillings.

No doubt grateful for this information, he proffered me a cigarette and even lit it for me. I was just settling in for more homespun Nazi wit and wisdom when he clearly decided the formalities were over.

"You'll never see London again!" he shouted and signaled to one of the goons behind me, who stepped forward on cue and slapped me across the face, sending my cigarette flying with a little trail of sparks. The interrogator pointed to the guard who had just struck me. "He will see it. He will be in London! Where will you be?"

I felt little need to encourage him by offering suggestions, and he obliged me by telling me anyway. "You will be dead today unless you give us some names. We are not unreasonable people. Just a few names and you will be treated as a pilot instead of as a spy."

Just like a compulsive eater or gambler, I knew that if I gave them even one name it would be impossible to stop, and with some advice from Monsieur Jean, I had become adept at trying to find out as little as possible about the people who had helped me.

"Just one name," he coaxed. "We already have many of them

in custody, so you need not worry about giving your friends away."

I thought, then reluctantly squeezed out one name. "Monsieur Joseph."

My interrogator was delighted. He leaned forward. "Ah, Monsieur Josef. And what does this Monsieur Josef do?"

"He's a teacher."

The interrogator wrote down this nugget officiously, then turned his cold eyes back to me.

"Where?"

"In Texas. He tried hard with me, but I was never much good at French."

He turned purple once more. I could tell I was going to pay a high price for stringing him along. But he seemed almost disappointed that our session was ending. He simply got up and left, turning to me at the door. "You had your chance. You will be shot tomorrow morning. Good day, Herr Ash."

As he left, he nodded to one of the guards and they commenced on giving me the beating of a lifetime. Blows and kicks rained down on me for what seemed like an eternity. A searing pain doubled me over as one of them punched in on the kidneys. As I started to lose consciousness, they dragged me back to my cell. I could no longer walk properly.

For the rest of that day, I lay aching and bleeding on the rough cell cot. This time I was in no doubt that they meant it, and the gradual erosion of one's sense of self and perspective at which the Nazis excelled was beginning to take its toll as my physical condition deteriorated. But instead of shooting me, they took me out later for another interrogation, and another beating, and another, and another. The days blurred into one long, bloody hell of pain, humiliation, and unanswered questions. I can no longer say how long it went on. Perhaps a week, though it certainly felt longer.

By the end of this period the Nazi techniques were starting to backfire. The mere thought of being shot no longer seemed quite so terrible. I lay, aching and bloody and wretched in my cell, listening to the click of military boots on hard floor outside my cell door. What this time? Perhaps the final bullet? Or just another beating? Or perhaps it was time for more Reich tea, to keep me alive until the next beating.

Instead, I heard a new sound. My captors loved shouting—shouting at me, shouting orders at each other, and shouting at anyone who did not do as they were ordered—but the tone of such shouting always had the same ring to it, a superior bawling out some unfortunate *Untermensch*. This was different. A blazing row outside my cell was being fought out by two equals. I recognized one of the voices as that of my interrogator, and even though he was no slouch in the screaming department, he was gradually getting the worst of it from whoever was on the other side of this argument. A final bark by his adversary was accompanied by an insistent thump on my cell door, rapidly followed by the reluctant clank and shuffle of the loser unlocking it.

By the time the door opened my interrogator had left already and I was faced with the stern but relatively friendly figure of a Luftwaffe officer and several soldiers. He seemed taken aback by my condition, but he saluted.

"We must leave now. You are now in the custody of the Luftwaffe as a prisoner of war and will be treated as such. But we must hurry. The Gestapo still dispute that you are a pilot, and we should leave before they get a chance to have our orders countermanded. Come!"

I needed no further encouragement, but I was in such bad shape after the endless beatings that I needed some help from the Luftwaffe subordinates as I limped my way out of that hellish place, which was something few of its unfortunate inmates ever lived to do.

As the heavy gates of the Gestapo closed behind me, I could almost hear the sigh of relief from my new captors. The fight for custody of prisoners between the Luftwaffe and the Gestapo was a recurring theme of their war, and a battle which the Gestapo would gradually win. But for now the Luftwaffe had the upper hand, which was fine by me. In general they wanted to abide by the Geneva Convention. On a less noble note, they knew that there were hundreds of Luftwaffe prisoners of war being held in camps in England and Canada. If word got out that the Gestapo was beating and shooting their prisoners, who knew what might start happening to the German prisoners.

I had plenty of time to ponder all this as I sat on a train, propped up between two Luftwaffe guards. The escort was a bit over the top, since I could barely stand up. As the train rumbled from France to Germany, a group of Luftwaffe pilots stopped by to take a look at me. They were based at St. Omer in the Pas de Calais, heading home on leave, and were delighted to discover that the strange, lone Spitfire pilot they had taken turns shooting at some months earlier was alive, if not very well, and in relatively safe hands.

I could not muster much enthusiasm for a chat. Any idea that this war was simply something cooked up by our superiors, and that the brave little men like us on both sides were simply doing as they were told, did not fit with my recent experiences.

The military might that allowed Hitler and his vile theories of racial supremacy to turn Europe into a giant slaughterhouse of innocent people was based on both military muscle and individual people doing as they were told, even when they knew in their hearts that it was utterly wrong. Such thoughts might be considered churlish, coming from someone who had, in effect, just been rescued from death at the hands of the Gestapo by the Luftwaffe, and I do not for a minute compare the actions of the Nazis to the average German soldier, but the truth is that their military actions were the only thing that made the Nazi outrages possible. Their well-meant camaraderie, like the dream of the humble foot soldiers on both sides getting together every now and again to play football in no-man's-land or sing a few rousing choruses of "Hurrah for the next man who dies" belonged to another time, another war, and another movie.

I settled down and stared at the countryside as the train rolled toward Frankfurt and my first prisoner of war camp, Dulag Luft—as it turned out, the first of many.

7. For You the War Is Over

My Luftwaffe escort deposited me at a sort of mustering camp
for new air force officer prisoners called Dulag Luft, just outside
Oberursel, near Frankfurt. It was the Luftwaffe's main interrogation center and a sort of transit camp from which captured fliers
were sent on in batches to the main prison camps. Apparently, at
some point in the war, a British airman prisoner carved a giant
sign that hung over the camp entrance, reading, "I told you it
wasn't a Spitfire," but if I saw it at the time, I must not have been
in a laughing mood. I was pretty battered after my brief stay with
the Gestapo, and for me it was one of the lowest points in the war.

I was put briefly in solitary confinement and paced my cell as
all the events from my crash landing to that very moment seemed
to well up at once and slap me in the face. I was physically suffering from weeks of beatings at the hands of the Gestapo, but men-

tally the strain of constant threats of death and the ultimate let-
down of months of tension and hiding resulting in only this—a
bare cell and an eternity of barbed wire ahead—was starting to
take its toll. A strange feeling welled up inside me, like a combination of food poisoning and utter depression. I felt increasingly
disgusted with myself—for allowing myself to be shot down, for
letting myself be captured, and most of all for failing the long
line of brave French people who had done so much to help me
get away, potentially at such a terrible cost to themselves. I
smashed my fist into the brick of the cell wall again and again until it was in just as bad shape as the rest of me.

As I watched the blood trickle down my hand, a metal tray
with some food was shoved through a hatch. As I stared at the
food something struck me mentally with more force than any
thump I could give the wall. The food! Every time I had a meal in
the cell I immediately started to feel even more low and strangely
passive. I started to wonder if they were putting something into
the food or drink, to make us more manageable. My next experience hinted that this was right.

A man in Red Cross uniform under a white doctor's coat came
in with a clipboard. He sympathized with my plight and offered
me a cigarette, leaning in closer to ask quietly if the guards were
treating me reasonably. He then encouraged me to fill in his detailed questionnaire so that he could get the information to
Switzerland as soon as possible and my worried family and former unit could be informed that I was safe and a POW. The way
I was feeling, I did not think anyone would very much care what
had befallen me, but as I stared glumly at the ground I noticed
that under the bottom of the good doctor's white coat a shiny pair
of jackboots peeked out. I took a look at his questionnaire, and

sure enough, it was crammed full of questions the answers to which would be of no use to a worried mother but very handy to German intelligence. I declined politely and told him that since I had fallen from the sky several months ago, another week or two before my family found out I was all right would not really matter. He stamped out in a manner that was much less sympathetic than his entrance, and the cell door clanged shut behind him.

In common with most prisoners arriving at Dulag Luft at that stage of the war, the spell in solitary was followed by a series of interrogations by Luftwaffe intelligence officers who spoke good English and some of whom had lived in America or Britain before the war. Their questions, though probing, were not too difficult to deflect, and they generally behaved in accordance with the Geneva Convention, which was a welcome change from my treatment by the Gestapo. I could see how this gentler approach might actually pay dividends when dealing with a frightened young bomber pilot, blown out of the sky on his first or second mission, who had just watched his closest friends burn up and for whom the terror of capture was replaced with a strange sense of security and the familiar warm tones of an accent he recognized from home. But I had seen the other side of the Third Reich and could still feel the bruises and loose teeth from my last chat with the Gestapo, so I was in little danger of being charmed out of any state secrets. Better still, I didn't know any.

Things started to pick up when, still at Dulag Luft, I hooked up with another downed Spitfire pilot I mentioned earlier. Paddy Barthrop's luck had lasted from before Dunkirk, right through the Battle of Britain and beyond, in fact, right up to a few days before our meeting at the Dulag. Paddy had parachuted when he was shot down over France, and a large German reception committee was waiting for him as he hit the ground and carted him off to a local jail. Some of the pilots who had downed him were stationed nearby and came over to inspect their catch. They were decent enough to give him some cigarettes and huddled together for a souvenir photo in which Paddy stands puffing enigmatically before being carted off to Dulag Luft.

Paddy was almost out of central casting as the young hard-nosed Spitfire pilot with a devil-may-care attitude to life and death and a passion for anything fast, including airplanes, horses, and women. Certainly that was part of Paddy, but underneath the persona was one of the kindest, most generous men I have ever known. Years after the war, if any one of our old colleagues from either operations or prison camp was in any kind of difficulty, they would always turn to Paddy for help or advice. His arrival was just the boost I needed, and I started to turn from wallowing in self-pity and recrimination to concentrating on getting out and getting back to the war. I was Prisoner Number 757 and Paddy was Number 759. We never did find out who was the mysterious 758.

Filled with newfound zeal for an escape, I approached a senior Allied officer who seemed to be stationed at the transit camp permanently. He had apparently been in the second-hand car business before the war, but I instantly had the feeling that no one in his right mind ever bought a car from this slippery character. Still, I pressed ahead and told him that I wanted to have a go at escaping from Dulag Luft. He waved his hand airily and told me in a rather patronizing way that this sort of activity was all well catered for in the main POW camp near Breslau, much as if he were talking about day-trip excursions from a holiday camp. After the war, I found out that he had been working for the Germans all the time, so it was a bit like a criminal going to a policeman to announce his intention to rob a bank.

Luckily, we were very quickly moved on from Dulag Luft to Stalag Luft III in eastern Germany, now a part of Poland. We were shipped out in a large batch by truck, heavily guarded and unable to see much on the long journey through Germany. Luft III was the main POW camp for Allied flying officers, located at Sagan, some hundred miles southeast of Berlin.

On arrival, we were given a fairly standard "For you the war is over" speech by the camp commandant, Von Lindeiner. As far as Paddy and I were concerned, it was just getting going, but it seemed rude to interrupt. In fairness, though, Colonel Friedrich Wilhelm von Lindeiner had an unenviable job. He ran the camp from the time it opened in May 1942, about six weeks before I arrived, right through to the aftermath of what became known as the Great Escape in 1944, when he was relieved of command and replaced by my old friends the Gestapo.

Von Lindeiner was in his sixties, a longtime military man who was already a seasoned soldier at the time of World War I, when he was wounded three times and won the Iron Cross twice. He married a Danish aristocrat and did his best to sidestep Nazi politics, but at the start of the war he was refused retirement and put in charge of a camp that eventually grew to house ten thousand prisoners, including a fair few like myself whose day job was trying to escape. It must have been the least welcome of all assignments—apart, perhaps, from the Russian Front.

The camp was divided up into several compounds—at that time one for officers, another for sergeant pilots or NCOs, and another area which was exclusively for the Germans, the *Vorlager*, containing both their barracks and the administrative buildings.

The camp was surrounded by a pine forest, and within, it was defined by wooden huts, barbed wire, and tall machine gun posts at regular intervals. We were shown the low warning wire that led to a sort of no-man's-land before the real wire, often twelve feet high. Even between the compounds there were double fences of wire, on the far side of which was the center compound for the NCOs and later my fellow Americans, though at this stage there were fewer than a dozen of us, all waifs and strays like me, with perhaps six hundred or so prisoners in all. The compound was later to be renamed East Compound as our captors built new ones to accommodate the steady supply of downed airmen.

Our accommodation in those early days, particularly in comparison to that given to me by the Gestapo, was pretty good. Men were divided into groups of six or eight housed in small rooms within larger purpose-built wooden huts. Those huts, the endless walking circuits of the exercise yard, ringed in every direction by barbed-wire fences and the ever present eyes and machine guns of the guards in their towers, were the defining landmarks of a tiny area that was to become our entire world.

Under the terms of the Geneva Convention officers were not expected to work, so the main things to fill time were studying, working with the camp entertainment through music or theatre, or simply trying to escape. As well as new surroundings and a microgeography of huts, towers, and exercise yard, there was an entire new language to learn. Guards were "goons" and the cry of "goons in the block" was used to alert anyone doing anything illegal as they approached. Specially trained guards used to sniff out tunnels and contraband became known as ferrets, while our own men, innocently lounging in a doorway while acting as lookouts for some escape endeavor, became known as stooges.

Walking through the gates of that massive barbed-wire fortress into the prisoners' compound was like finding I had died and arrived in the feasting halls of Valhalla, where a previous generation of warriors was already at home. Over there was Bob Tuck, a truly brilliant fighter pilot who flew both Spitfires and Hurricanes. He had been based at Hornchurch during a remarkable career in which he shot down thirty enemy aircraft before he ended up "in the bag." And over there by the wire was former 242 Squadron Leader, the redoubtable Douglas Bader, a legend in Britain, who had lost his legs in a prewar crash but taught himself to fly again with artificial ones. Nearby, standing in the doorway of one of the wooden barracks huts, was Norman Ryder, another Spitfire ace, and a sea of other faces I did not recognize but was soon to get to know.

Some of the inmates had been prisoners since the early days of the war. One navigator had been flying around in a Blenheim over the North Sea in September 1939 when he was suddenly blown out of the sky by a ship's guns. A German E-boat fished him out of the cold water, which had failed to dampen his anger. He shouted at them that they were fools and that actions like this could even start a war. They gleefully told him it had already started and that his stay as a POW was going to be almost exactly the same length as the war itself.

Among the many prisoners I got to know around that time was Bill Stapleton. He had been shot down back in 1940 flying from the same station as me, at Hornchurch. While most of the acres of print about the camps have focused on the obsessive escapologists among us, Bill is a great example of someone who helped many of us get through those tough years in unexpected ways. He had a great streak of humanity in a place where it was in short supply. Bill was the proud owner of a rare and valuable thing in Stalag Luft III, an old windup phonograph with a small but treasured hoard of classical records. Back at his first camp, Stalag Luft I at Barth, he had begun a tradition after lights-out. Lying in the darkness, even among so many other prisoners, men turned over in their minds all the things they missed and the loved ones they did not know that they would ever see again. Into this loneliness crept some of the most beautiful music ever composed. It would waft out from Bill's phonograph, out across the camp, making us feel just a little bit more free and a little less forgotten.

Bill, who also contributed to the famous "wooden horse" escape, was able to continue his good musical work at another camp in Poland, then in Luft III again, a good training for a job he is still doing sixty years later, helping to organize the annual prisoner-of-war dinner at the RAF club in London.

Paddy and I quickly gravitated to that small knot of prisoners who headed up the serious or at least serial escape artists. It might seem strange that this was something of a minority pursuit, but it is hard to overemphasize just how much the average pilot had been through even to get there in one piece. Virtually every prisoner dreamed of escaping, and most were willing to help others get away, but the chances were so slim of making it home, and the dangers of being shot even before you were out of the camp perimeter were so great, that most decided to wait it out.

Every single pilot in the camp had been through some catastrophic shootdown, parachute experience, or crash landing in enemy territory, the odds being usually ten-to-one against survival of such an event. I remember a rear gunner in a Whitley that had been hit and forced to land at night in Germany. The crash landing was incredibly rough, and the gunner had crawled forward in the shattered fuselage to give the pilot an earful for such a duff landing. He discovered that he was utterly alone in the plane. His intercom had been shot away earlier, and so he had missed the order to bail out. The rest of the crew had done so, leaving him oblivious at his gun post as the plane drifted lazily down and crash-landed itself.

As a result of all this shared experience of crash and capture, most prisoners were understandably not overly keen on pushing the odds even farther by escaping in the heart of Germany. Then there were the slightly crazier ones like myself and Paddy, determined to escape from the start. Even some of the more adventurous characters tended to think better of it after they had escaped once and survived but been recaptured and put in a punishment cell, or "cooler." But for those of us who undertook a second escape attempt, there was usually another and another. Escaping is quite addictive, and like all addictive drugs, it is extremely dangerous.

Even for the most ardent escapologist, there was a period of adjustment to life as a prisoner and an exploration of the strange world of a prisoner-of-war camp that took some time. True to form, I started by looking for food. Cooking facilities were spartan, with dozens taking turns cooking on one little potbellied stove in each hut, but the real problem was finding something to put in the pot.

The early days after my arrival were before the advent of regular Red Cross parcels, which transformed our diet for the better. Before that, rations were very bleak—a virtual starvation diet of black bread and a scraping of jam plus the occasional potato. Later, we would rejoice in the contents of the Red Cross parcels, which varied with where they came from. The Canadian and

American ones tended to contain coffee, which was good for bartering. The British ones contained such delights as tinned bully beef, raisins, tinned salmon, and always-sought-after chocolate. While these were administered individually, we tended to pool them among our group of roommates and try to make them last all week. But those days were still ahead, and at first we had to make do with the barest of rations from our captors.

The atmosphere in the camp was a bizarre mix of prison and British boarding school. Before the war the RAF recruiting policy had favored bright young men from fairly upper-class backgrounds, many of whom had been boarders at the expensive but spartan private schools. Some of my more delicate British upper-crust officer colleagues obviously found the grim fare on offer very tough, while I on the other hand, brought up in the more hungry and precarious environs of Depression America, could munch my way through most things. Still, one particularly well brought up pilot once challenged my theory, saying that anyone who can live through several years of the cooking at a top-drawer British boarding school could handle anything the Third Reich threw at us, even if on occasions we felt like throwing it back.

Paddy and I were determined that our stay at this particular eatery was going to be a short one, and we would leave without paying the bill. We decided that before we could escape, we should be a bit fitter and a bit fatter to cope with the demands of our journey. We needed food, and lots of it. But there were only two items that could be classed even vaguely as food that were not immediately wolfed down by the hungry masses. One was a green, slimy, vile-smelling substance that pretended to be cheese. Most people could not even approach it, never mind put it in their mouths. I manfully munched my way through buckets of the stuff, with a sort of grim fascination and amusement at how each mouthful was worse than the previous one. But man cannot live on green liquid cheese alone, and I was soon on the lookout for something with a little more substance. I found it in the form of *Klippfisch*.

Clipfish, a delicacy virtually unknown even to my generation, was made of those parts of a fish that would be best kept to itself, pounded into a sort of paste. This had then been dried out some decades earlier, at the time of World War I, into something resembling wood shavings. Some enterprising Berlin bureaucrat had rediscovered it in his quest to find the cheapest possible way to feed the growing number of hungry Allied pilots who seemed to be dropping out of the sky, and so it reached Stalag Luft III in prodigious quantities. If it started out looking like sawdust, things got even worse. It had to be soaked in water for about a week, by which time it developed both the consistency and smell of wet dog hair, but it tasted much worse. The next step was to cut it into slabs, fry it, and then, in most cases, hurl it out the door in disgust. And that was its one great advantage.

I requisitioned a big basket and went from hut to hut collecting the stuff from people grateful to get it out of their sight. I collected basketsful, barrel-loads, and bushels of the stuff. Other prisoners used to huddle around just to watch me, in much the same way that passersby in Detroit had peered in at me as I ate stew for two weeks in an attempt to bulk up enough to end up here in an enemy prison camp. Because I had been through some fairly tough times, I honestly did not find conditions all that bad in the camp, and some of my more sensitive colleagues used to accuse me of being unreasonably cheerful just to annoy them. I agreed that the food was lousy, but pointed out that the prices were very reasonable.

Once we had padded ourselves out a bit with the Luft III diet, Paddy and I knew that the next step was to get fit enough to attempt an escape. The easiest way seemed to be to kindle a bit of interest in team sports, so about a dozen of us set off for an exercise area with a rigged-up ball. The only problem was, we seemed to be playing several different games at once. I was familiar with the wild world of American football. Paddy seemed to be playing Gaelic football. Some of the Brits were playing rugby, while the Aussies were playing their own version and I think there were a few soccer players, too.

As the game progressed the players and ball were passed, thumped, bounced, and tackled in every way possible, with heated disputes about whether a goal was a try or a try was a touchdown. Best of all, most of the players were in pretty bad shape from the lack of food and the experience of being shot down. Quite often, while making a charge down the wing, I would pass the ball to someone, only to discover that he had fainted from hunger and exertion and was already lying on the ground without suffering the indignity of being tackled. I thought it was a salutary tale of not eating everything that did not try to jump off your plate, but did not say so, in case they asked for their clipfish back.

Finally, we judged that we had eaten enough clipfish and returned to some sort of fitness. Our ponderings about what method of escape to try might have gone on longer but for an event that gave us both some inspiration. A month or two after our arrival, I stood with a crowd of others and watched as Douglas Bader, who, though he had no legs, had the heart of a lion, was carted off by the guards to Lamsdorf, then Colditz. Ever since being shot down and having to leave one of his artificial legs behind in the crashing plane as he parachuted, he had taken the same sort of attitude with the enemy as he had taken to the loss of his real legs. Nothing was going to beat him. I once talked to him about the Battle of Britain, and his analysis was as brisk and straightforward as his attitude to his physical state or the importance of resisting: "We couldn't have the bastards flying over England, attacking our own land and people, now could we?"

When the RAF was permitted to parachute him a new false leg just a couple of days after he crashed, he had already thanked the Luftwaffe by attempting to escape from the hospital. Once he got to Luft III, he had missed no opportunity to attempt escape and encourage others to do the same, all the while tormenting and outraging his captors at every opportunity.

Bader's personal war on the Third Reich soon gained two new recruits. Shortly after Paddy and I arrived, there was an attempted escape. The next morning the entire camp was standing outside on parade for hours while the guards took a roll call to figure out how many had got away. Bader decided on guerrilla warfare. That included waiting until the guards had almost finished counting, then telling about twenty of us in the dwindling uncounted rank to run over and mingle with those already counted, forcing the guards to start again. Paddy Barthropp and I, being the keen new boys, led the charge.

With a whoop we set off racing from the uncounted herd to the counted one, and others joined in. The guards at first reached for their guns, thinking it was a mass breakout, but quickly realized that our objective was to make them restart the count.

Anyone who has ever been cross at being distracted and "made to lose count" in the middle of a long sum can imagine the effect multiplied a thousandfold on irate guards in a prisoner-of-war camp trying to find out if anyone has escaped. Paddy and I were grabbed by a group of soldiers and marched off into the guards' part of the camp, and then out of the camp gates at gunpoint.

Normally, leaving the hated wire that caged us and suffocated all hopes of returning to the wider world would have been cause for jubilation, but in this case, as the camp receded behind us and we were shoved and prodded forward at rifle point by seething enemy soldiers, there seemed to be little cause for celebration. Our spirits sank further as we saw where they were taking us—off the path and deep into the murky pine forest that surrounded and isolated the camp.

We marched deeper and deeper into the forest, into the gloomy permanent twilight caused by the thick pine branches blocking out even the smallest rays of the sun. Each tread of a jackboot on a twig sounded like a gunshot as we marched forward with a row of guns trained on our backs. Then, in a clearing carpeted by pine needles, we were ordered to halt.

We were roughly pushed to our knees, side by side, as our unseen captors stood behind us, their guns pointed at the back of our heads. The ground felt soft and cold beneath my knees, and we could hear our own breathing. I had learned in the Gestapo cells in Paris just what it felt like to be waiting for my own execution, but this was different. Waiting for the end, I felt the ceaseless, powerless gnawing of time passing with almost glacial slowness yet seeming to hurtle forward as it ticked away the last few precious seconds. Waiting for a Gestapo cell door to swing open seemed easy in comparison to waiting for a bullet in the back of the head. Paddy was praying, and I was relying on his rather better relations with the Almighty, whom I did not correspond with much, to work for both of us. After a few minutes that stretched like an eternity, the soldiers told us to stand up. They herded us back to the camp.

We were almost glad to see the welcoming barbed wire as they marched us back in, at least for a few seconds, after which our attitudes returned quickly to business as usual when we were hauled before the camp commandant. Von Lindeiner tore us off a strip. In order to discourage such adventures in the future, particularly as we were relative newcomers whose bad habits he thought might not be as solidified as those of our mentor, Douglas Bader, he gave us each two weeks in solitary confinement in a punishment cell, or cooler, on iron rations.

The punishment cells were simple concrete affairs with nothing but a bare bed, sometimes not even that. The ones at Luft III then had a small, high window with bars, through which interesting noises of the world outside sometimes wafted in. After what I had been through, my first stint in a cooler seemed strangely tranquil for a day or two, but the twin evils of boredom and gnawing hunger soon made me long for a return to the camp. Gradually, over the coming years, I would get a lot of practice in ways to survive such spells in solitary, to make the bliss of silence last a little longer, and managed to pass the time by living more in my own head than in the grim reality of isolation and semi-starvation.

When we got out of the cooler we bumped into Bader, and Paddy expected at least a pat on the back. Instead, Bader asked us where we had been as he hadn't seen us around. Luckily, he smiled before both of us exploded. Bader appreciated anyone who was willing to bring the war to the enemy. He was an inspirational leader and really practiced what he preached.

Not everyone in the camp was as fond of Bader as we were. There were many who felt his constant goon-baiting risked losing us much more valuable privileges that helped us plan bigger, better escapes. Equally, there were those who just wanted a quiet life, people for whom any of us escapers were at best a necessary evil.

Eventually the authorities had enough of Bader's incessant warfare and effectively admitted defeat by hustling him off to the Lamsdorf camp then to the ultra-high-security Colditz castle. At first it looked like he would not go quietly. The commandant marched in about forty armed guards, and we and other Bader supporters lined up in our droves, ready to do anything he told us, even if it resulted in a bloodbath. Some of the cooler heads in the camp prevailed on him not to start anything when there were so many trigger-happy guards aiming at us, and he satisfied himself by knowing that he was demonstrating a valuable lesson to us as he left. Here was one man, without even the use of his legs, and his actions had diverted at least forty enemy soldiers from the war effort. We might not be able to fly anymore, but as he would put it, we could still bloody-well fight.

As he was marched out, he stopped momentarily in front of the lines of menacing guards with their guns at the ready. The enemy troops were baffled as he then walked along the line scrutinizing them—until they realized that in an ultimate act of defiance he was taking an inspection of them. We stood around the barbed wire at the gates, cheering him and saluting as he was taken away. That was it. Paddy and I decided it was time for us to escape.

8. This Drain Leads to Poland

The only problem with thinking up an escape scheme and acting on it was that such activities were not organized on the sporadic, freelance basis that has been the hallmark of so much of my life. Even in those early days, the camp had a well-organized escape committee. Four stony-faced escape experts would listen to and evaluate harebrained escape plans and either give the OK or forbid them. We waited nervously outside a hut for our audience with the committee, covered by a range of prisoners casually lolling at strategic points against nearby hut walls, operating an invisible lookout system to warn of any enemy presence in the vicinity.

Compared to selling this hard-nosed bunch on an escape plan, getting past the guards was thought to be relatively easy. Almost any scheme, even one that sounds brilliant at its invention, starts to sound faintly demented when you are pitching it to an audience that looks like it is trying you for your life. And in a way, that's exactly what the committee was doing. Escape from a German camp was, even at the best of times, a risky business. If you were not shot on the way out of the camp, there was a considerable chance that an enterprising German civilian or policeman would regard you as easier to capture if dead.

Then there were the dangers of traveling across foreign territory. The senior member of the committee that was listening to our escape plan, Lieutenant Commander Jimmy Buckley of the Fleet Air Arm, later made a brilliant escape himself, which ended in a tragedy we will come to later. He was a tough career navy man with an unblinkingly honest eye and a strong sense of humor. He was older than most of us, and his job was to ensure that some of us had the chance to live to be a little older than we were. Only one in about one hundred made it back to England, and even those prisoners who were recaptured undamaged often fell into the hands of the Gestapo. I did not fancy my chances with them a second time.

Paddy and I outlined our scheme. It is said most great ideas come to people when they are in the bath, a long tradition presumably started by Archimedes when he shouted "Eureka!" after having discovered that an object immersed in water displaces an amount of water equal to the object's weight. In Stalag Luft III we did not have the luxury of baths. We stayed relatively clean by dousing ourselves under a coldwater tap, and once a week the guards herded us into a *Vorlager* shower block for a welcome warm wash. And that is where the idea for the Great Shower Escape was born. Unlike Archimedes, we did not want to displace a volume of water—we just wanted to displace ourselves. The escape committee listened in silence, then asked a few questions and kicked us out while they discussed it. They called us back and, much to our astonishment, agreed. The escape was on.

The first step in our escape strategy was to become "ghosts." That was the camp code for someone who had managed to disappear within the camp and evade detection so that eventually the authorities decided he had really escaped and gave up looking. Admittedly, this type of escape had the rather obvious drawback that the ghost was still inside the camp, but the theory was that once you were a ghost, you could escape at a more leisurely pace, unencumbered by roll calls, head counts, bed counts, and curfews.

Our plan was to disappear into thin air during our weekly shower. We had noticed that inside the shower there was a small drain and trapdoor leading to a compartment where the water could be turned off at the mains. It would be a bit snug, but the two of us would squeeze into the compartment and hope that the guards did not notice two fewer coming out than went in. If we could go undetected until that night, we had just to avoid several hundred guards in their own part of the camp and cut our way through the *Vorlager* fence to become real escapees rather than ghosts. Whether we graduated from POW ghosts to real ones would depend on what the Germans did if they caught us.

Support from the escape committee meant a great deal more than mere permission to put our plan into action. We were kitted out with a compass, a hand-drawn map of the area that used the experiences of previous escapees, and—most important to us in those hungry days—a generous supply of "the Mixture." This was a sort of cereal concoction of oats, chocolate, and sometimes dried fruit, all of which were considerably more valuable than gold dust to us prisoners. Much of it came from other prisoners

pooling their gifts from home or making donations from bartering one food source for another. It was used as an easily portable
high-energy food for those on sanctioned escapes. Some of my
more cynical brethren who knew of my ever-hungry appetite
even suggested that getting my hands on a prodigious amount of
the Mixture was my primary motive for risking life and limb on
an escape.

On the appointed day, we marched into the showers as usual,
and in the commotion of steam and everyone removing their uniforms, Paddy and I quickly dived into our soggy hiding place under the shower grating, clutching our clothes, and waited. All
would now depend on the ability of the others to distract the
goons long enough for them to miscount or not count at all as the
sweet-smelling squad was returned to the compound. After that
there would be further roll calls, but the bigger gatherings were
easier to fix.

As we hid in our soggy roost, the rest of our colleagues took
their time with their weekly shower, which we experienced
second-hand until one of them had an argument with a grumpy
guard. Our colleagues knew that one of the best ways to distract a
guard was to irritate the hell out of him, and unfortunately they
decided to start the process rather early, when they were in mid-
shower. Normally they got two blasts of hot water—one to soap
up and one to rinse off. One of the prisoners opened up an interesting conversation about Adolf Hitler's parentage with a guard.
Starting off by being merely rude, he progressed to calling Hitler
so many choice names that the guard did exactly what they wanted
and lost his temper. To punish them for bad-mouthing the Führer,
the goon withheld the second blast of hot water and our colleagues
were herded out, still covered in soap, back to the compound.

At this stage, everything depended on our colleagues' ability to fix the head count that ensured the same number of prisoners returned, soapy or otherwise. When it came to the bigger parade-ground count, or *Appell*, there were all sorts of stunts that could be pulled. Men would wait until they had been counted once, then duck down and crawl to the end of the row so they would be counted again, covering for someone who was hiding or had already got out and needed time before the alarm was raised. One amazingly effective tactic was to occasionally line up one of the sections of men in four rows instead of five, with the goons simply counting the neat front rows and multiplying by five as always. This only worked if there were a neatly divisible number of escapees and gave the prisoners as many head-count headaches as the guards.

Another brilliant ruse at another camp was the creation of a papier-mâché life-size dummy known as Albert RN. He was very realistic, dressed in an old Fleet Air Arm jacket with his elbows out and his hands shoved in his pockets, designed so he could be held up between two real prisoners who would link arms with the dummy to keep him upright and then choose a sleepy place at the back of the parade where a German head counter in a hurry was not likely to notice that the stony-faced Albert never seemed to blink.

But these were all scams for bigger parades. Our comrades were being marched back from the *Vorlager* to the compound by their grumpy guard. But the sentry on the compound wire was neither grumpy, sleepy, nor dopey, nor any of the other Seven Dwarfs. Like many of the camp's eagle-eyed ferrets, he was a worthy adversary, on the lookout for any manner of wickedness which we might try. The best we could hope for was another distraction that would make him lose count, or that a bored guard would not bother to count in the first place. Instead, the prisoners were counted meticulously. Their efforts at distracting or enraging were met by prods from a rifle to keep quiet. The sentry was puzzled and counted again. Then again.

Paddy and I waited in our cramped, soggy roost, every second seeming like an eternity. Then the game was up. The steamy shower air was filled with the noise of running jackboots. Whistles blew, sirens blared, and guard dogs barked themselves into a frenzy.

A squad of guards with guns at the ready burst into the shower room but missed us at first. Then we heard the dogs arriving, sniffing and snarling, and we knew it was only a matter of time. Paddy and I looked at each other. We could shred the map to stop the searchers finding out what we knew, but our pockets were crammed with the Mixture. With minutes to go before we were caught, we adjusted our plans. Escape would have to wait. The best we could manage was not to let the Mixture fall into enemy hands.

As more and more goons, ferrets, and growling Alsatians descended on the shower block, I and Paddy were cramming mouthful after mouthful of the Mixture into our gullets. Then it was all over. The trapdoor was flung open and we found ourselves looking up at a ring of rifles pointing at us and snapping Alsatians straining at their leashes. We emerged soggy, with our hands up and our faces covered in chocolate, which I think they took to be some kind of ingenious camouflage. I dropped the last of the Mixture for one of the Alsatians, hoping that he might remember the good deed when we met again on some future escape attempt.

From there it was a short, sharp march to the solitary punish-

ment cells of the cooler. In the coming years I was to become a
regular resident in cooler cells, in this camp as well as others in
Poland and Lithuania. Some kind souls have even suggested that
I was one of the half-dozen real-life role models for the Steve
McQueen made-up character of Hilts the Cooler King in the
film *The Great Escape*, but if I was, no one told me. It is true that
at this stage in the war there were not too many American pilots
in the camp, and fewer still that ended up in the cooler on a regular basis, but the reality was that no Americans got away in the
Great Escape. By then I was in a different compound, not to
mention being locked up in the cooler. Anyway, my skills at riding
motorcycles over barbed-wire barricades might have left something to be desired.

As further punishment for our shower-escape attempt, Paddy
and I were added to a list of about ninety other incorrigible escape artists chosen to be purged to an army-run camp in Schubin,
Poland—Oflag XXIB, where conditions would be harsher and we
would not be able to corrupt the minds of our more docile colleagues. So without much ado, Paddy and I joined Jimmy Buckley
and what seemed like half the most accomplished escapologists
from the camp as we were loaded into train carriages and trundled in the general direction of the Eastern Front.

Our transports read like a who's who of recidivist escapees,
many of whom later became the nucleus of the Great Escape
team. Alongside Lieutenant Commander Buckley and fellow
navy flier Peter "Hornblower" Fanshawe were senior British officer Wings Day, who had asked to be moved with us, Major John
Dodge, known as the Dodger, and Jimmy James. Then there was
escape intelligence officer Aidan Crawley, who went on to become a member of Parliament. Aidan had shared our salubrious

surroundings at Luft III, so Paddy and I felt that we were in very good company, or very bad company, if you happened to be a ferret.

It must have been around October 1942 when we rolled through the bleak landscape of Poland on our way to a new home. It is worth giving an idea of the reality for most prisoners of war facing a new camp. We were not daft enough to think that just because we got out from behind the barbed wire we would get home, but we knew it was our duty to tie up as many enemy troops and resources as possible to divert them from the war effort, and there was always the thought that, just like winning the lottery, a few people occasionally did get home.

There cannot have been a single POW, or "kriegie" as we called ourselves, short for the rather more unwieldy *Kriegsgefangener*, meaning prisoner of war, who did not think about escaping. Yet out of the total pool of all prisoners, maybe only a third in an average camp would have been actively involved in escape-related activities. Most of the other two-thirds would assist if possible behind the scenes and undergo some hardships to help, while a small rump simply waited the war out and took the Germans at their word when they announced to each of us, on arrival, "For you the war is over."

The majority of nonescapees concentrated on filling their time with education, sport, and reading, with the biggest enemies being hunger, cold, and the crashing boredom that comes from being a prisoner with no release date other than the end of the war. For some, survival after a terrible flame-filled air crash, often in the case of bombers with the loss of other crew members, had so scarred them that keeping their heads down and surviving the war was about all they could manage.

But the third of the population which comprised the pro-escapers and their helpers was more than enough to keep our jailers fully occupied. Even of that number, maybe only 5 percent were committed to getting outside the wire themselves at all costs, but none of us would have done so without the help of the remaining 25 percent that was involved in keeping an eye on the guards over long, dull shifts as "stooges" or helping prepare anything from documents to clothes and maps to digging implements. Even among that last 5 percent of die-hard escapers, one attempt was usually enough for most sensible people, and on its failure, or its success but their recapture, some decided to concentrate on supporting activities in the future rather than tempting fate. But for the last one or two percent, escaping became a way of life.

For nearly every one of us crammed in those third-class carriages on the way to Schubin, escape was an almost all-consuming addiction, a full-time job. While others worked on concerts or education, we ate, slept, and breathed schemes for escape, from the ingenious to the insane. Of the whole prisoner population, less than one percent ever got to the other side of the wire, and less than one percent of that number made their escape and reached all the way to England. But we all dreamed that we might be the one to accomplish the Home Run, that rarest of achievements.

Even before we arrived in Poland, the effect of having so many career escapologists together in a few train shipments was starting to be felt. The Dodger was fearless almost to the point of comedy. Nothing was going to stop this remarkably brave man escaping, short of a bullet. Later in the war he even survived

Sachsenhausen concentration camp, but at this stage of the conflict he was just another of our small group of serial escapees.

American-born John Dodge was old enough to be the father of most of the other prisoners. Just five days after the start of the 1914–18 war, and three years before the United States got involved, Dodge sailed for Britain to join the fight. He emerged from the carnage of the Western Front as a colonel with the Congressional Medal of Honor, still only twenty-five. Like most experienced soldiers, he was called back into service at the outbreak of World War II. In the chaos that followed Britain's defeat in France and the Dunkirk evacuation, Dodge was captured but managed to escape, and the second time he was caught happened to be by the Luftwaffe, a twist of fate that saw him spend the rest of his war as a rare soldier among fliers. He was tall, remarkably good-natured, and very well liked, yet despite his calmness and the fact that in his midforties he was a lot more mature than some of us, it was often the Dodger who led the charge on escape attempts.

On the day of his transport, as the elderly locomotive wheezed its way toward the new Polish camp at Schubin, Johnny Dodge got permission to use the lavatory as the train paused at some signals. Modestly leaning over the door, he set to work levering off a few planks with a hidden implement in order to enlarge the lavatory window. When the noise of the flushing toilet had subsided he was off and running. Unfortunately, he was in the middle of a vast open field through which the railway line sliced, with not so much as a lettuce leaf to hide behind. He was spotted in a matter of seconds. Prisoners who saw him making his mad dash cheered him on, but guards started to open fire. Still nowhere near any cover, he knew the game was up and turned, hands up and smiling, as if he had been struck out in a baseball game rather than being two seconds from death. Afterward he played it down in his amiable way, telling friends that the guards were not aiming quite accurately. As he was marched back to the train, to be dealt with at our destination, he shrugged at one of his captors and said, "No harm in trying!"

The trains rolled on for thirty-six hours, as we squirmed in our third-class wooden seats, not allowed to move, stand, or even lie down on the floor. Occasionally the train would wheeze into some quiet station and we would study the civilians, getting tips on how to dress to blend in on future escapes. At this stage the locals were still bustling about with no sign that they expected to lose the war. The Russian Front had reached what would later prove its high-water mark for Germany, and it would soon be downhill all the way. But for now soldiers on leave from the *Ostfront* still proudly wore the red insignia from the Russian campaigns, and the civilians stared at us with a mixture of curiosity and contempt.

After two days of travel in the cramped carriages, with rather more attentive guards, we arrived at a sleepy station called Altburgund and were marched down the deserted main street of a village, eventually reaching the gates of Oflag XXIB, the Schubin camp. It was situated about 150 miles west of Warsaw, the Polish capital. The invaders had declared it part of a new German province called Warthegau, which the Poles did their best to ignore.

A ragged line of prisoners and their Luftwaffe escort were kept waiting outside the gates like unwelcome door-to-door salesmen. One of our senior guards eventually argued his way in, and we waited. Feldwebel Hermann Glemnitz, one of the senior ferrets who had accompanied us from Stalag Luft III, left the compound looking irritated, while the rest of our Luftwaffe guards had still not even been allowed inside the camp. It looked like relations between the army and the air force in the Reich were not all that rosy. But Glemnitz was not a man to shirk his duty. As the senior German NCO at Luft III he was the leader of the attempts to keep us in. He was generally well respected, even if his name, when spoken by any of us prisoners, was always preceded by the epithet "that bastard." This was partly because he was depressingly smart at sniffing out tunnels, partly because he treated us with some respect, and partly because he had been an experienced pilot himself in the Great War, which seemed to give him a little understanding of how we felt.

As Glemnitz stomped out of the compound it was obvious he had been given short shrift by our new warder. After months of trying to stop us leaking out of Luft III, Glemnitz was obviously having a little difficulty letting go. When the army had said a frosty farewell after the handover at the gates, he had insisted on going inside to attempt to tell the new army management about the wicked ways and wiles of the new arrivals. The duty officer in the camp, a pompous and thoroughly nasty fascist Germano-Czech we called Simms, had taken great umbrage at a mere fly-boy such as Glemnitz daring to tell the army how to run their prison and had virtually booted him off the premises, sending him on his way back to Luft III with a Wehrmacht flea in his ear.

So angry was Glemnitz at this treatment that as he was saying farewell to some of us, he confided the whole sorry exchange between himself and our new masters, complimenting us by saying that if he were a gambling man, he would be laying bets on a mass breakout within a month. It would serve the army blockheads right for not listening to him. He did everything but wish us luck, and we assured him that we would do our best to make his dreams come true. Our Luftwaffe guards soon became small smudges of blue-gray uniforms hurrying back to the railway station to return to Luft III before the prisoners still there decided to start their own spree. We were handed over to some nervous-looking German soldiers. They herded us into the camp and left us to our own devices.

9. New Country, New Tunnel

The grim camp at Schubin, Poland—an *Offizierlager*, or Oflag 21B—was built around the grounds of a former girls' school, centered on a big building called the White House, with a host of smaller ones dotted around. To these had been added the ubiquitous barracks to house the captives, though unlike many of the other camps, they were made of brick. There were twelve barracks, six on each side of the school's former playing fields. These huts were little more than huge shells, lacking even ceilings, just bare rafters through which the Polish wind whistled day and night.

Because of its previous function the camp looked strangely attractive, with trees and gardens dotted about a few old, scenic buildings, including the big white house and a chapel, but the reality was very different. Despite the landscaping, the surrounding rings of barbed wire and guard posts were very real.

Inside the barracks there were two-tier bunk beds and a table and benches for every twelve prisoners. This resulted in one giant room, partitioned by lockers, with a central aisle. A wall of conversation and cross talk between prisoners along the length of our communal barn made it one of the loudest prison camps in the history of war. Despite the cacophony, grim conditions, and lack of privacy, morale at the time of our arrival was remarkably high.

The place was run by Wehrmacht units, rather than the devil-we-knew Luftwaffe, and although conditions were spectacularly grim, we felt as if we had arrived in an escapers' paradise. These guards, some elderly, some invalided out of units on the Eastern Front, and others simply trying to avoid any front whatsoever, had none of the Luftwaffe's hard-earned expertise in stopping our escapes.

We were delighted to see that there were about two hundred RAF and British army prisoners already installed, the remnants of an equally grim camp at Warburg, and for a while the area buzzed with reunions between men who had last seen each other over a pint of beer in a sleepy English pub some years and a few lifetimes earlier.

Then it was down to business. Once we had studied the camp as a place to live, we took a long, close look at it as a place to leave. Paddy Barthropp commented that the designer must have had a drop of British blood, since some of the buildings were conveniently close to the prison wire, some of the huts only about seventy feet from the outer perimeter, making tunnels shorter. The basic fact was that the camp had not been built as a prison, and it is always harder to guard a place that was not specifically designed to keep people in. The layout of the buildings created several blind spots where the goons in the watchtowers could not peer, while clumps of trees and some steep slopes gave us more chances to hide.

Best of all, we were in Poland, and that meant that if we got out and managed to knock on a door, we were just as likely to be helped as not. This was in stark comparison to Luft III in the heart of Germany, where every Nazi Boy Scout was on the lookout for escaped fliers and every blond, apple-cheeked lass would sooner stick a *Jugenddolch* in your ribs than help you. To discourage such collaboration the occupiers had the simple remedy of shooting anyone, including the family of those who helped escaped prisoners, no matter how briefly or ineffectually. Despite this threat, thousands of ordinary Polish people risked their lives to help escapees.

On arrival at Schubin, I found myself in an utterly alien position—invited to become one of the hard-faced veterans on the escape committee, whose job was to stress-test the mad escape ideas of people like me and decide which should be allowed and supported. Luckily, Paddy was soon on the committee, too, and our friend Aidan Crawley was in charge of security, so we could all be astonished at the same time.

By this stage I was really feeling the one profound truth about our escape activities—very few of us ever got out, and only a microscopic percentage of those succeeded in getting back to England. During the course of the war only about thirty Allied pilots made Home Runs to Britain. The best most of us could hope for was to tie up as many enemy troops as possible in searching for and recapturing the escapees. Still, even if the odds on getting home were not ones any bookmaker would care for, at least our escapes added to the general sense of unease among the population, with the thought that even in the heart of the Third Reich, there might be a scruffy, hungry American lurking behind every hedge.

On the escape committee, the idea that I should tell other people what to do or what not to do never came very naturally to me. I think people tend to do their best work when they are working together following their own instincts. But in a war, sometimes we do not always have the luxury of walking our own path. Effectively, by joining up I had recognized this, however instinctively or on whatever emotional basis. I agreed to serve on the escape committee though secretly I planned to escape as soon as possible, and be too far away to have to make tough decisions about who should stay and who should go.

Crouching down in the compound, I examined a handful of the rich Polish earth. It was well drained, allowing more freedom to tunnel, though requiring decent shoring to avoid collapses in tunnel walls. I took a trip into one of the vast huts, already filling up with prisoners grabbing bunks and a few trying to give themselves some feeble privacy by hanging up their spare clothes like curtains beside their bed.

One bunk was as good as the next, so a group of us, including myself, Paddy, Aidan Crawley, and a French Canadian named Eddy Asselin, picked a corner of the barnlike Hut 6, barricaded off by a few lockers, and set up shop. The first thing I looked at was the construction of the beds. The bed boards were perfect, not perhaps for sleeping on, but for use as sturdy tunnel supports. At the end of each hut was a bare concrete wash area, and some distance away, in a nasty black shed, were the latrines, a grim row of thirty-six holes in a wooden bench, located above a reeking pit.

Bill and his sister Adele prepare for a quick getaway, Dallas 1925.

Bill's childhood friend George Coe, pictured in 1926, rode with Billy the Kid. *(Courtesy of Haley Library)*

Bill got a day off from school to watch Lindbergh's parade after the first transatlantic flight in 1927.

Early Canadian training in 1940 was mostly on lumbering Fairey Battle bombers.

Bill in the cockpit of a Battle while training in 1940.

The *Georgic* brought Bill to England in early 1941. It was bombed at Suez later that year. *(Courtesy of George R. Frame)*

A formal portrait that Bill sent home to his family in 1941.

Bill flew with legendary "Cowboy" Blatchford who was killed in action in 1943.

Fellow U.S. pilot John Gillespie Magee wrote the poem "High Flight" shortly before his death.

Commanding Officer Stan Turner of 411 Squadron would light his pipe in the cockpit after a successful engagement. *(Courtesy of 411 Squadron)*

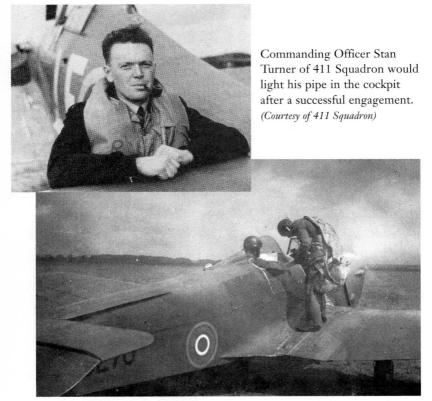

The duel-control Magister that Bill flew and from which "Buck" McNair jumped. *(Courtesy of 411 Squadron)*

Buck McNair spins Bill another tall tale. He went on to become one of Canada's fighter aces.
(Courtesy of the Public Archives of Canada)

Waiting to scramble outside the dispersal hut in Digby, 1941. Bill is at the right, pen in hand.

Don Blakeslee, later a USAF fighter ace, Bill, and Gordie Chamberlain, who was killed in action 1941.

Bill gets an unexpected handshake from Canadian Prime Minister Mackenzie King in 1941.

Bill took part in the ill-fated Channel Dash attack on the battleship *Scharnhorst* in early 1942. *(Courtesy of John Asmussen)*

Victor Beamish was the fist to spot the *Scharnhorst*. He was killed in action in March 1942.

Bill's friend and mentor Wilfred Duncan Smith, father of U.K. politician Iain Duncan Smith. *(Courtesy of Richard Smith)*

Bill in flight in his beloved Spitfire DBF in late 1941.

The cover of Bill's prisoner-of-war file from Stalag Luft III.

Marthe Boulanger saved Bill and later survived Ravensbruck concentration camp.

A mug shot of a battered Bill, shortly after his time as a guest of the Gestapo in Paris.

Bill stands on the spot where he crash-landed in March 1941, Vieille Eglise, France.

The guard post and exercise circuit in Stalag Luft III. *(Courtesy of USAFA)*

Bill's friend Paddy *(right)* pictured soon after his capture with the pilot who downed him *(second from the left)*.

One of the dummies used to cover for escaped prisoners during parade head counts. *(Courtesy of RAF Escaping Society)*

The entrance to Schubin camp in Poland, where leading escape artists were sent in 1941.

John Dodge, "Hetty" Hyde, and "Wings" Day were senior escapologists at Schubin.

Eddy Asselin was Bill's partner in the Schubin tunnel escape. The tunnel was called Asselin. *(Courtesy of Nicole Asselin)*

John "The Dodger" Dodge is captured while attempting to escape from the train on the way to Schubin.

Friends killed on the Great Escape *(from left to right)*: Ian Cross, Danny Krol, Tom Kirby-Green, and Roger Bushell.

Schubin comrades Jørgen Thalbitzer and Jimmy Buckley who were killed on the tunnel escape.

George Grimson escaped Hydekrug but stayed to help others. He went missing and was presumed to have been shot.

The wire between compounds, which Bill had to vault in daylight.
(Courtesy of McDermott Library, U.S. Air Force Academy)

Stalag Luft III Commandant Von Lindeiner, with Bill peeking over his right shoulder. *(Courtesy of the Imperial War Museum)*

Jimmy "Dixie" Deans, elected leader of the NCO prisoners at Hydekrug. *(Courtesy of Cal Younger)*

Fellow Escape Committee member Joe Kayll.

Bill's friend "Legless," legend Douglas Bader, was briefly incarcerated in Stalag Luft III. *(Courtesy of Hulton Getty)*

Specially trained guards ("ferets") hunting for tunnels at Luft III. *(Courtesy of USAFA)*

No man's land between the barbed wire of compounds that Bill crossed three times. *(Courtesy of USAFA)*

The Sagan "death march" in early 1945 as the Third Reich crumbled. *(Courtesy of USAFA)*

The three POWs in 1942 are still friends today: *(standing)* Bill Stapleton, Bill Ash, *(front center)* Paddy Barthropp.

Bill *(right)* with friend and fellow escapee Paddy Barthropp at a recent reunion.

Before we could do any further inspection of our no-star accommodation, the German army decided it was time for them to take a look at their new inmates, and they called an Appell.

The event was a near riot. We met the man who had ruffled Glemnitz, Captain Simms, a caricature of Prussian pomposity with a vicious streak that he took out on both his own subordinates and any prisoner who caught his eye. At that first Appell, Simms was appalled that we were not turned out like new recruits on a parade ground. He screamed and shouted at us and at the guards, who screamed and shouted at us again. Much to their surprise we screamed and shouted back. Over the following months Wings Day, as senior British officer, attempted to work with the pompous Simms and his laconic camp commandant. It was not love at first sight. Once Wings had introduced himself as the senior officer and stood at ease, the commandant had barked at him to stand at attention, despite his being the same rank as Wings and the two being therefore on an equal footing in accordance with both military custom and the Geneva Convention. He didn't care what rank Wings held, he was just another British prisoner, and he was not to speak unless ordered to do so.

If he had known Wings a bit better, the commandant would have realized that he just made a very big mistake. Wings simply told him not to shout at an officer of equal rank, saluted, turned on his heel, and left. From then on the two had their own private war, which Wings was determined to win. Addressing a group of us a short time later, he declared his intention to get men out of the camp not just in ones or twos but in large numbers. He would have done it anyway, but he told us that the camp commandant had been "damnably rude" and refused even basic requests on food, parcels, sanitation, and mail. So, in return, Wings was going to ensure that as well as giving the Third Reich a headache catching us, his secondary aim would be to chop the commandant down like a tree.

Wings Day, a tall, angular man, had a special place in escape history. While he was in effective charge at Stalag Luft III, given free rein by his superior, Group Captain Herbert Massey, Wings had taken the disparate freelance efforts of a bunch of quirky runaways and tunnelers and turned them into a coordinated escape force. As one wag put it during one of our frequent debates about politics and the future of Britain after the war, Wings Day had already nationalized tunneling.

Wings, though very likeable and extremely popular with the men, was also a bit of an old-school officer, hence his indignation at his treatment by the commandant. He expected his own people to behave with a certain amount of military discipline, which was often lacking among us civilian-volunteer types as opposed to the career military men with whom we rubbed shoulders. One day, some time before Christmas 1942 at Schubin, Wings gave a somewhat routine telling-off to a group of NCO orderlies who had been transferred to the camp with us, including one called Wareing. Wings did not think that just being locked up was a good enough reason for them not to apply themselves to the job of orderly with the same spit-and-polish zeal expected of them in a barracks at home. Even Wings had to see the funny side when Wareing, on a trip with other orderlies to get coal supplies from the local village, managed to slip away, steal a bicycle, and pedal all the way to Danzig, where he hopped a ship bound for Halmstad, Sweden. Ironically, his ticket to freedom was a coal boat, and he was back in London in time to celebrate Christmas 1942, the first successful Home Run from Schubin. He was awarded the Distinguished Service Medal.

For the rest of us, it was business as usual until we could follow in his footsteps. One excellent reason for cranking up our escape activity was to get away from the appalling conditions, which made Luft III look relatively like a five-star hotel. We were assailed by a novel version of the biblical plagues, our main ones being Famine, Pestilence, and Ice.

Hunger was a constant presence in our lives. A normal day's ration would consist of a thin slice of black Reich bread for breakfast, with margarine, sometimes jam, and a cup of boiled confetti pretending to be tea. Lunch would be a few sad leaves of cabbage boiled to oblivion and called soup, with an evening meal of either another slice of the grim bread and maybe a few small potatoes. Gradually we dwindled to a fraction of our former weight.

Those of us who made frequent visits to the cooler for two or four weeks of solitary punishment were treated to a bread-and-water diet for the duration, making the incorrigible escape artists even thinner. If this kept up, I once confided to Paddy, we might be able to slip between the strands of barbed wire or perhaps disappear altogether by turning sideways. In another of our endless food conversations, shortly after emerging from another stretch in the cooler, I suggested a great plan that had hatched as I lay on the floor in solitary. Paddy leaned in eagerly to hear the details. My plan was to lure some of the more vicious guard dogs into Hut 6, where we could do away with them, eat them in a feast, and then dress up in their skins as very large guard dogs and wander out the front gate, stopping for a pee on the commandant's trouser leg. Paddy was up for it, but the dogs must have got suspicious and stayed away from our hut for a few days.

Our constant enemies of Famine, Pestilence, and Ice were ever present, and the Polish midwinter could certainly get pretty bleak. The pestilence mainly surfaced in the form of jaundice, which spread rapidly in our poor living conditions, reinforced by the inadequate diet. At one point almost half the camp was down with it. An even more common pestilence came in the form of lice and bedbugs, which infested every corner of the barracks, from the concrete floors to the rafters where the ceiling should have been. The lice were huge brutes with a red V on their heads, and we spent a good deal of time every day finding them and crushing them with a satisfying pop against a thumbnail. A combination of tunnel dirt, sewage, and the ubiquitous lice made us less than the most fragrant of guests, but the guards still insisted on hanging on to us.

As for ice, bitter arctic winds whistled in from the Baltic. As winter of 1942 arrived, snow fell in vast drifts, and temperatures plummeted to minus fifteen and below. The football pitch now doubled as an ice skating rink. This had an added advantage. The Germans had underground microphones to listen for tunneling activity, but the noise of fifty ice skaters on rickety homemade skates drowned out even the noisiest burrowing.

Wings Day continued to demand better conditions. Our thin uniforms failed to keep out the cold, and we huddled around the brick stoves, half numb and unable to think straight with the mixture of chill and hunger. The commandant was as unhelpful as ever, though he finally cracked and rustled up some moth-eaten greatcoats taken off the Polish cavalry when they surrendered.

His one other gift was a huge supply of badly made French

wooden clogs, which were no use for keeping our feet warm and which were clearly designed to stop us escaping, or even walking more than a few yards at a time. As I studied one in the chill of the barracks one evening, I thought back to the foolish young man on the run in France who had chosen a pair of clogs for his quick getaway. How long ago was that? Nine months? Or maybe a lifetime? Studying the clogs, I and my colleagues had a brainstorm. They might not be much good to walk in, but they could still keep our feet warm. I opened the brick oven door and threw them in.

The only other way to keep out the cold was to find more food, and once again we were back to the famine part of our Famine-Pestilence-Ice cycle. On good days we were able to share the contents of a Red Cross parcel, though we tried to save as much of these as possible for "escape food."

At Schubin, our basic escape concoction of the Mixture evolved into two entirely new subspecies. These were called Fudge and Goo. Fudge was built around cocoa, while Goo's main ingredient was dried cereal with vitamins. Other key ingredients from our Red Cross parcels that ended up in our escape concoctions included milk powder, sugar, and dried fruit. Both versions had the consistency of fudge or caramel, depending on the individual batch, since producing the stuff was not an exact science. Many of the veterans from Stalag Luft III called all such mixes dog food, which baffled some of our newer arrivals, since it tasted so much better than anything else we got to eat.

The origins of the term "dog food" came from a time at the Sagan camp when some overzealous cooks made such a prodigious batch of the stuff that supply of the mixture temporarily outstripped demand for escaping. To avoid the surplus falling into enemy hands, those responsible dug a hole under Hut 62 and hid it for future use. That night the hungry inhabitants of the hut could do nothing but listen as a guard dog on patrol sniffed out their hidden treasure, dug it out, and started wolfing in down with loud slurping noises and grunts of delight. From then on it was dog food.

The basic recipes at Schubin were devised by David Lubbock, a Fleet Air Arm officer who had been a dietician in a previous life, and his basic aim was to make the best use of the food from the Red Cross parcels without leaving escapees with the headaches or nausea that came from eating relatively huge quantities of sugar and fat after months of our virtual starvation diet. By the end of the war, like old wine connoisseurs, some of us used to debate the relative merits of the escape mixtures from half a dozen camps. In comparison to our usual fare, they were all like nectar.

The fact that there was a dietician in the camp is a good clue to one of our greatest strengths. Many if not most of us had joined up after some other experiences in life, and if you looked hard enough, there was every possible trade, skill, and profession represented in the camp, from engineers to medics and artists to accountants. In the world of an escapee, every single one of them had a skill that could make the difference between discovery and a Home Run. They were all forgers, scroungers, tunnelers, surveyors, and tailors in waiting. This camp would be the first to function as a pure escape factory, building on what the inmates had learned from Luft III, Barth, and Dulag Luft. In turn, the hard lessons we learned at Schubin were later put to good use by those involved in the Great Escape, including many of my Schubin accomplices.

We all made sure we teamed up with the prisoners from

Warburg—including some very experienced escape artists—and we also welcomed the increasing number of my fellow Americans who were being shot from the skies in bomber crews on a regular basis. The Prussians might let their interservice rivalries surface, but for us the only enemy was whatever kept us on the inside of the wire. The senior officer among the Warburg veterans was "Hetty" Hyde, who was rarely seen without a pipe clenched between his determined jaws. He knew Wings from their mutual time at Dulag Luft, and soon an unholy alliance was born, with both elements contributing all their escaping experience.

The army, as you might expect, was keen on team-effort assaults on the outside world, and our first joint effort was based on a brilliant escape they had managed at Warburg. Not long after our arrival two teams were put in training for Operation Forlorn Hope. The groups hid at the ready after lights-out, one inside the barracks, the other huddled in a blind spot between the machine-gun posts. The boundary lights shone brightly around the perimeter fence as always. Then there was a loud bang and the lights went out. Our enterprising colleagues had fused the electricity generator, and seconds later both teams were charging for the wire, neck and neck, like some competition at a military show. They were carrying scaling ladders like some medieval horde besieging a castle. Both teams got their ladders up against the wire. Then, with another muffled bang, the lights came back on.

My friend Aidan Crawley groaned. As the man in charge of intelligence for escapes, a job at which he generally excelled, he knew what this meant. The Germans had an emergency secondary lighting system that we had failed to spot. Suddenly, the wacky race to the wire was run in reverse. Amazingly, the would-be escapees made it back to safety, mostly unscathed. The guards did not know this, and on discovering the ladders were convinced that some of us had got away. There followed a long, cold night in which we were turned out of our barracks and counted and recounted. As a small crumb of comfort for our failure, we all tried to make the counting as difficult as possible. Even those who did not normally share our passion for goon-baiting joined in, and one missing prisoner was only discovered after some hours perched in a pew in the camp chapel, apparently having a quiet word with the Almighty.

But if a mass escape had failed, there were a thousand smaller schemes afoot in those first weeks and months. Our initial approach to escaping from Schubin was less than subtle. As our eyes roved the camp we saw dozens of potential ways out—under the wire in tunnels, over the wire by vaulting or climbing, through the wire with cutters, or through our main gate by hiding or in disguise as anything from a guard to a Red Cross inspector. We went off like a wayward bunch of schoolkids who find themselves let loose in a chocolate factory.

What our army guards lacked in experience, a few of them made up for in thuggishness, in stark contrast to the majority of Luftwaffe guards at Luft III, as I discovered on one of my first escape attempts that winter.

I had decided to diversify from my usual tunneling and wire-cutting habits to try strolling out instead. A work detail of nonofficers and Russian prisoners was being herded out to some unknown destination for the day. Sliding alongside them, my uniform hidden under a long coat, I waited until the guards were distracted and then slipped into the column. I marched along with my head down until I got to our destination—a local railway station. There we were detailed to unload a goods train while several bored guards had their guns trained on us, just in case we got any ideas. When the guards were looking the other way, I managed to roll myself under the train. Looking up at the sooty, oil-smeared wheels, I prayed that the train would not move and rolled as quickly as I could to the other side of the line. I ended up crouching on the far side of the train while the bustle of the loading continued a few feet away on the platform.

I looked into the distance. There was about half a mile of desolate open ground and then a line of trees marking the edge of a wood. I looked back toward the guards—that was a great deal of open terrain in which even a bad shot could pick off a fleeing prisoner. But the woods were calling me. It was too tempting, and I set off like a greyhound at a racetrack.

Seconds later a shout went up, and what I hoped were warning shots whistled over my head. The German officer surveyed the distance I would have to run to escape, evidently with some amusement, and ordered several soldiers with bicycles to cycle around either side of me. There are few experiences more depressing than racing as fast as you can for an unattainable target while your enemies overtake you in a leisurely manner and are waiting for you, guns at the ready, just in front of your objective.

They expected me to give up meekly, and indeed, if I had been smarter, I would have, but as I had got that far, I decided I might as well really go for it. I attempted to charge through them as if I were an American fullback, determined to score the winning touchdown. I was brought down by a rifle butt in the face and got a very severe beating for refusing to halt.

I was thrown, battered and bruised, into the Schubin cooler. Like many things at the camp it was not in the most logical place, being outside of the inner wire in which we usually lived. The guards had been so busy battering me that they had not searched me very well, and so I unpeeled the piece of adhesive tape I had patched on my leg and took out a very tiny file that I had hidden in it. I started to work on one of the three thick iron bars that covered the small window.

Part of my punishment was a bread-and-water diet, and the bread was Reich bread, which was to bread what Reich tea was to tea—one step down from baked sawdust. Every time I was left alone, I would saw for hours on end with my tiny file. When I took a break for my Reich bread, I at last discovered a good use for the stuff. If chewed enough and mixed with powder from my cell walls, it blended in brilliantly with the cement that held my cell bars in place. Each day I was able to cover up my handiwork with Reich bread putty and, when the coast was clear, continue with my sawing.

After a week, I was through the bottom cut on one of the bars and about to start on the next. But by this time the goons were starting to learn how to keep us on the hop, and for no apparent reason they changed my cell. I started on the bars in the new one. A few days later a guard noticed my handiwork when cleaning out my old cell. I was searched, and my file, by then pretty blunt anyway, was confiscated. I was sentenced to another two weeks in solitary, without the aid of escape equipment.

But the one thing they could not confiscate was my mind. There was hardly a night when my dreams did not take me soaring back to London—to the kind people and the theaters, the music, and the last train to Hornchurch. To kick-start my nocturnal adventures, my brain imagined every possible type of escape. I catapulted myself over the wire on a giant rubber band. I burrowed out through the walls like one of the mites in the German cheese. I soared on homemade glider wings, and sometimes the guards kindly left the gates open. But no matter how brilliant or bizarre the escape, I still woke up in solitary.

During the day I passed the time by remembering poetry I had learned at school in Texas. I got so good at it that I could start a day knowing only a fragment of a poem and end it by being able to visualize the entire page in the poetry book where I first read it. Whether this was evidence that we are all gifted deep down with a well of memories of even the smallest things that happen to us, I do not know. I was certainly glad that the Gestapo did not subscribe to the theory. Alternatively, it is perfectly possible that the bits of poems I was conjuring up had very little to do with what the poets had written, but with no books allowed and no one to challenge me, the versions in my head were word perfect.

I got out one lunchtime after my double stretch and was enjoying wolfing down as much Red Cross food as possible in my hut when two of my friends, Mike and another Bill, started telling me about a break they had planned for that same night. I really could have done with a rest, but the one thing time in the cooler does for you is to make your priorities very clear, and mine was escape.

As soon as darkness fell, we slipped out of our hut and made our way down to an area where a natural hollow and a small vegetable patch gave a little cover from the searchlights that swept back and forth from the guard towers all night. We wriggled through the vegetable patch, smelling the earthy night smells and listening to the nighttime noises, fearing that every little sound was a guard on patrol.

I found myself trying to huddle under a potato plant that was about six inches tall, and I began to wonder just why I kept on doing such stupid things, reasoning that I would probably have another month in the cooler to figure it out. Then the other Bill cut the wire. It was stretched so tight that the tension made it go off like a gunshot as the wire whipped around and nearly caught us. An incredibly loud twang, like the first note of a crazed bluegrass banjo solo, filled the air and echoed away along the fence.

A dozen lights snapped on, sirens wailed, and all three of us dived in different directions. There was no way to get out without cutting more wires and no time to do so. We tried to make it to cover, and I lay still, camouflaged again as a very unlikely potato plant. A light shone directly on Bill and Mike, and they were carted off at gunpoint for a long stay in the cooler. But amazingly, as I lay still, a guard examined the minimal damage to the fence and walked away, almost treading on me as he passed by in the darkness. When the commotion had died down, I crawled very slowly back to our hut and fell into a long sleep in which I was too exhausted to escape, even in my dreams.

Soon after this disaster, several of the hastily started "blitz" tunnels which were under way almost from the day we arrived were discovered. A mixture of overzealousness, not enough planning in the construction or security aspects, and a large dollop of bad luck meant that one by one they were nearly all discovered. The ferrets were a bit shocked that one of them started underneath the altar in the chapel, but just because the enemy had *Gott mit Uns*, or God Is with Us, written on their belt buckles didn't mean that we could not look to the same source for inspiration.

Another of the tunnels, as yet undetected, says a lot about what sort of leader Wings Day was. The tunnel started underneath his own senior officers' mess table. Perched at the table,

Wings had determined that our future tunnels needed to be bigger and better and with cast-iron security. Instead of a couple of hopefuls scooting out the second the tunnel broke, we would aim to get people out in the dozens, maybe even the hundreds. We could keep so many Germans occupied looking for us that we would make our own small contribution to the war. It was the thinking that sowed the seeds for a later breakout from Luft III— the Great Escape.

But having dozens of people on the outside meant dozens of sets of civilian clothes, escape rations for more people than ever before, mass production of everything from compasses to maps, and, most important for those hoping to travel in style, forged documents and passes, or *Ausweise*. Our pool of talent from all walks of life was suddenly called on to produce in overdrive.

In order to maintain security, each part of the operation was known by the name of a shop in Britain. The people who turned blankets and spare uniforms into anything from bogus German uniforms to business suits or peasants' garb were known as Gieves, after a famous gents' outfitters in London, the same with Gamage's, which was our security network. The mapmakers were known as Cook's Tours, and those in charge of concocting escape food were named after Lyons's celebrated Corner House restaurants. Those who specialized in dying cloth were named after Pullar's of Perth, a big dry-cleaning company in Scotland. The Germans were baffled, as, of course, were any of us from America.

The denizens of Pullar's of Perth, under the leadership of John Paget, needed incredible coordination and the support of almost everybody in the camp. The only way to dye the volume of cloth that would be needed for so many sets of clothes for escapees was to do it under the cover of our regular laundry day. Each week on one day the huge cauldrons used to prepare our communal soup were requisitioned and used to boil our flea-ridden clothes. The regular washing went on all over each of the barracks, giving cover for the contents of the cauldrons, but every time a couple of guards appeared, any of the heavy overcoats that were being dyed would be hastily bundled up and shoved in kit bags which were then smuggled to the tunnels or hidden in the barracks. In some cases it took weeks to get them dry.

The world of the dyers and tailors was fraught with problems. There were only two main sources for cloth used to make civilian clothes—old uniforms and blankets. The tailors were delighted at first when a consignment of blankets arrived from Britain which had encoded instructions on how they could be turned into rather natty suits, but a quick look at the results presented an obvious problem. They were too good. This was, after all, wartime, and strolling about the Polish countryside dressed like a Piccadilly toff was not much better than wearing an RAF uniform. Instead, old threadbare Polish blankets, smoothed down with a sharp knife, led to a much more credible wardrobe for next season's well-dressed escapist.

We were fortunate to have one of the greatest forgers of the war with us at Schubin. Eric Shaw would produce apparently typewritten letters with a tiny paintbrush and magnifying glass, knowing that a single slip on a single tiny letter could cost a man his freedom or maybe his life. His passes and letters of authority to travel on business from companies like Krupp Engineering were truly works of art, a far cry from my job of burrowing in the mud but just as important. And so, for those above and below ground, days turned into weeks and weeks to months as my first Christmas in captivity approached.

Christmas is always one of the toughest times for any prisoner. It is a time to spend with family and loved ones, and not isolated in freezing conditions with a few hundred men even more glum than oneself. It was a time when bad news from home—whether of death or of marriages disintegrating under the strain of enforced separation—could hit very hard.

Every POW camp in the war had its own stories about suicides or virtual suicides as men pushed beyond endurance finally cracked. Sometimes the trigger was a letter from home. While we Americans knew these as "Dear John" letters, the British called them "Mespots." At first I was interested in this—it sounded like "mess pot," which in turn sounded like something that might involve food, my only main interest apart from escaping. In reality, the name came from the British interwar campaign in Mesopotamia, a place so miserable and far away from home that it prompted a flurry of long-distance breakups.

Many of the most remarkable Mespot letters became almost legendary, the stories moving from camp to camp with the prisoners. One told of a wife who wrote to a prisoner that she now had two babies by an Italian prisoner of war at a local camp at home, but she added that she would make it up to him by buying him a motorbike after the war. Another told how a complete stranger rushed up to her under cover of the blackout and presented her with a bouncing baby that she had decided to keep. In some camps such letters were even pinned up on the notice board as a way of sharing the misery and avoiding individuals suffering alone or being whispered about.

Not every letter from home brought such news. Most helped keep prisoners going, reminding them what they were fighting for, and giving them something to work for. Some of the most welcome Christmas packages included board games and playing cards. It was not just that a few rounds of the Monopoly board helped remind us of strolling down more interesting streets at home: The boards themselves contained escape materials from home, ranging from maps to blank passes. These helped to supplement the painstaking work of our forgers and cartographers.

Perhaps our most remarkable piece of news that December was a message from Buckingham Palace. The letter was brought in with a certain amount of reverence by one of the senior guards, Rittmeister Reimer. Reimer was a rather rotund and jolly-looking former cavalry officer who would have made a good Santa Claus compared to most of us half-starved inmates. He was amiable and did his best to look wounded if we were not quite as jolly in return, but anyone who took him for a fool was badly mistaken. He was eventually promoted to head of security, and despite his mannerisms and appearance—or maybe because of them—he was extremely effective.

He handed the letter to Wings. It was a Christmas card from the king and queen, with a photo of them and the two princesses in London. It probably had wound its way through the Red Cross or other neutral diplomatic channels, then though the more chivalrous sections of the Luftwaffe, to somehow arrive safely in the heart of enemy territory.

As we passed it gently from hand to hand, I thought back to meeting the king on that rain-sodden airstrip in Lincolnshire, exchanging a few words as the rain dripped off our noses to form an egalitarian puddle at our feet. He was a naturally shy man, who had no desire to be king, but ended up with the job after his brother abdicated, just in time to hand him the crown and a one-way ticket to a world war. He and his wife stuck it out in London during the blitz, despite a direct hit on Buckingham Palace, and earned the respect and affection of thousands who were also suffering from the equally egalitarian bombs. I also thought of the parties in London and my boisterous city nightlife being interrupted by an unexpected introduction to his wife, Queen Elizabeth. It all seemed like events that had happened to someone else, in another century or on another planet. I've never been much of a monarchist, and always figured the Boston Tea Party was a good idea, but getting that card did wonders for our morale. In some strange way it was a little civilized gesture that said, even in the wilds of Poland in the bleak midwinter, we were not completely forgotten.

But for every letter from royalty, there were a hundred Mespots. In Schubin, whether because of bad news from home or just from the strain of captivity, physical or mental, there were some poor men who only escaped the wire when carried out in a pine box.

Poor old Flight Lieutenant "Pissy" Edwards had been very badly shaken by a particularly traumatic crash before his capture and during his time in captivity had become less and less stable, gradually becoming what we called "wire-happy." His unhinged arguments and nervous ticks could be irritating to men already cooped up and spoiling for a squabble, but he was harmless, and most of us did our best to look after him. When he announced one day that he was "fed up with this place," no one paid much attention. Minutes later, when he strolled over the death wire, a low warning wire some yards in front of the main fence, and started to climb the perimeter barbed wire in broad daylight, it would have been an easy job to take him down and lead him somewhere to lie down for a while. Instead, an army guard called on him to halt, just once. Edwards climbed on feebly, not getting very far up the wire. The guard shot him in the stomach, and he dangled briefly on the wire like a broken doll.

When I and some others who had rushed to the edge of the death wire protested, one particularly vicious guard—known as the Blond Beast—was all in favor of mowing us down, too. Machine guns and rifles were clicked at the ready as a menacing crowd of prisoners gathered to support us, and the fatally injured Edwards was taken away. Some of the more moderate guards cooled the situation, and we were spared. I, however, was marched back into the cooler as punishment for raising my voice and fist against a guard.

Years later, when watching the film *The Great Escape*, I noticed there was a similar, tragic moment portrayed in which an officer is shot down on the wire and a protesting American is led away to the cooler. As far as I know, such an event never took place at Luft III, but the real-life tragedy at Schubin was burned into the minds of anyone who saw it.

Back in the cooler, I tried to conserve my strength. Iron rations and isolation were the main forms of punishment. Each evening the Blond Beast would come into my cell and remove my shoes. There were now so many guards around during the day that escape from the cooler was impossible, and just to make sure I didn't try something during the less well-guarded night shift they would take my shoes, returning them, sadly unpolished, along with my Reich bread in the morning. Sometimes it was difficult to tell the two apart.

Every evening, as he stole my shoes, the Beast would play a little game. "Who is winning the war?" he would ask me, amiably. On the first occasion I replied, "We are," and got a mighty backhander in the face, which sent me sprawling to the floor. The next night he was back for more. He asked the same question. This time, showing that I might be stubborn, but not entirely stupid, I changed tack. "You are," I replied. I got an equally hard punch in the mouth, apparently for lacking sincerity in my delivery. This continued night after night. Each night the same question, and each night I tried a new victor in the war, including the Chinese, the Patagonians, and the Whirling Dervishes, but none of them seemed to make him happy. My bruises multiplied.

Things were pretty grim, but with some really creative thinking, I managed to make them even worse. If I jumped up and clung to the window bars, I could peer out at the road that ran alongside the camp. One day I heard a commotion. Whips were cracking and men were shouting. I had not heard any noises like that since my childhood vacations in Texas and New Mexico. It was the sound of a herd being driven. Yet the one sound that was missing was that of the cattle.

Hauling myself up by the bars, I saw that instead of cattle there was a moving mass of about two hundred young women. Members of the local fascist militia and some German soldiers were driving them along the road with whips and sticks, herding them like animals toward the nearby railway station. I am not sure whether they were Jews destined for the extermination camps or young Polish women destined for the brothels on the Eastern Front.

Not since I had sat with my blood boiling while I watched American newsreels in the 1930s showing the Nazis' treatment of

Jews and Communists had I felt such a red rage welling up inside me. And this time it was no purely abstract experience. I had indeed organized my war badly, and now I knew just what I was fighting against, and just what I would fight against while there was breath in my body, whether by escape or sabotage or back behind the guns of a Spitfire if I could manage it.

Something inside me snapped. The year of abuse, captivity, beatings, and a thousand tiny humiliations boiled up into one overwhelming desire to fight back and to defend these poor women who were going through everything I was and probably things a hundred times worse. Through that tiny barred window, I screamed at the fascists herding the women. I shouted and swore and cursed, throwing every vile word I could at them. Some of the women looked up, and I like to think that this small voice of defiance gave them a little comfort in the human hell which the Nazis had created for them. The Blond Beast and the other guards came running into my cell to see what all the commotion was about and tried to pull me away from the window, but my grip was like iron on the bars. I continued to pour out abuse at them, at the fascists, and at the whole corrupt system that was reducing Europe to rubble. I was so enraged that I hardly felt the blows raining down on me and the gun butts smashing my hands until I finally let go of the bars and fell to the floor, where the kicking continued.

As I lay curled up and semiconscious on the bare concrete floor, the guards returned with wood and nails and boarded up even the tiny window. Then they left me, clanging the cell door locked behind them. My face ached and my back and stomach throbbed from where I had been kicked on the ground. I was badly bruised, but I knew I would have time to heal before they let me out. I felt the cold concrete against my battered cheek as I lay utterly alone in the darkness, but I was glad I had raised my voice. Human beings are surrounded by a universe many sizes too big for them, and the ability either to shout out in anger or to laugh in the face of chaos are the only truly noble options available to us. That shout, or that laughter, even in the black infinity of the universe is an absolutely new and pure thing, filling the void and going on, echoing off among the nebula, with an entirely human significance.

10. Digging for Victory

When I emerged from my latest stint in solitary I was even thinner, but even more determined to get out. Christmas was nearly upon us. In fact, it was the night before Christmas and all through the house there were scruffy, uniformed creatures stirring. Down by the vile latrines, a group of us were engaged in activities other than the obvious ones. Reasoning that even the most diligent guard would be reluctant to rummage about in an open sewer, we decided that this would be the ideal place to start a tunnel. It was the closest building to the wire, though still a long way from the perimeter—about 150 feet—but that could not be helped, so we just got started.

At first we worried about the German defenses against tunnels, the most prominent being their network of microphones planted in the ground at varying depths designed to pick up any digging sounds bigger than the local moles. Through Aidan Crawley's excellent intelligence network we soon found out that this was not a big problem. The microphones were, in fact, too sensitive, and anyone tromping around aboveground would more than drown out any tunneling noises far below. We decided to be on the safe side by taking the tunnel depth down to seventeen feet belowground, while scores of our helpful fellow prisoners took long walks and stamped their feet to keep out the cold, all deafening some unfortunate guard given the tedious job of listening to the soil for eight hours at a stretch.

If the authorities could think up some tedious jobs, we were not to be outdone. The first job we needed was the unenviable post of "throne stooge." This involved sitting on a particular toilet seat for hours on end, guarding our tunnel entrance, and ensuring that our fellows did not unwittingly add to our miseries when we were working below.

Eddy, Paddy, and I, along with perhaps a dozen willing helpers, chose the end toilet hole of the communal latrine. This last seat was beside a wall that divided the latrine building in two. Under the concrete floor, the wall continued, dividing an underground sump on one side from a huge sewage pit on the other. We chipped away around the toilet seat until the "throne" was effectively a removable tunnel entrance. Below it, we made a hole in the dividing wall and made up a removable dummy wall in case the ferrets ever held their noses and peeked in. The hole was just large enough for a man to squeeze through, and in the sump we hollowed out a huge working chamber. The best thing about the latrine is that all of our normal convoluted antics to get rid of soil from the tunnels, whether by storing bags in the huts or acting like "penguins" by shuffling small amounts into the ground from bags hidden in our trousers, were no longer needed. We shoveled the dirt from the sump into the latrine pit on the other side of the wall.

Once we had a big enough chamber to work in, we started the tunnel, which was to become one of the most successful in the war. Since Eddy Asselin was in charge of the operation, the tunnel was called Asselin, and if any ferrets overheard the name rather frequently in the following months, they must have assumed that Asselin was a particularly popular man, which indeed he was.

Edmund Asselin was only about twenty-one, but had as much nerve as style. He was a French Canadian from Quebec with my own squadron who had been shot down shortly after I arrived in Britain. He was an outstanding planner and organizer, and the organizing genes seemed to run in his family, since on news of Eddy's capture his mother Beatrice set up and led the Canadian support organization for prisoners of war, which helped to keep us alive with very welcome food and clothes. I had encountered Eddy briefly as a fellow RCAF Spitfire pilot, but he had been shot down before we had much of a chance to get to know each other. By the time we renewed our acquaintance in Stalag Luft III, Eddy was a charismatic veteran of all aspects of life in Kriegie-dom, from tunneling to playing poker for back pay. Before the war he had been a star college football player for Loyola College in Canada. He was immensely likable and tried to be helpful to his fellow prisoners, but he also had a very well-developed streak of ambition, and we all had an unshakable sense that no matter what happened, Eddy Asselin would come up smelling of roses.

Unfortunately, roses were not what we smelled of as we started the Asselin tunnel. The entrance to the tunnel was a daily horror experience as I wriggled through the hole where the toilet seat was and my face came to within a few inches of the great stinking lake of sewage. I thought back to France and the day I was shot down when I found myself wading through a river that turned out to be a sewerage ditch. I seemed destined to spend a great deal of the war swimming in unsavory seas, which is how I generally regarded the Third Reich and all its works.

After getting past the grim, stinking lake, a wriggle through the wall brought us to the working chamber and the tunnel entrance. We dug with scoops made out of old tins with wooden handles cut off brooms. Virtually every prisoner in the camp was persuaded to relinquish at least one bed board, though a small minority whined about even this assault on their comfort. By now there were thirty of us working on the project, and we were expected to lead the way in all such sacrifices. As the tunnel progressed, every single bed board from my own bed was cannibalized as tunnel props, and I ended up sleeping on a crisscross web of string.

We were now working on the tunnel in three crews of eight men each. I mostly dug, along with Eddy Asselin and some of our other close associates. The next crew dispersed the earth, mostly into the latrine pit, and the third concentrated on shoring up and securing the tunnel after each digging session. Day after day we progressed, sometimes only a few inches a day, depending on the saturation of the ground and the number of interruptions as the goons patrolled or inspected. We celebrated after ten feet, then after twenty-five, inching our way toward freedom like the mites in the German cheese.

Emerging blinking into the early evening sunshine one day from a long shift underground and trying not to look as grubby as I felt, I saw an animated debate going on in a Slavic language between an old Polish worker and one of our comrades, who was Czech. It turned out that the old Pole was the driver of the tanker vehicle that had the unenviable job of pumping out the latrine and departing with the contents every few weeks. His tanker had the euphemistic nickname the "honey wagon," and he was complaining bitterly that his tank was half full of gravel from our tunnel every time he emptied it. Luckily, he turned out to be a Polish patriot, and instead of giving us up to the guards, he agreed to help in another escape.

The Czech pilot, whose real name was Josef Brycks, but who had changed his name to Joe Ricks to avoid retaliation to his family, explained to me is his excellent English that he had just persuaded the driver to allow him to get inside the honey wagon and drive to freedom. We brought the idea to the escape committee, and Wings Day and the rest of us considered it a good plan, since the Germans were no more keen on poking around in a tanker full of sewage than they were on sticking their head down latrines. Still, we worried about the old man, who would certainly be shot if the plan went wrong. We decided to approve the escape, but only to take place at the same time as our mass breakout from the tunnel, which would be how the commandant would assume Ricks got out, leaving the honey wagon driver in the clear.

Joe Ricks, a short and immensely tough man with the broad face of a prizefighter, was quite a character. As well as being invaluable because he spoke Polish, Czech, and German as well as heavily accented English, he was something of a Romeo and was carrying on a long-distance romance with a farmer's daughter who passed by each day on the road outside the camp. Somehow he persuaded a Polish worker who came into the camp to carry his messages of affection, and she sent hers by return. Ricks had more reason than most of us to want out of the camp, but perhaps less reason to get as far away as possible.

As the entire camp turned into a hive of activity above and below ground, the ferrets started to get suspicious and threatened to lock us up earlier in the evenings to stop us lurking around in the early evening darkness of a Polish winter. Loud protests about the effects on our already failing health were heeded, partly because the camp authorities knew that if we came down with something like typhus, the germs would democratically decide to infest their men, too. But our freedom was curtailed in another way. Simms, the unpleasant security officer, ordered in an extra company of guards and from then on our two Appells a day rose to three, four, and even five. Whatever we were doing, we had to stop, cover our tracks, and show ourselves in a matter of minutes.

Underground, when not disrupted by the cry from above of "Goons in the block," we were making steady progress, now at the rate of two or three feet a day. We had turned an old army kit bag into a bellows, pumped by a man in the entrance cave pushing a wooden handle in and out for all he was worth. The pump was joined to an air pipeline made of dried Klim milk tins from our Canadian Red Cross packages. Luckily, the tins were slightly smaller at the lid end, so if you cut out the bottom they fitted into each other like ready-made tubing. Despite these efforts the tunnel, as it grew longer and longer, passing sixty feet, became a suffocating place. Each trip down it required a little more courage, and the need to blot out the thought of all those tons of earth pressing down on you and the certain knowledge that a cave-in would leave us trapped, breathing mouthfuls of mud and unable to go forward or backward. The presence of light became important, not just to work by, but to steady our nerves and to remind us that there was a world above with sky and fresh air, waiting for us to return.

We experimented with different forms of light and settled on a sort of lamp fueled by margarine with a wick made from a bootlace. The margarine had been slowly simmered for hours to get rid of the water content, but as we clawed away at the dirt, the air would become worse and worse, until eventually even the margarine lamp would go out. After that, we worked on in stifling darkness, trying not to think about the amount of unstable earth directly above our heads.

It is hard to convey the real sense of claustrophobia that comes from an hour of stabbing away at a wall of Polish mud in a tunnel so narrow that you can only get one arm forward to work at the face and so long that it takes half an hour to wriggle back to safety and sanity at the tunnel start. The experience assaults every sense. We felt the cold clay around us, pressing in on us and seeping into our bones until we almost became part of the tunnel. The darkness when the lights went out was total. No glimmer of light had penetrated that wall of mud in a million years. Even when the margarine lamp flickered, it only served to emphasize the blackness around it, what Milton once called "darkness visible."

The sense of smell was overpowered not only by the stench from the yellow and brown clay through which we wriggled, but also the nauseating waves of filth which sometimes flooded in from the latrines. The sense of taste was only hit when a shower of earth fell from an unshored roof, filling the mouth of an unfortunate digger who had been gaping wide for oxygen in the stale void of the tunnel. The only sound was the slapping and snapping of homemade knives and scoops, digging into the mud, or the wheezing noise made as some heroic character pushed for all he was worth to keep the bellows operating far behind as the air circulated feebly in our Klim milk tin pipeline. Sometimes, when you stopped for a rest, the silence was so deafening that it made you want to shout just to hear a sound, but the knowledge that, a few feet above us, the guards had hidden microphones reaching into the ground like inquisitive, greedy fingers made us stifle any sound and return to our digging.

We moved the dirt back in a big bag tied to a long piece of string. After hacking away at the tunnel face, I would scoop the dirt into the bag and give a sharp double tug on the string. Somewhere, far back in the opening cavern, I would get an answering double tug on the string, and the heavy bag would start to be hauled back along the tunnel. At the other end another team would dump the cans of dirt into the main latrine and prod the unpleasant contents around with a pole to avoid any telltale blockages.

As our work progressed the strain on our string grew greater. One day there was an ominous snap and a loud curse from far back in the tunnel. Unable to turn around, I had to wiggle back yard after yard to find the bag and then to grope around for both ends of the broken string to make a running repair before crawling back to the tunnel face. When the string snapping became a regular event, we realized that we actually needed men positioned in the middle of the tunnel, hauling back to that point, and another at the end. As the tunnel grew, there was a gradual, almost imperceptible change in our own attitudes. The grumbling and cursing about the grim conditions continued, but now it was tinged with excitement and an unspoken feeling that maybe this time we would not be discovered. Once we passed the hundred-foot mark, instead of measuring how long the tunnel was so far, we started to talk about how far we had to go.

Apart from lack of air, the terror of collapse, and the fear of discovery, a surplus of sewage was sometimes a more immediate problem. The proximity to the latrine certainly helped to get rid of the tunnel dirt but when the latrines flooded with winter rains or a blockage, the resultant vile liquid would pour in on us as we dug. One of the toughest jobs was making sure that all the diggers were slightly clean after hours of working naked in cramped, dangerous conditions in the dirt. Those same smells made our tunnelers less than popular with their roommates in the big, open barracks, and there were rumors that those left behind planned celebrations after we escaped.

The tunnel was only two feet square, and cave-ins were a constant fear, despite the sacrifice of so many bed boards from so many prisoners. Working in the suffocating, stinking world of a claustrophobic tunnel, hacking my way through yet another six inches of what seemed like an eternity of muck with a bent tin, I had plenty of time to ponder. I wondered sometimes why I did not just settle down to life as a kriegie. Then I could have been clean, lying back on the lumpy straw mattress, staring at the place the ceiling should have been in our hut, with nothing to worry about but the fleas. Better still, the mattress rather than the tunnel would still be supported by bed boards. But then I would remember all the bravery of the Londoners, and of the French men and women who risked their lives to save mine. I would remember the beatings I got at the hands of the Gestapo and from thuggish guards. Most of all I would remember that, without resistance, this was all the world could look forward to and that the fate that was already befalling the Jews, socialists, gypsies, and trade unionists would sooner or later be waiting for all of us. And so I dug.

At about that time we had another casualty, but whether depression or accident was the cause we will never know. A young officer called Peter Lovegrove was involved in the attempts to map our surrounding for the tunneling teams. He had just had some bad news from home when he climbed up to the very top of the biggest building in the camp, the White House, which housed our command staff. There was a sickening thump as he plummeted to his death some forty feet below. I like to think he simply slipped, but there were few of us who did not at least think about ending it all at some point in our captivity. The life of a prisoner of war is full of strange ironies, and when Wings Day was permitted to attend Lovegrove's funeral with military honors in the nearby village, he was able to see and memorize the very details that Lovegrove had been trying to map when he fell and died.

Week after week we burrowed in the muck and the mire, expecting every day that the ferrets would find the Asselin tunnel and for all of our work to come to nothing, but still we dug. One of the hardest parts of digging the tunnel was that we were on virtually starvation rations, so any physical exertion was twice as tough. Eventually, by the start of March 1943, it was almost ready, more than 150 feet long. All but the last few feet had been clawed out by tired, impatient hands over three months. Eddy and I would dig the last section out on the night of the escape. If the calculations of our engineering and surveying comrades were right, we should emerge in a small ditch containing a potato patch on the far side of the perimeter fence.

Our plans to take our time and wait for the perfect moment were given a sudden jolt. Wings had got news on the intelligence grapevine that plans were afoot to send us back to Luft III. We had our own methods of bribing guards to find out what was happening, sometimes even before the commandant knew, and there was also word from the secret services back in London, often though our intelligence officer Aidan Crawley. He had several prisoners who agreed to encode messages into their letters home, which were then intercepted by the War Office, who would reply using a complex code based on the specific page numbers of a German-English dictionary. One of the code writers was the young Dane Jørgen Thalbitzer, a fellow tunneler who was to team up with Jimmy Buckley on our escape.

The news was stark. If we did not act right away, all of our weeks and months of eating dirt would be wasted as we were carted back to Luft III. It was time to make a decision about who was going and when. The tunnel was completed on the third of March and we decided to make our move on the fifth, using a relatively moonless night for cover.

The decision about who should go was fairly simple. In order to have any hope of avoiding alerting the guards, the escapers would have to be sealed in the tunnel for several hours after curfew but before the breakout. That meant that the maximum number who could go equaled the maximum number that could be shoehorned into a damp, airless hole in the ground and left there for several hours without suffocating. The final number of thirty-three was arrived at, half to be nose to toe along the tunnel, the other half crammed into the cavern at the start of the tunnel. Some of the tunnelers worried that the air would give out and that the result would be thirty-three prisoners who killed and conveniently buried themselves for the Germans, but our semi-scientific calculations suggested that we would be OK.

Most of those chosen were the team who had helped to make the tunnel. To this group were added some senior escape personnel, including John Dodge, the Dodger who had tried to jump from the train on the way to Schubin, as well as the Senior British Officer Wings Day himself. Wings figured that since he was going to be thrown in the cooler for presiding over our escape anyway, he might as well give them a run for their money.

Our security chief, and later a member of parliament in Britain, Aidan Crawley, was also on the list. In fact, had we but known it, we were in very august company as we squeezed into the tunnel to await our fate. Among the other escapers were Anthony Barber, a future British chancellor of the Exchequer, former bomber pilot Robert Kee, who went on to become a world-famous historian, squashed alongside the first and greatest leader of escapes during the war, Jimmy Buckley from the Fleet Air Arm. Those of us who had done the tunneling were given priority. We decided to go in pairs, with Eddy Asselin and I being numbers one and two, because ours was the job of completing the last few feet in the hours before breakout. Paddy and his escape buddy, Wilfred Wise, were just a few people back in the horizontal conga line at numbers seven and eight. With characteristic modesty, Wings Day awarded himself the last place out alongside his escape partner Squadron Leader Dudley Craig, who was also no slouch in the escape department, having earlier attempted to stroll out of the camp at Barth dressed as a guard, clutching a rifle made entirely of wood.

In addition to the real escapees, ten other prisoners volunteered to hide in the attic of the main building, the White House, so that if we got away, the Germans would think they were looking for even more runaways. If they could remain undetected until the camp was evacuated in a few months, they could then slip away when it was deserted. In the meantime they would be kept supplied by the small number of their fellows who would know they were hidden inside the camp rather than far away.

Earlier on the last day before our nighttime escape, the bouncing Czech Joe Ricks and his escape companion, a Squadron Leader Morris, clad head to toe in hooded overalls, had waited in a quiet corner behind a building, out of the line of sight of the guard posts. The brave old Pole had parked his honey wagon there as promised, and the two men squeezed through a specially adjusted top hatch. Mercifully, the driver had done a good job of washing the interior out, and a large bucket of sewage was hung under the inside of the hatch, just in case some zealous ferret decided to peek inside. As always, they were not so inclined, and the honey wagon drove out of the camp, taking the lucky Joe straight to an assignation with the local farmer's daughter, hopefully by way of a bathtub. Normally, our escape kit was kept as small and light as possible, but Joe had special dispensation for an extra piece of vital equipment—a huge bottle of eau de cologne, which was an expensive trophy from our bartering system, unwittingly donated by some unfortunate guard.

After the last Appell at about five o'clock we sauntered a few at a time to the latrines, since we thought that even the doziest guard might raise an eyebrow if confronted by a delegation of thirty-three men all heading for the latrines at once. For added cover there was one of our frequent POW rugby matches on the exercise ground above, England versus Australia. As we ambled in a few at a time on a strict rota, no one noticed that more people seemed to go in than came out. Wings Day allowed himself one of his wry smiles as a junior escape officer chose his words badly when he came to say, "It's time for you to be put down, sir."

Eddy and I went in through the latrine first, and we prayed it would be for the last time. We were followed one by one by the rest. Being wedged at the front of 150 feet of dark, cramped tunnel was bad enough, but with the men lying head to toe all the way back behind us, even a slight tunnel collapse would mean the end. It would take hours for each man to wriggle backward to allow the one ahead to do the same. At least Eddy and I had the last bit of tunneling to occupy us as we spread the dirt back on the tunnel floor. Soon, with thirty men in dyed greatcoats clutching bags and laid end to end in a tunnel, the air became stifling. Naturally, until we broke the tunnel, it would be worst at the tunnel face. The air pump was working overtime with exhausted men taking turns pushing the kit-bag bellows in and out like galley slaves at the oars, but the air it pulled in was from the latrine pit next door, so it almost made matters worse. Then came the next torture: There was a leak from the cesspool next door and we were further soaked by the vile concoction. If ever I wanted to escape, that was the moment.

While Eddy and I dug like demons, the rest could do nothing but lie there suffocating, wondering what was happening. Hissed messages were passed forward from one man to the next in a giant, smelly version of Chinese Whispers. A message that started off as "Hurry up, we need more air," after passing through fifteen whispered versions would come out as something like "What's happened to the bear?" and an equally confused question would make its way back until someone, worried about the level of whispered hubbub, hissed, "Shut up!" His message was duly muttered noisily all the way up the line.

But if our entry into the outside world was going to be less than glorious, at least we were prepared for the possibilities.

Never before had an escape attempt for so many provided the es-capees with such good equipment. An entire camp had worked nonstop. We had civilian clothes, forged documents, accurate maps, compasses, escape food, and more. The escape would also be something of an experiment, with every possible mode of travel and strategy being applied. If we managed to get all thirty-three out, we would be able to see which techniques worked best outside the wire. Not all of us wanted to travel in comfort on trains, exchanging pleasantries with some Gestapo officer check-ing tickets, and those of us who intended to evade by tramping across country while avoiding contact with the enemy were col-lectively known as the "hard arses."

At last, with a triumphant shove of his homemade trowel, Eddy was through to the surface. He passed me a lump of earth to dispose of on the tunnel floor, and I felt a clump of grass on it. The scent of living plants joined the wonderful rush of cold air that will forever be linked in my mind to the smell of freedom. Men further back along the tunnel gasped and gulped in great lungfuls of fresh air. We had reached the outside world.

Eddy carefully cut the roots of plants out of the way, handing down the debris to me, which I trampled into the tunnel floor. Then came the moment of truth. Eddy cautiously poked his head up, and we both blessed the mathematical geniuses who had helped survey the tunnel route. It came out exactly where it was supposed to in the potato ditch, just outside the wire. Eddy froze as a guard on his rounds inside the perimeter strolled past. He didn't see a thing. The reality was that all the lights pointed in-ward to illuminate the camp, and as we had hoped, his entire at-tention was focused on the inside of the wire, looking out for prisoners scurrying from the huts or making for the perimeter fence. The only things likely to be outside were stray cats. Eddy made his move, squeezing out and spraying tunnel dirt down the vertical exist shaft as his feet scrabbled on the walls.

Then it was my turn. The guard was on his way back, so I waited, feeling that my head sticking out of the tunnel must look as big and luminous as a pumpkin. When he had passed by on the far side of the wire I squeezed out of the tunnel mouth and commando-crawled from one potato ditch to another, inching my way along under the cover of the ditch until I was nearer the woods. The silence held, and I waited for the right moment to make a last terrifying dash into the trees. I scurried forward, half-crouching half-running. My every footstep sounded like someone dropping an entire set of crockery, and every twig snap sounded like a rifle being cocked to finish me off, but seconds later, panting from the exertion, I made it to a stand of trees where Eddy was waiting.

Then we were up and off, the first two out of a successful tunnel at Schubin, with the camp eerily illuminated behind us.

As the remaining thirty-one started to emerge, Eddy and I took off, heading in the general direction of the Baltic Sea. Not far behind us Lieutenant Commander Jimmy Buckley, astutely teamed with a young Danish pilot who spoke fluent German, was aiming to make for Denmark, then Sweden. I knew the young Dane with a broad, likable face as John Thompson, but his real name was Jørgen Thalbitzer, and he had risked his life at the start of the war to escape to Britain and become a pilot with the RAF, changing his name to avoid retaliation against his parents in occupied Denmark. Danny Krol and Otto Cerny, a Pole and a Czech, were going to "hide in plain sight" as laborers heading back to Warsaw. Danny was short and incredibly hardy, a former fencing champion who caused some consternation among guards and prisoners alike by regularly washing naked in the snow outside the huts. After the fall of Poland he had made his way to France to fight on under Polish General Wladyslaw Sikorski, but after the fall of France he had made it to Britain to continue the fight from there. Even after his own fall, like mine from a Spitfire over France, he continued his war on both sides of the wire. He was one tough customer.

Aidan Crawley, as befitted an intelligence officer, was planning to stroll onto a train, waving a letter introducing him as a traveling engineer working in a Krupp factory. The letter was on beautifully headed paper, forged by our fellow kriegie Eric Shaw. Nearby, but pretending not to know him, would be German-born Flying Officer Stevens. He was a brave man. His advantage was that he spoke native German. His disadvantage was that he was both Jewish and a German fighting for the British. If he was captured and either of these interesting facts came out, he knew he would be tortured and executed. Others who let the train take the strain included future historian Robert Kee and Tommy Calnan.

Then there was my pal Paddy Barthropp and Wilf Wise, hard arses on foot like myself, as were Wings and Craig, though an hour passed before it was their turn to make the dash for the woods. Person after person scurried out of the tunnel, until all thirty-three were clear, though one unforeseen problem was that each of the men kicked some dirt back down the tunnel as he scrambled out. By the time Wings had done his final job of extinguishing the margarine lamps and had wriggled his way forward, the end of the tunnel had narrowed alarmingly, and he was barely able to squeeze out, covered in mud. It was midnight, and everyone was out.

As Eddy and I scurried away through the woods, we listened for the telltale firing of shots and the mournful wail of the alarm siren, but the night was as quiet as it was dark and cold. By the next morning we were far away, but with one small part of us wishing we could be a fly on the wall for the next Appell, just to see the expression of the face of pompous little Hauptmann Simms.

We were off and running. The feeling you get from being free, after so many months when the barbed wire at the edge of the camp represents the limits of your horizons, is like no other freedom. It is sharpened by the fact that you are in enemy territory, hundreds of miles from home, with nothing but a few handfuls of the Mixture in your pocket and half the guard dogs in Germany hot on your heels. Never, before or since, have I felt more alive.

Eddy and I managed to evade capture for about a week, hiding in hedges and sometimes sleeping in barns. We wolfed down our escape supplies, drank from streams, and occasionally liberated some vegetables. On the first night we hid in some woods and sat perfectly still as what seemed like half of Germany passed within a few feet of us, shouting and beating bushes, waving flashlights. They came within inches of finding us, but when they had passed by we quietly moved on. The nights were cold, and we sought some shelter in a particularly large barn, hoping that the inhabitants would not find us, or that, if they did, they would be patriotic Poles.

One of the most frightening moments came when we were forced to cross a bridge at night. We knew that the Germans had thrown a cordon around the camp and that every road and bridge had sentries posted on the lookout for us. Normally we would have skirted around to find some quieter spot to cross, but the river was deep, and there was little cover, so we decided to risk the bridge. There was one sentry at each end, luckily huddled in a sentry box to keep out the cold and only occasionally marching up and down the bridge to keep a lookout. We crawled along the side of the bridge in the shadows. Every tiny noise we made as we scrabbled across sounded to our frightened ears like someone dropping an entire dinner set. At one point a guard stood peering over the opposite side of the bridge, no more than ten feet away from us as we kept perfectly still. When he went back to his box we continued our crawl and breathed a long, quiet sigh of relief when we reached the shelter of the woods on the far side.

We woke one morning, about six days after our escape, to find ourselves held at bay near a railway crossing by a group of ethnic German farmworkers brandishing pitchforks. A farmer's wife returned with some soldiers and shouted at them to shoot us there and then. When they refused, she tried to wrestle the gun from one of them so she could do it herself. They restrained her and searched me. One, who spoke some English, found a letter from my mother. He translated it for the amusement of the others. It told how my mother in Texas was baking apple pies to send to the local prisoner-of-war camp for the German boys, because she felt sure that the German moms would be doing the same for me.

What with the chaos of thirty-three prisoners running around and being recaptured, returning us to the camp was not a top priority. In fact, while our escape was a great success in terms of getting what felt like half the German army out looking for us, the downside for anyone hoping to get home was that we had become such a sensation because of our large numbers that every Hitler Youth, German farmer, and spare soldier for a hundred miles was spending every waking hour looking for us. Reports of how many troops were tied up in the search for that first week vary greatly, from the modest to the near impossible, but the most common one is that we were being hunted for by three hundred thousand regular troops, police, militia, civilians, and Hitler Youth. It is a very satisfying thought to have tied up so many enemy troops, even for a week, though for that one week I would have been much happier if they were looking for someone else.

We were thrown in the civilian jail in a little town called Hohensalza. I added to what was already one of the most bizarre groups of prisoners gathered in any jail in history. There were Polish pimps and mobsters, petty thieves rubbing shoulders with those who had resisted the invaders, and Jewish people trying to stay out of the death camps. Alongside them were German deserters and Axis soldiers whose papers had been lost, and now two stray escapologists.

Eddy had been pretty shaken up by what we had been through and our rough treatment. I had the advantage of being a serial escaper who regarded such treatment as an occupational hazard, but for Eddy, the man who guided and masterminded every aspect of the tunnel, all those months of pain and planning and dirt had led only to a dusty jail full of deserters a day's truck ride from where we started. Eddy was a practical man, and he confided in me as he lay on his bunk that he wanted to get home, if not now, then eventually, and he felt that if he continued joining the small band of obsessive escapers he was unlikely to see the end of the war. Modestly, he described his mother, who was running the Prisoner of War Association in Canada, as "the only hero in the family" and suggested that he might try his hand at some of the nonescaping activities to fill in his time in a less life-threatening way, if ever we were lucky enough to be returned to the camp without being shot or interrogated by the Gestapo. He was interested in many things—politics and poker being his favorites.

I did not press him. Each man had to decide for himself what was right in terms of the balance between suffering and defiance, between risk and foolhardiness. For me the equation was simple. I had joined the war to resist, and I would keep resisting with every breath until I escaped or until the enemy helped me to get away from it all on a more permanent basis, six feet underground, and not in a tunnel.

Eddy was a survivor, a philosopher, a helper of others, but also someone with a finely developed sense of when to push and when to step back in the cause of self-preservation. Maybe that's why he made such a great poker player. Having decided on his strategy for the rest of the war, he yawned, stretched, and joined in a game of cards with the motley group of pimps, deserters, and refugees with whom we shared our cell. Very soon, as always, Eddy Asselin was winning.

Once he got back to Schubin camp, Eddy did as he had said, both there and later in Stalag Luft III, where he ran a vast and never-ending poker game, racking up huge amounts of money in back pay from those just as willing to wager but less sharp of mind. He also participated in the frequent political debates about the future of the world after the war, and when he went back to Canada, he became hugely successful as a leading light in local politics in Quebec, then for a time as also a member of parliament in Canada and finally as a lawyer and judge.

I, on the other hand, was a more straightforward organism. My escaping gene was just as much a part of me as my instinct to keep breathing. I particularly remember one character from the jail, Stefan, who I fleetingly got to know and like. He was a German soldier and something approaching a deserter king. I think Stefan had too much of the sun in North Africa and decided not to bother with the rest of the war. He was amiable and ruled over a kingdom of demoralized and cynical jailbirds as if the prison were the only sanctuary of sanity in a world gone mad. He enjoyed music, and I taught him a few of my cowboy songs, such as "Blood on the Saddle." Toward nightfall, the warders would go off duty, leaving the prisoners to their own devices.

Then came one of the most surprising sights of the entire war for me. Stefan casually got up, stretched, took out a hidden key, and let himself out, locking the cell door behind him. I tried to coax him into letting me out, too, but he informed me that the guards would not have to look too far for the guilty party, and he had a point. He said that as long as he was back in his cell by morning, and kept the guards well stocked with contraband and cigarettes, he could come and go as he pleased.

For someone who had spent more than a year risking his life to get out of prisons, the thought of escaping nightly only to lock oneself in again each dawn was a tough one. I asked him why he did not leave for good. Stefan just smiled through the bars at me and shrugged as he headed off for a night on the town, calling back, "Where to?" Before I could think of a reasonable answer, he was gone.

Next morning, while Stefan was back in his bunk, sleeping off a busy night, the soldiers came to take me and Eddy back to Schubin camp, and a long spell in the cooler, which was doing a roaring trade.

By the time we were returned to our rightful box, virtually all the other prisoners had been recaptured. Of the thirty-three of us—actually thirty-four, since an enterprising South African squadron leader named Don Gericke had seen the morning after our escape that the tunnel was miraculously still undiscovered. He had grabbed his escape kit, popped out the other end of the tunnel in broad daylight, and strolled along trying his best to look like a Polish workman. He did not get very far, but he gained high points for initiative from us, and even Eddy Asselin admired the fact that he was smart enough to get someone else to do all the digging.

The rest of my fellow escapists had some equally hair-raising travels to report, but always in the great low-key way that was one of the hallmarks of much of the courage I witnessed in the war years, where coming within inches of death was usually retold as "a spot of bother."

Paddy and Wilfred had made for the railway line, where they planned to jump the train, but the only thing on the track was one of those strange hand-pumped contraptions that resembles a see-saw on wheels that featured regularly in comedy chase scenes in old Buster Keaton movies. It was manned by four railwaymen heading west, and the escapees decided not to risk hitching a lift, so they slept in a cold, damp quarry.

After wandering about the next day but not getting far, they crept into a farmer's barn for the night and slumped exhausted in the hay. They woke with a start as the entire floor of the barn was apparently moving. It was a shoal of huge rats, attracted by the rare allure of the Mixture, and they did not seem to care much which brand of escape food was on offer. The men thrashed out and chased off the apparently fearless creatures and were preparing to flee when an elderly couple came out of the farmhouse and presented them with hot tea and bread. The old folk were clearly terrified of German troops finding the escapees, since they knew that while Allied pilots would probably just be put back in prison, they or any locals who helped would be shot on the spot. Paddy and his companion moved on, heading in the general direction of Warsaw.

They had made Warsaw their objective because they had a contact with the Polish Resistance who was hoping to get three crews out of the country. The other two crews were Poles and Czechs, who had already made the rendezvous, and Paddy and Wilfred would be the last. As it turned out, they were lucky they did not make the rendezvous, since all four of the other pilots disappeared without a trace, probably found and shot by the Gestapo as part of their no-quarter war on the Polish Resistance.

Increasingly tired and bedraggled, the two moved through a forest plantation and spent a third cold night in an old and long-deserted graveyard as wolves howled in the forest around them. By this time Paddy was suffering from a bad case of trench foot and was having difficulty walking as it ate away at his left heel. The next morning they were delighted to discover the railway line again, and this time they had more luck, jumping a slow freight train where they shared a box car with two nervous and untethered horses.

Ironically, the train rolled into Hohensalza, where I was to be jailed myself just a few days later. The men hid while the train carriages were shunted around and found to their dismay that they were left in a single carriage in the middle of the station. They knew that they would be discovered if they stayed, but the station was alive with people, including German guards, soldiers, and pro-German civilians. They made a dash for it, but were soon cornered by armed men. They were paraded as the town's prize catch by Polish collaborators and Hitler Youth, then interrogated by the local Gestapo. After that, much to their relief, they were returned to Schubin camp. They were driven there, and one event along the way was seared into Paddy's memory.

As they drove toward the camp, the car was slowed to a crawl by an old man walking down the middle of the road at a snail's pace. The car horn honked and the soldier driving cursed at him, but either he was deaf, or senile, but for whatever reason he just ignored the driver and kept on walking. The soldier jumped out and started to beat the old man, who crumpled to the ground. The guard dragged him to the side of the road and continued to kick him viciously until he stopped moving. Paddy has never ceased wondering whether the old man survived the attack, and to both of us, it always summed up the Nazi brutality and arrogance we were fighting against.

Two others of the footslogging hard-arse variety, Wings Day and his partner Dudley Craig, after they became the last of our group to struggle out of the ever-narrowing tunnel, made south in the direction of the town of Gneisen. They were perhaps less well equipped than our urbane friends on the trains. All they had were a couple of cigarette cartons with phrases scribbled in Polish declaring them escaped British officers and asking for help.

Wings was already suffering from a bad case of jaundice, and he said afterward that the whole escape seemed like a sort of semisurreal dream in which he faded in and out of focus, and felt little of the usual mixture of excitement and fear that were part and parcel of an escape, only the need to keep stumbling on in the hope of freedom. On their first day out they thought they were captured when a group of Polish farmworkers found them hiding in a haystack, but the Poles, instead of handing them over to the

Germans, risked their lives by sharing their lunch sandwiches with the escapers. Wings thought that the chunky bread and sausage he shared with those Poles was one of the best meals of his life. That night they were again discovered by Poles on another farm and awarded four fried eggs each. They might not be getting very far, but at least they were being better fed than in many months.

They walked most of the night, through swamps and over barbed-wire fences, to reach Zinn railway station, intending there to hop a freight train south, but even at night the freight yard was floodlit and a hive of activity. They stumbled on in the dark.

Just as they were going to go to ground for the day, they ran headlong into a young blond boy and had no chance but to show him their cigarette carton phrase book, which by now was getting well thumbed but seemed to have done the trick with a variety of brave Poles so far. The boy beamed when he found out who they were and gestured urgently for them to follow him. He installed them in a safe, warm barn and departed as they collapsed exhausted in the hay. Wings's jaundice was getting worse, and he shivered and sweated uncontrollably as they waited for the boy to return, hopefully with food and help. Gradually they fell into fitful sleep. They were awoken by the jab of fixed bayonets, surrounded and captured by German troops. The angelic child who had helped them turned out to be a fervent Hitler Youth, living in an all-German enclave. At first they received rough treatment, but when it transpired they were British and not, as the German troops had thought, escaped Russians, they were treated a little better.

The highlight of Wings's escape was something he learned as he was being driven back to the camp. The police chief in the town of Posen had ordered roadblocks thrown up all over his jurisdiction to catch the escapees, but being in a hurry he had driven through one of his own men's barriers, assuming they would recognize him. They didn't, and he was shot dead. When Wings and Dudley arrived back at camp and were thrown in the cooler, it was already so crowded that Wings had to share a single cot in "solitary" with Aidan Crawley, a big man who snored like a buffalo.

The other escapers had their own stories to tell. Those who spoke German and traveled by train got farthest. My friend and our escape security supremo Aidan Crawley got all the way to Innsbruck in Austria, a distance of some five hundred miles. He had the supreme satisfaction of resting back in his comfortable train seat as he stared out the window at the hundreds of troops fanned out across fields looking for us. Others traveling by train reached the Ruhr, and one got as far as Hannover. The quality of the forged documents from Schubin was such that two of the train escapees had got through five identity checks along the way, including some by the beady-eyed Gestapo, while Aidan managed to get through seven checks on the long ride to Innsbruck, using sleepy local trains where possible.

Train hoppers Robert Kee and Tommy Calnan did well to get to Bromberg railway station, where they bought tickets for Berlin and beyond, though Kee had fallen in a water-filled ditch along the way and did not look very presentable. They had forged documents declaring them to be foreign workers and managed to pass several checks until they had a narrow escape. They made the mistake of having a whispered conversation in a railway station toilet, not realizing that one of the cubicles was occupied. The eavesdropper came out, washed his hands casually, then reported them to a Gestapo man on the platform, but their cover story and forged paperwork held up, and they were allowed to go on. Finally, they were caught at Cologne, where they were spotted by the smallest of details. They were wearing leather bootlaces rather than the normal German cloth ones.

Ironically, the man who stayed out longest from our escape was probably the honey wagon Romeo Joe Ricks, who—once he had climbed out of the wagon and liberally doused himself with his escape-kit eau de cologne—decided to stay in the vicinity of the camp for a few days, enjoying a romantic interlude with the farmer's daughter whom he had fallen for through the barbed-wire fence. After that, he hooked up at the farmhouse as planned with Otto Cerny, who had escaped via our tunnel. Ricks set off with a spring in his step that allowed him to walk all the way to Warsaw in a few weeks. The pair managed to stay free there for more than three months. They joined the Polish Resistance, but they were eventually recaptured when enemy forces surrounded their safe house after a tip-off, and they fell into the hands of the Warsaw Gestapo, where they had a predictably rough time. They were only saved by the intervention of the commandant at Luft III, who sent a letter saying they were escapees, and they were shipped back to our old alma mater at Sagan.

In another way, there were two men who did stay out longer. They stayed out forever in fact. Lieutenant Commander Jimmy Buckley of the Fleet Air Arm was the first and perhaps the greatest of all escape leaders in the RAF camps. He had been shot down during the defense of Norway but managed to get back to British lines before the evacuation, and then flew Coastal Defense operations until shot down and captured in summer 1940 over

France, gaining the unenviable job of setting up an escape committee at a point in the war when defeat looked more likely than victory.

The first time I faced Jimmy as a new arrival at Luft III, eagerly pouring out my slightly half-baked escape plans, he had seemed like a man chipped out of granite. He was small and dark, older than the rest of us at about forty, a tough navy flyer to his bootstraps. But when not weighing up the life-and-death matter of which escapes to support or forbid, his eyes always had a spark of humor, and in any waking moments not occupied by escape plans, he would write brilliant comedy sketches for the prisoners' theatre groups to perform.

Jimmy's sense of humor sometimes even crept in to the serious business of escaping. When they were discussing the plans of my friend Roger Bushell, later the leader of the Great Escape, to slip away by hiding in a sort of kennel which was home to a goat mascot just outside Dulag Luft, someone inquired, "But what about the smell?" To which Jimmy replied, "Oh, I'm sure the goat won't mind."

Jimmy had become the first "Big X" or chairman of the escape committee at Dulag Luft, then at Barth, at Luft III, and finally at Schubin. Along with Wings Day, Jimmy Buckley had dug the very first RAF tunnel while still at Dulag Luft transit camp, a year before I dropped in to the same mustering point. It was the first successful RAF tunnel of the war.

Jimmy and his Danish partner Jørgen Thalbitzer, a.k.a. Thompson, made their way north on foot, hoping to reach the port of Stettin. The pair were great friends, though utterly different. Jimmy was an older, tougher senior officer with a wry sense of humor, while Thalbitzer was a brawny, amiable youth of twenty-one, with a great appetite for both adventure and laughter. While Jimmy had been blown out of the sky, along with five of the planes under his command, defending the evacuation at Dunkirk, Thalbitzer had an even more spectacular tale of how he had "bought his ticket" for the Schubin escape.

When he was only nineteen, in April 1940, he had watched silently as the Third Reich marched in to his native Denmark. He had recently gained a sports pilot license from a Danish flying club, and he decided the best thing he could do to get the invaders out of Denmark would be to fly for the RAF. Since the route from Denmark to London presented a few problems, he decided to take the scenic route. He landed himself a job as a refrigerator salesman and accepted a posting to far-off Turkey. He made the perilous trip through Axis Europe, arriving in Istanbul in January 1941. There he made contact with British officials. They helped him plan an even more extraordinary route to London, traveling south around the entire coast of Africa by tramp steamers and sailing vessels, somehow eventually reaching England.

At about the same time I was shot down in spring 1942, young Thalbitzer was visiting Winston Churchill at Downing Street, where he presented the prime minister with a check for some $80,000 raised by Danes in Britain, enough to buy three Spitfires, one of which would be flown by the newly appointed Pilot Officer Thalbitzer. When he first told us the story in the camp, I remember thinking that while as an American I certainly was unusual in volunteering early for this war, Jørgen had gone one better by volunteering *and* buying his own airplane.

Just three months later, Thalbitzer was forced to cash in his new Spitfire for a lifetime supply of free barbed wire when he was shot down over France. He crashed into overhead electric cables and barely managed to escape being fried as his Spitfire lost a wing and crashed upside down to the ground below. He evaded for about two weeks before a French farmer handed him over to the police when he asked for food. Some weeks later he rolled into Stalag Luft III, where he immediately fitted in with our small group of enthusiastic escape artists and quickly earned himself a ticket to the camp at Schubin alongside Buckley.

After the escape Jimmy and Jørgen marched north, avoiding all contact and making their escape supplies last as long as possible, guided by a compass made out of a bottle cap and a piece of pen. About a week later they were spotted by a group of farmers waving shotguns, and they took off, with shot whistling over their heads. Luckily the shot missed, but the farmers cornered them in a field. Jørgen explained in fluent German that they were Danish sailors whose steamship had been sunk by a mine in the Baltic. They were heading for Stettin to get another ship back to Copenhagen. Jimmy Buckley added an indignant *Ja* or *Nein* where it seemed appropriate, which probably exhausted his entire repertoire of German phrases.

The farmers were die-hard German settlers who had heard on the radio that escaped pilots were traveling in pairs in the area and gave their story little credence as they sent one of their number off on a bicycle, peddling furiously in the direction of the local police station. He soon returned with a policeman who examined their papers, including *Ausweise* and Danish passports, all forged in the Schubin camp.

The policeman examined the documents in detail and listened to their story. He read a letter, brilliantly forged in Schubin, from a Seaman's Mission in Danzig urging the reader to offer every assistance to the stricken sailors. He took a second look at the official German eagle stamp in their passes, counterstamped with an ornate and very impressive but entirely fictional seal of the Danish consulate in Warsaw, then saluted and handed them back before rounding on the unfortunate farmers and yelling at them for frightening innocent Danish sailors in their mad pursuit of stray prisoners. The farmers slunk off, and the helpful policeman escorted Buckley and Thalbitzer to the local train station where he made sure they got tickets to Stettin for free and waved them off.

Their luck started to wobble when they reached the port, since there were no Danish vessels and none expected in the near future. They set off walking again and then jumped a freight train to Rostock, where once again there were no Danish vessels, so they moved on again. Their remarkable forged documents, Thalbitzer's fluent German and plausible story, and Jimmy Buckley's nerves of steel saw them through numerous checkpoints and past inquisitive locals. Finally, two weeks after their escape, they reached the small port of Flensburg and found two schooners heading for Denmark. They picked one, which proved to be the second to leave, and were cursing their luck when the ship's captain got word that the other earlier ship had hit a mine and exploded en route. They stopped cursing their luck.

They made it safely to port in Copenhagen, and Thalbitzer, knowing that Jimmy Buckley would be safest out of sight, left him on board and headed for his family home. He found his father, Billy, buying a ticket on the local railway station platform, tapped him on the shoulder, and appeared, as his father remembered, "like a sunburned sailor." Billy hugged his son like a ghost returned from the dead, and Jørgen was able to spend a few remarkable days with his family as plans were made to get him and Buckley away to neutral Sweden. Thalbitzer sent friends for

Buckley on the boat, and he almost made a run for it, mistaking them for Gestapo men, but they persuaded him they were friends and took him to a safe house where they gave him fresh, clean clothes, which he said "make me feel like a gentleman again."

With help from the Free Danish forces the pair were taken up the coastline and given a two-man canoe made of wood and canvas for the short crossing to Sweden. They pushed off from the shore at ten P.M. on March 28, 1943. It had been raining all day, but that night was still and perfectly calm as the armed Resistance fighters waved them off. They were never seen alive again.

Some months later, Billy Thalbitzer got a call from his Free Danish contacts to say a body had been washed ashore. He was able to identify a signet ring on the left hand as one he had given to his son some years earlier. Jimmy Buckley's body was never found. It is possible their canoe was hit by a large vessel in the dark, since Thalbitzer still had on his heavy overcoat and gloves, so it is unlikely he ever had time to swim for it.

Somehow, even in occupied Denmark, the RAF managed to get a wreath of flowers to Thalbitzer's funeral, marking the passing of brave young man with a sense of fun and an even greater sense of freedom, but Jimmy Buckley had to make do with a different memorial, in the minds of those who survived. I and every other person who ever escaped from the camps in which he was our first leader or "Big X," thanks to his blend of caution, courage, and humor, owe him a great deal, probably our lives.

Some of these stories trickled back to me in the cooler as other escapers were recaptured, while other stories only reached us long after the event. I stared at the concrete walls and bars and wondered if it was all worth it. Eventually, all good things must come to an end, so one day the cell door of the cooler was flung open and I emerged squinting and covering my eyes from the bright sunlight. The Blond Beast looked surlier than ever when I was released, and I quickly found out why. We were all soon to be transferred back to Stalag Luft III. For me, this meant reunion with my many former friends, even if it was in a camp where escape was much harder. For the Blond Beast, in disgrace since our mass breakout, it meant an inevitable transfer to the Russian Front, where things were not going all that well for them.

The one advantage to being back in Schubin was that eventually I was able to relish the exact details of what had happened inside the camp after the escape. When I emerged from the cooler, a group of friends including Ollie Philpot, who later made one of the greatest escapes of the entire war himself as one of the Wooden Horse team at Stalag Luft III, welcomed me back to the "real" world. They told me the story of the morning after our escape. That night they had lain awake waiting for the telltale siren or the noises of shouting guards and growling guard dogs and they had heard the most amazing sound—total silence. They could hardly believe it when the eight A.M. Appell was called and the alarm had still not been raised.

The newer, more excitable prisoners hastily threw on their clothes to hurry out for a good place at the show, but the camp veterans knew better. They methodically put on layers of clothing and shoved what food they could into their pockets. An Appell after any escape, never mind one in which more than forty prisoners would be missing, either as escapees or "ghosts," was liable to last all day, with endless hours being spent in the process as the guards tried to work out how many prisoners they had and how many had been mysteriously subtracted.

As luck would have it, the camp security officer, the obnoxious

Simms, was taking the parade, along with one of the most hated and bullying young guards, an Aryan giant known as the Butcher Boy. Simms strutted toward the line of senior officers, in which the senior British officer, Wings Day, and his deputy, Major Dodge, were conspicuous by their absence. At first Simms thought it was another of these strange British jokes, but gradually it dawned on him that they had escaped. He barked orders to the Butcher Boy, who scurried off, much to the mirth of the assembled prisoners. About eight hours too late, the sirens sounded, telephones rang, and sleepy guards were turned out of their beds.

Meanwhile Simms counted the men. He furrowed his brow and counted again. Now trembling with rage and confusion, he stamped back to the stand-in British senior officer, Wing Commander Ryder.

"There are too many! How is this?" Simms voice rose along with his blood pressure, and Ryder shrugged as if he were just as baffled as Simms. The irritable little Czech fascist who had made our lives a misery with his pomposity and lack of humanity started counting again. This time he saw something different. Appells, since time immemorial, had consisted of men standing in rows five deep, making counting easier for the more mathematically challenged of the guards. On this morning the prisoners were in neat rows of four. On discovering our ruse, Simms, now ready to have a heart attack, barged back to the senior British officer.

"You know we count in fives! We *always* count in fives! Why have you put your men in fours?"

Ryder took his time, looked at the men, and then, almost apologetically, turned back to Simms. "Well, there seemed more of them that way."

The rows of prisoners erupted into the loudest cheering and laughing that had ever been heard in that godforsaken camp. Their delight helped keep out the cold as they were forced to stand in the open for the rest of the day while every available guard tore the camp and the surrounding grounds apart looking for the missing prisoners or evidence of an escape.

A guard searching the perimeter found the tunnel exit, but the ferrets were so afraid of booby traps and cave-ins that they sent a reluctant Russian prisoner down at bayonet point with a rope tied around his waist. Much to the ferrets' surprise, he emerged quite some time later inside the latrines. Meanwhile the content of the latrines was hitting the fan for the unfortunate German officers. Both the pompous Simms and the camp commandant were taken away to a court-martial and a one-way ticket to the Russian Front. The commandant may have had time to ponder the irony that when Wings Day had come to him six months earlier to complain about the state of the latrines, he had sent him packing with the reply, "They are latrines. What do you expect them to smell like? Anthony Eden's hair?" To every prisoner in the camp, they now smelled like victory. Wings may only have escaped for a few days, but he had won his war with the commandant.

The even more unpleasant Gestapo took over the running of the camp for the following weeks, and later on that first day after the escape, a huge fleet of buses pulled up outside the camp. Hundreds of SS troops and Gestapo intelligence men marched into the camp in single file. Here was proof positive that our theory about tying up German troops and resources by our escapes was true.

The Nazis shoved the confused and leaderless guards to one side and kept the prisoners out of the huts while they rummaged and ransacked, but since they were not trained ferrets, they had little idea of what exactly they were looking for. Ollie Philpot told me of how the SS troops discovered an illicit barrel of home-brewed beer in one hut. Instead of smashing it, they asked how much it was for a glass. They were charged fifty pfennigs each and a roaring bar trade was soon under way until the barrel was drunk dry. One of the most difficult things to get inside a prison camp was German currency, and to be caught with even a single German banknote meant a long spell in the cooler, but here the SS were only too eager to form an orderly line to meekly hand it over. It was lucky for the POWs that they were only interested in the beer, since a more careful search might have revealed that the barrel had a false bottom in which were concealed all the remaining forged documents in the camp. Pressing our advantage, other prisoners opened up a thriving retail outlet for chocolate and cigarettes, and more useful cash rolled in.

Some hours later, after finding very little, but laden with chocolate and cigarettes, the SS marched smartly back to their buses to continue the search in the surrounding countryside.

The Gestapo ran things for a few weeks after the commandant and Simms disappeared to their court-martial. As well as a new commandant, the camp needed a new Abwehr, or security, head to replace Simms, and the jovial Rittmeister Reimer found himself promoted. Despite his amiable and jolly nature, he was all too effective from our point of view, and in the final months of our stay he found several of our remaining tunnel projects.

The replacement commandant, a rather Gothic-looking Austrian, was only in place for a few weeks or a month, but he seemed a more reasonable character despite having rather theatrical tendencies. No doubt knowing that he was next in line for the Russian Front if any more tunnels succeeded, he took to strolling around in the evenings after we had been locked up, like an extra in a Dracula movie. He wore a black officer's cape buttoned at the neck that then flowed open down to the ground. In his hands he usually carried a mysterious black device, and he looked for all the world like one of those cartoon drawings of an anarchist clutching a black bowling ball with a fizzing fuse, helpfully marked BOMB. Strangely enough, that was exactly what it was. He would stalk around the open areas and then choose a nesting place for his device, which must have been some kind of small mine. He would then scratch a hole with his highly polished jackboot, deposit his mysterious object and stroll to a safe distance, with his minions getting as far away as possible. Then he would stand, head forward as if he were praying, cape flapping, peering at the ground like an old crow waiting for a worm. There would be a muffled boom and a small shower of earth would fly in the air.

The commandant would then step forward and inspect the small crater he had made, perhaps disappointed that he had not created a new and unexpected entrance to a tunnel, but nonetheless would stroll off, apparently satisfied, to repeat the whole process a few days later. While the unexpected bangs were not good for the nerves, most of us agreed that if he was busy engaging in theatrical but harmless gestures while we got on with the humdrum business of escaping, then his interest in fireworks was only to be encouraged.

Our mass escape had made the Wehrmacht look foolish. The army was meant to be showing the Luftwaffe how to deal with us, but their camp was leaking like a sieve. The date for our departure was brought forward, and the German High Command was glad to give the Luftwaffe another go at keeping us in our place.

A fleet of army trucks was waiting to take us back to Stalag Luft III, and there, grinning like a Cheshire cat at the downfall of his Wehrmacht foes, was our old Luftwaffe jailer, Feldwebel Glemnitz, just to make sure that we went "home" without any detours.

When he had us marched out of the camp and into the town, he discovered that the army had laid on trucks for our journey back to Luft III. Knowing our propensity for escaping from such vehicles, and assuming quite rightly that many of us were armed with files to saw our way out of the trucks, he had us marched back to the camp. There he argued with the army once more until we were all put into nice escape-proof third-class trains.

"You are officers," he smiled. "You will be so much more comfortable this way!"

11. Over the Wire

By spring of 1943, the tide of the war seemed to be turning both in the East and in North Africa. The invincible tone of all Nazi propaganda boomed out over the camp loudspeakers began to have just the faintest trace of doubt lurking somewhere in the background. It was starting to strike the smarter soldiers of the Fatherland that their Thousand Year Reich might not be around quite as long as planned. This was to have repercussions for us prisoners of war.

Since the early days of the war there had been a power struggle between the Luftwaffe and the Gestapo for control and running of the camps. In a way, my rescue from the Gestapo in Paris had been a microcosm of this bigger battle. In the early days of the war, the Luftwaffe won most of the skirmishes, but as the tide of war turned, the Gestapo started to make its move.

It might seem strange that two such forces would fight over the privilege of trying to keep tens of thousands of young men against their will in camps all over Germany and the East, but the High Command recognized our value to any negotiated settlement. If things were going badly for Germany, we prisoners turned from a liability into an asset in the form of a large body of hostages who could be shot or freed, depending on how negotiations were going. Nearly every Nazi at this period, or at least those who were not so deluded as to still be convinced of victory, thought that the most likely scenario was a truce in the West with their old Anglo brothers, swiftly followed by a joint Holy War against the Red Menace in the East. They, like the so-called appeasers of the 1930s in Britain and America, who were perfectly happy for Hitler to rampage as long as he did it in the East, underestimated the determination of the people of both West and East to finish what the Nazis had started. Those same ordinary people who had joined up in their droves to fight Hitler did not think of the Russians as anything other than an ally, and it took years of cold war rhetoric to replace that friendship with mutual fear.

So it was back in the creaking trains for us, and back to the Fatherland. At Stalag Luft III, business was booming, with the number of prisoners there having risen from about two thousand to a peak near the end of the war of ten thousand. In my absence they had opened a new RAF compound as well as a third compound for downed airmen of the USAAF. It was good to be near so many Americans, even if divided by two layers of barbed wire and the deadly no-man's-land in between that was covered by the machine gunners in the watchtowers.

I was reunited with many of my old friends and started to help with a tunnel which, like most in Luft III, was a triumph of meticulous planning and engineering skill. Aboveground, camp life went on, but was now more structured. There were amateur drama groups and debating societies as well as all the usual sports groups and an army of gardeners supplementing their diet with homegrown vegetables. Yet even in these gentle pursuits the world of escapology was never far away. The gardens were liberally sprinkled with tunnel dirt to get rid of the mountains of the stuff we had to shift, and later, during the north compound Great Escape, much of the tunnel spoil was tipped into a huge cavity under seat number thirteen of the prisoners' theater.

By this time Red Cross parcels were arriving more regularly, and a flourishing commodity market had opened up. A few shrewd but greedy prisoners traded in the futures of Canadian butter or British corned beef and bribed guards for information about what would be in the next Red Cross shipment so that they would be well placed to have the right things to swap. It seemed sad to me that some people would spend their time hustling other prisoners rather than trying to escape or just to get on with life as a prisoner, but they were always in the minority. Similarly, there was a handful of sharks that specialized in long-running poker schools where the more foolish players ended up owing literally years of back pay. Luckily, the majority of prisoners, if not anxious to get themselves shot while escaping, were more interested in helping other escapees than in being reduced to the miserable state of preying on each other. Myself and my old escape buddy Eddy Asselin never did manage to see eye to eye on that one, yet we stayed friends.

While my first love remained escaping, I was really missing the music that had been such a part of my life since being stopped in my tracks in Texas by that wonderful first time I heard classical music seeping out of a church hall into the night air. It reminded me of the other times it had played a part as the backdrop to my adventures—listening to the cello solo by the woman I was in love with but never talked to at the National Gallery while the sirens wailed and the bombs fell, or staring at the ceiling in my room at the airfield as the sound of Bach or Schubert mixed with the noise of Spitfire engines.

Apart from the welcome serenades by Bill Stapleton at lights-out that I mentioned earlier, there was not much chance of hearing classical music in Luft III. There were few records and even fewer phonographs, and while we had a few hidden radio receivers, using them was much too dangerous to do so for entertainment, or indeed for anything but brief bursts to grab the news from the BBC in London. In every camp, there was only one place that classical music was sure to be played, and that was on the phonograph or radio in the German officers' quarters. I remember risking a long spell in the cooler, or even being shot, by slipping out of my hut after curfew and crawling and running between the huts until I reached an internal fence that separated us from a hut full of off-duty German officers. One of them listened to classical music radio broadcasts from Berlin, and I would crouch by the wire, spellbound as the music would drift across, an unwitting gift from my captors. I was always puzzled by a culture that could produce and appreciate Bach or Beethoven also being responsible for the chaos and atrocities of wartime Europe, but if music was the one thing on which we could call a truce, that was fine by me.

During my years of captivity, I started to realize just how much the creation of Hitler was owed to the terrible conditions imposed on Germany after World War I that resulted in economic collapse and mass unemployment. Not for a minute do I condone the people who sought salvation through Hitler or his crude, vicious political theories, but it is too convenient not to see the role that the victorious West played in helping to create the monster in the first place. The Western leaders, with exceptions such as Churchill, were not too bothered about Hitler so long as his hostilities seemed to be pointing east toward the "Bolshevik peril" or aimed at weaker countries such as Poland or Czechoslovakia, a place that the prewar British prime minister cynically called "a faraway country about which we know little."

By the time I got back to Stalag Luft III, it also felt like a faraway country. If the camp and the Allied prisoners had changed in my absence, so, too, had the guards. The ferrets were now even more sophisticated at discovering tunnels. There is now some evidence that they did not always act immediately to shut a tunnel when they detected it. If it was still a long way from the perimeter, they would let us slave away oblivious, knowing that we would otherwise only be starting a new one that they might not detect. Then, when it looked like we might be getting somewhere, they would pounce and cart the diggers off to the cooler.

The ferrets used listening tubes to detect the sound of digging underground. They measured soil levels under the huts to see if we were dumping spoil from the tunnels there. They even took to driving heavy vehicles over the area between our huts and the perimeter fence to collapse our underground earthworks. Despite all of this, the tunneling continued. When one was discovered, we would "break" another one.

Paddy and I both got involved with the tunneling plans and covering for other people's escape activities, but after my spending so much time in the cooler and being a rather obvious serial escapologist, I started to find that it was difficult for me to even go for a stroll around the perimeter fence without attracting attention from the guards. This made working toward escapes even more difficult, and I did not want my own unwelcome celebrity with the ferrets to make matters worse for my comrades.

For a while, I was not quite sure what to do. Maybe I should throw myself into some worthy educational project or start scribbling yet another unpublished masterpiece. One thing that always stayed with me was my hunger for news.

In a prisoner-of-war camp there are only a few possible sources of news. There was the rumor mill. Someone had heard that the Allied invasion was about to happen. Someone had heard that a senior American officer had been captured and the Allies were going to stage a daring commando raid to rescue us all along with him. Someone else had heard that the SS was going to shoot us all, or that there was a new batch of Red Cross parcels at the local train depot. Virtually all the rumors turned out to be untrue, particularly the good ones, so kriegies developed a sort of split personality, eagerly adding to the output of the rumor mill while regarding all such "sure things" with healthy skepticism.

Then there was news from home. Every letter from loved ones was eagerly pored over, and those bits that had not been obliterated by the censor's pen were read and reread. They opened a door to a world we had almost forgotten. It was a world in which people went to parties and children made things to bring home from school. Other people got married, sometimes to the wife of the letter recipient. Part of us delighted in being able to at least peer into a world that felt very far away, but the effect could also be to make us feel more forgotten, if not by the letter writer, then by the rest of the world, which seemed to be getting along just fine without us.

My own letter writing, not prolific at the best of times, gradually dwindled in the course of the war, with the exception of occasional overly cheerful replies to my mother's worried letters. Because I read books more than I wrote letters, a girl who worked at one of the charities that sent books to us from Switzerland started to write to me. Apparently in an attempt to keep my morale up, in addition to sending crateloads of improving classical literature, she would always enclose a letter giving the details of her weekend, spent in the pawing embraces of her boyfriend. No detail was regarded as too steamy for inclusion, and with the letters I could probably have started a thriving black market in second-hand pornography. Instead, since I've always thought making love was not much of a spectator sport, I buried my head in some volume on medieval romance and pretended not to be thinking about escaping.

The next source of news was the Nazis themselves. They would blare propaganda on a regular basis over a wheezy loudspeaker system. Usually the details were nonsense—all Nazi triumphs and heroic repelling of the Russian hordes—but if you listened carefully for place names in each broadcast, you could usually follow on a map the rough reality behind the lies, watching which way the place names mentioned in each bulletin seemed to be moving—east or west.

Slightly more reliable broadcasts could be obtained from the BBC in London, but this involved building and hiding a secret radio receiver. Luckily for us, expert radio operators on bombers were being blown out of the sky on a regular basis, and several of these clever people dedicated their entire time in the camp to the simultaneous pursuit of the news and evasion of the ferrets.

The secret radios—there was usually at least one hidden in every compound—were ingenious contraptions. One of the earliest was put together at the Barth camp and brought in pieces to Stalag Luft III. It was mostly made from scrap materials, but the tubes usually had to be bought from bribed guards.

Hiding places had to become ever more ingenious. In Luft III, one radio was smuggled in inside a football and another hidden under a toilet, while at Schubin one had been hidden inside the phonograph belonging to Wings Day, the senior British officer. Later, in the central compound at Luft III, some enterprising Americans stole a radio from the infirmary and reassembled it to fit inside a table leg, which was nailed under the tabletop with four long nails. Two of the nails were used as terminals for the power supply, and the others were used to connect the earphones.

There were different methods of disseminating the news, but since it was clearly impossible to bring the listeners to the radio without also bringing a lot of interested ferrets, the most common network was one of reporters and readers. Each night a radio operator would listen with headphones, often quietly repeating the news for another prisoner who was an expert in shorthand. These men would then ensure that the news was read out to groups of prisoners the following day, usually under the guise of some education class. Sometimes, when those whose job it was to stand on a chair and tell a huddle of prisoners the news were unable to make notes or write it down, the news was a bit sketchy, but at least most of them refrained from adding to it to make it more exciting.

On one occasion the guards unwittingly obliged in the transfer of news from one compound with a radio to another where the radio had been found and confiscated. One of the shorthand experts was allowed to give classes to the prisoners in the other compound, and each day his sample shorthand exercise bore a remarkable resemblance to the previous day's news from the BBC.

The prisoners who devoted their days to supplying news to thousands of isolated and information-hungry kriegies played a vital role in stopping the camps turning into little inward-looking worlds. Many of them went on to very successful careers in print journalism or broadcasting.

As I listened to the progress of the war in the outside world, my old desire to get out and see what I was missing started to return. I heard a rumor that sergeant pilots from the central compound beside us were to be sent to a different camp at Hydekrug in Lithuania, for noncommissioned officers. The fact that I was not an NCO sergeant did not deter me. If I could get to a different camp, I could use the period of chaos at the founding of any camp as a happy hunting ground for future escapes. I hatched a plan and found a plucky New Zealander, Don Fair, who was more than willing to swap identities if it meant he did not have to get sent to the wilds of Lithuania. He would get a free promotion to flight lieutenant into the bargain. The only trouble was that Don Fair was in the central compound next door, on the other side of two tall barbed-wire fences covered by guard posts and machine guns.

I said my farewells to Paddy and my other friends and, with their help, prepared for an escape from one compound to the next. The guard towers and walking patrols had the area covered, but most of their attention was directed to the outer perimeter. My friends caused several distractions—a mock fight and a noisy football game—while I loitered on one side of the fence and Don Fair strolled innocently on the other.

When the guards were looking the other way, we raced for the fence, crossing the warning wire that meant you would be shot on sight beyond that point, then over the barbed-wire fence that was ten feet tall, but felt more like a hundred feet while I was clambering it, waiting at every second for a bullet in the back.

Meanwhile Don was doing the same from the other compound. We both made it to the no-man's-land, which spanned perhaps three or four yards between the fences. We crouched down, hastily shook hands, and swapped identity papers. Then, with a quick look around to make sure the guards were still distracted, we were off again, climbing the wire into the other man's compound, across the terrible open space and over the warning wire to safety and the continuation of our innocent strolls. I never got to see or speak to Don Fair again, but for the best part of a year, my parents got letters from someone called Don whose handwriting looked very much like their son's, and who seemed to know rather a lot about their son's former life in Texas. Meanwhile, somewhere in New Zealand, the Fair family was probably getting letters from someone they had never heard of called Bill Ash, telling them he missed them and was looking forward to coming home.

12. A Tour of Lithuania

The departure from Stalag Luft III was made more interesting when the camp commandant, Von Lindeiner, turned out in person to see us off. Since he had several occasions to have a close look and a shout at Flight Lieutenant Ash, usually when I was en route to the cooler, I shuffled to the back of the parade in case he got curious about the uncanny resemblance between one Don Fair and the roving prisoner Ash. In fact on one occasion he had even furtively congratulated me on a previous escape, but I think he would have been less than supportive of my current efforts. I remember in his farewell speech he called us his "boys" and urged us not to escape, hinting that the days of chivalry were coming to an end. I think he was a decent man and was genuinely worried about what would happen to us when we left the relative safety of Luftwaffe jurisdiction for a world full of Wehrmacht and

Gestapo types. Still, I smiled to myself, thinking back to Paris, since as far as I was concerned, the world of chivalry had apparently ended some time back in 1933.

As we marched out, I could see some of my old friends in the other compound standing by the wire to see us off. There was Paddy, and over there was Bill Stapleton. Even the senior British officers, Wings Day and Group Captain Herbert Massey, were there. Wings took off his cap and waved it at us. I found my hand reaching up to wave back but shoved it resolutely back in my pocket. This was not a good time to draw attention to my unauthorized departure.

As we passed the senior German officers, we were marching in pretty impressive formation for a ragtag bunch of prisoners. The senior British NCO barked the order "Eyes right!" and we marched out like soldiers. The Luftwaffe officers held their salute until the last man had left the camp. I marched along trying to look inconspicuous, hunched within a huddle of my tallest new NCO friends as the wire gates were shut behind us and we marched under the watchful eyes and machine guns of our guards to the local railway station. As Stalag Luft III receded behind me, I hoped that I would never see it again. If I had been able to see into the future, I might have been surprised at just how glad I would be to be back there.

Many of my new NCO colleagues had originally come from another camp, Stalag Luft I at Barth, and they were a very interesting mix of career soldiers and a majority of wartime volunteers, a mix which had previously led to some lively differences of opinion about discipline and democracy. The attempts to run their previous camp along rather rigid lines of King's Regulations by some career senior NCOs had met stiff resistance among some of the more dogged individuals who had only recently left civilian life and were determined to fight on their own terms. Some of them came from families who had lost a previous generation of obedient soldiers who charged to meaningless deaths in the trenches of the previous war, and these men were not about to do the same.

While knowing that an army without rank and regulations will never get anywhere, I naturally felt a closer affinity to these characters. They could be tough and disciplined when they needed to, but they did not need to be shouted at by those for whom barked orders on parade grounds and spit-and-polish regimentation were the order of the day. So the NCOs had achieved a remarkable thing: Despite several hundred years of army tradition, they had effectively voted in their own leader to run their affairs. This man was recognized not only by the prisoners but by the German authorities as what they called the "Man of Confidence." He was the remarkable Jimmy "Dixie" Deans, a sergeant who the men decided was a general.

Jimmy was a brave but very low-key man from Scotland, and a brilliant example of someone who could use his head as well as his heart. He spoke excellent German and was always turned out very neatly in regulation uniform with a collar and tie. He tended not to waste words, but said what he meant and meant what he said. Jimmy was proof positive that you don't have to shout to be a commanding presence, and the camp authorities knew it as well as we did. He viewed his job as being to make the place run as well as possible so that the escape committee could work in peace, and despite incredible hardships and dangers, he never lost sight of both of those at times contradictory necessities. In a world where most people liked to pretend that the war would be over in

a few months, or at least could not bear to face the thought of
further years behind the wire, Jimmy was prepared to look the
possibility in the eye. When he was captured in September 1940,
he had made a calendar for himself. It ran from the day he made
it to the end of May 1945.

There was one other truly remarkable character eventually
destined for the Hydekrug camp. As the prisoners sat on the train
with our guards and a shouting German officer ran about issuing
orders, some of my new NCO colleagues stared goggle-eyed at a
smartly dressed German civilian guzzling down a tankard of beer
in the station cafeteria on the platform.

The man got up from the café and approached the hyperactive
German officer in charge of the train. He had a stern conversation with him, and the officer seemed to cringe and nod. One
man on the train muttered, "Gestapo," but another man replied,
"No, it's not. It's bloody Grimson."

George Grimson was perhaps the most remarkable figure in
the NCO camp, which was crammed with amazing people. He
was a stocky man with close-cropped fair hair, and he had a pugnacious manner that put some people off, but was actually quite
reserved underneath. He had been shot down in 1940 and had
started to gain a reputation as a man of great nerve when he was
at the camp in Barth. There his escape attempts had included im-
personating a guard as he strolled out the gate, with the advantage that he spoke good German and could use his natural
manner to bark at guards and distract them from searching him
or checking his identity. He had escaped a few times but had been
recaptured.

How he came to be drinking beer and was able to convince the
train officer that he was a Gestapo man while the rest of us were

being herded off to the Hydekrug camp is a typical Grimson story. Back in Luft III, in the NCO compound we had just left, he had dressed as an "engineering ferret," one of those who wandered around the camp testing telephone lines and repairing the lights. With his German forage cap set at a jaunty tilt and a ladder slung over his shoulder, he had shouted a warning to a machine gunner guard in a tower, then stepped over the death wire and marched up to the perimeter fence.

Grimson had borrowed the ladder from the camp theater and, equally theatrically, was carrying a large box with electrical cables dangling from it and a gauge that looked like an ammeter. Once he reached the fence, he put up his ladder and started testing lightbulbs. When he was at the top of the wire, he dropped some tools down the other side, accidentally on purpose. He swore loudly in German, then asked the guard in the tower if he could climb over to pick them up and then walk around the perimeter to the entrance to come back and continue his work. The bored guard nodded, and that is what Grimson did, although he forgot about the part where he was supposed to come back. This got him into the German part of the camp, where he hid out for several hours before marching through two gates and presenting his forged papers. Suddenly, he was outside the camp. When he was in a quiet spot, he peeled off his ferret costume to reveal a smart suit underneath as he changed into a new identity of roving Gestapo man. In an act of spectacular chutzpah, he had booked himself as a security representative on our train. He hopped on at the back, and the train pulled out.

The trains they loaded us on were cramped but otherwise not too grim. Each coach was divided into three wired-off sections, with the middle section containing a half dozen nervous German guards armed with machine guns and grenades, though any idea that they could have thrown one of them without themselves becoming what the bomber crews liked to call strawberry jam was at best unlikely.

Our captors took us on a wandering route of minor lines to the north and east, possibly because the more straightforward routes were disrupted by Allied bombing, which was really starting to pick up. At one such stop Grimson alighted and saw the train off, looking stern and Gestapo-like, before continuing his journey. He made it to Stettin on the coast and made some useful contacts among the slave laborers from many countries, but while he was still searching for a neutral ship that would take him, he was caught up in the hunt for an escaped Russian prisoner who had killed a German NCO during his escape. The Russian and Grimson were both captured and spent what Grimson later described as a very enjoyable night locked in a filthy cell, passing the time by having races and jumping contests with the bedbugs. They became so engrossed in the bedbug Olympics that the Russian protested loudly at his game being cut short as he was led out to a courtyard where he was executed. Grimson was put on a train to Hydekrug, this time traveling third class without his swastika lapel badge, where he joined us a few days later and immediately became active in our fledgling escape committee.

By nightfall on our own train journey we were shunted into a marshaling yard on the outskirts of Berlin. Soon we heard the heavy throb of aircraft engines overhead as Allied bombers rolled over the city. The sky was illuminated by swiveling searchlights and antiaircraft fire lit up the sky. The dull crump and shrill whistle of bombs falling and the louder crash of closer hits filled the night air. Many of the NCO prisoners were bomber crew, and they clapped and cheered from this unexpected ringside seat as the German capital took a pasting.

As the prisoners got more boisterous and jubilant, the guards got more nervous, their fingers twitching close to their gun triggers. The guards were not just nervous about us. They had rather more experience of being on the receiving end of such bombing, and they knew that a railway carriage on a Berlin siding was not the safest place to be when Bomber Harris's men were dropping explosives all around them.

Some of the prisoners started to goad the guards, inquiring whether they were from Berlin, and not surprisingly machine guns were starting to be cocked as fear turned to menace. The quiet, commanding voice of Jimmy Deans told the guard baiters to pipe down. Jimmy did not hate fascists any less than the rest of us, but he knew that a carriage full of dead prisoners due to a guard who had been pushed too far would hardly help the war effort. We would wait until we got to the new camp and then carry on our war with all the skills we had built up over years of escape attempts.

So, in the summer of 1943, we arrived at Hydekrug camp in Lithuania, Stalag Luft VI, not far from the town of Memel on the Memel Peninsula. The place was a strange, swampy, mist-shrouded backwater, not far from the Baltic coast. Like a Promised Land for escapologists, it indeed afforded better opportunities for departing suddenly than at Luft III. When we entered the camp, many of the prisoners flopped down in the long grass and lay soaking up the sunshine, grateful to be anywhere but Stalag Luft III, but within weeks the grass had been trampled by a thousand captive feet into the prison yard dust with which we were all too familiar.

Hydekrug was a converted barracks, and as such was a bit more solidly constructed than most of the German camps, which, from POW enclosures to concentration camps, were mostly built along very similar lines of communal one-story huts and barbed-wire fences. In Hydekrug the four long accommodation huts were built of brick and whitewashed on the inside. There were big, old brick ovens at each end of the rooms which helped to stave off the bitterly cold Baltic winters. However, it was summer 1943, and personally I planned to be far away long before the stoves would be needed for heating. The commandant had other ideas and was already building two new compounds alongside us to accommodate the vast numbers of American and British bomber crews who were now raiding Berlin both day and night and being denounced as *Luftgangster* in the Nazi media.

At first I was regarded with a mixture of amusement and bafflement by some of the down-to-earth and hard-nosed NCOs in the new camp. The idea that an officer would willingly muck in with the ranks to the extent of deliberately swapping identities to join them in the wilds of Lithuania struck some as funny and others as slightly demented. Luckily, word quickly went around that I was an experienced if not altogether successful escape artist, and I quickly found myself once again in the reluctant role of veteran escapologist for a new generation keen to learn.

Alongside a small group of experienced escape artists, forgers, tailors, and Allied escape trades stood an increasing number of new arrivals, mostly survivors of horrific crashes or bailouts from burning bombers shot down during the city raids of preceding weeks. Some of them looked to the veteran escapers for advice on anything from tunnel construction to surviving the loss of colleagues or the separation from loved ones. Our escape committee, which included me, Jock Alexander, George Grimson, Paddy Flynn, and several others, gave a new name to escape activities—the Tallyho Club. This sounded terribly upper crust and English to me, so naturally it was a club I was proud to join, even if it was one I hoped to get thrown out of by escaping.

Inside, I still felt like the same young Texan, hardly up to such tasks, with no idea where I was going or how to get there. The only thing I was certain about was that wherever "there" was, it lay on the other side of the wire.

The guards at Hydekrug were tough. Major Peschel, their security officer, and his team of ferrets worked ceaselessly to uncover our tunnel and other escape preparations, and at first they had considerable success, mainly due to overenthusiasm and lax security on our part.

Despite their little victories over us, the guards' morale was low and getting lower. The war was starting to turn, and the Eastern Front was gradually becoming a quagmire for the Germans. As things worsened, our meager rations got even smaller, and gradually it became harder not to suffer from some kind of malnutrition as weeks turned to months.

The news of Russian advances redoubled my resolve to get out and stay out. I even pondered some plans of heading east rather than west, conveniently ignoring the fact that to reach the Russian front lines I would have to somehow get through the German rear.

While I was pondering my options, I and the rest of the escape committee were also making preparations for the bold Grimson to make his next bid for freedom, only this one would be different from almost every other escape of the war. Grimson was not going to try to get away, but to set up an underground railroad for future escapees. It took some courage to attempt to escape, but to deliberately stay in occupied Europe to help others took a very special man.

The first part of the plan was to get Grimson out of the camp, and several schemes failed without the guards even knowing they were happening. Then Grimson hit on the idea of using his skills of deception to get him out disguised as a guard. In good weather the roll calls took place on the football field, and a dozen guards would take up positions around the field. When the counting and shouting were over, they would walk back across our compound, through the gates to the German area, or *Vorlager*, where the guard room was. On the day of Grimson's bid for freedom the prisoners managed to keep the count going until dusk, and at the end of the parade there was one more guard than at the start. He was resplendent in a German greatcoat, and his rifle looked menacing—if you did not look too closely to see that it was made entirely of wood carved from bed boards by a talented sergeant called Webster.

Grimson strolled out with no problems. He changed in a lavatory beside the guard room, then made his way to a storeroom where we had all his supplies and paperwork waiting for him. He ambled out of the camp as a well-dressed civilian and was soon on board a train to Innsbruck. He made it all the way to a village south of Danzig, where he was looked after by Polish patriots, and from there he set out to build an escape route through the Danzig docks to Sweden.

He stayed out for several months, snatching a few hours of sleep in railway stations and moving from one rented room to another, constantly in fear of capture, but along the way he made contact with the Polish Resistance and with those who were willing to help escapees either for moral reasons or for money. Bravest of all, he made several trips back to Hydekrug, where he met intermediaries who carried messages back inside the camps. He helped another prisoner called Paddy Flockhart escape and got him on a boat bound for Sweden. Ten days later, Flockhart was back in Britain, while Grimson continued his one-man war in the Baltic. But such bravery alone is not always enough, and good luck never lasts forever.

One of our brave Polish helpers on the outside was uncovered following a shootout between German troops and members of the Resistance. Afterward, Poles were tortured and shot and the Gestapo trail started leading back, through Poles and guards who had assisted him in the camp and on the outside, to Grimson. The escape committee sent him a short message: "Get out of the country. Position hopeless," but by then it was too late. Rumors of Grimson's arrest circulated, and then—nothing.

It is almost certain that Grimson was captured, interrogated, then taken out and shot by the Gestapo, but no trace of him was ever found, during or after the war. In a strange way this gave him an immortality that fitted very well with his bravery. Like a Robin Hood or a ghost, for the rest of the war both the Germans and more than a few escapers would look over their shoulders, half expecting to see Grimson, on the loose again.

In the months leading up to these events, a group of us had started a long tunnel, aiming for the edge of a grove of birch trees beyond the perimeter fence. Our experience had taught us that half the battle with a tunnel was keeping the entrance concealed despite searches for long enough to allow the tunnel to reach cover outside the camp. We had learned from our successes and failures at Schubin and Luft III, so we chose another latrine as a good starting point, both to discourage the ferrets from snooping and to give us somewhere to lose several hundred tons of tunnel dirt.

We started with the same sort of arrangement, a tunnel entrance underneath one of the toilet seats, then a precarious tightrope walk along a brick wall underground just a few feet above a cesspit of sewage that led to another underground foundation wall and another hole. Climbing though this brought us to a vast, hollowed-out chamber and the start of the tunnel. But we had hardly got started when we realized there was a fundamental problem. The high water table meant that as we added tunnel dirt to the latrine, the sewage level rose until it very quickly reached the entrance to our tunnel and flooded it with unmentionable liquid. We thought we were at a standstill until someone, I think it was a kriegie called Jack Catley, came up with one of those indecently brilliant ideas that can turn any situation around.

At the end of the long line of toilet holes was a wall, and on the far side of the wall was a small laundry room with three huge hot-water boilers. They weighed a ton, but could be deconstructed into three parts, a base, a boiler, and an outer metal sleeve for insulation. We moved the lot out of the way, dug a manhole through the stubborn concrete beneath, and excavated a new cavern as the starting place for our tunnel. Up above, we reassembled the boiler so it could actually be lit and working while I and the other diggers were toiling below. Even the most suspicious guard, peering at a huge bubbling vat of clothes, would not dream that it covered the entrance to another world. Best of all, having worked in half a dozen stifling holes in the ground by now, I knew that ventilation was one of the most important factors in how long and how efficiently we could dig. With this new arrangement, the tunnel acted as a flue to the boiler fire. We poked unobtrusive air holes to the surface from the tunnel and the draw of the fire sucked the air from the surface and through the tunnel to the boiler, giving us the first air-conditioned escape tunnel in the Third Reich.

There was no shortage of willing diggers, but despite the secure entrance and better air, the work was hard and seemed endless, marred by cave-ins and flooding in the soft swampy loam of Lithuania. The water table was very high, so we could not dig down too far, yet we could not make the tunnel too shallow either, since the German microphones would pick up the noise of our burrowing.

Our shoring to prevent further collapses was once again based on purloining bed boards, and once again the majority of the camp showed willing and donated at least one each, while the escapers were again expected to lead by example, by sleeping on a bunk bed apparently held up by air and string, defying the laws of gravity. To make sure that the tunnel roof was also defying gravity by staying up, the amount of shoring needed was calculated by former mining engineers and several university lecturers in mathematics who happened to be among our diverse talent pool.

While this work went on, Dixie Deans had his hands full as the leader, or Man of Confidence, in the camp. We desperately needed both information on the new locality and materials for escaping, from clothes to documentation. The passes, or *Ausweise*, changed with incredible frequency and there was no point in spending six months of incredible hardship working to get out if let down by a forged pass that turned out to have expired a week earlier. There was only one way to get such information, and that was from the guards. Some of them were incorruptible, either out of loyalty to the Fatherland or a healthy fear of being shot by the Gestapo if discovered helping the enemy in even the mildest of ways. But others were susceptible, mostly to greed, a few to excitement, others to getting their own back on some superior officer who had just bawled them out, and toward the end of the war an increasing number recognized that it might be a good idea to be in the Allies' good books if it came to swapping places, with them ending up as the prisoners.

Whatever the flaw, Dixie Deans knew that the way to a guard's heart, or at least to his *Ausweise*, was through his stomach. Our Red Cross supply of chocolate and our relatively generous supply of cigarettes were the envy of all the guards. Some would supply nonsense information in an attempt to get their hands on a few squares of chocolate, but it quickly became obvious who was supplying useful items and who was just a chocoholic. Looking back on it, I see that some of the guards took insane risks for the sake of a handful of cigarettes or a mouthful of chocolate, but the war did strange things to people on both sides.

Our biggest problem in this respect was not the ferrets, but a few of our own. Just like Stalag Luft III, a few prisoners with access to money or influence had managed to set up thriving industries as prison commodity brokers. They bought and sold everything from chocolate and cigarettes to musical instruments and paper, trading with the enemy for personal profit. Some of them used their influence to bribe guards to discover the main ingredients in Red Cross packages that had not yet been distributed. That way they could stay ahead of the curve and buy up whatever would become scarce while off-loading whatever would be plentiful. Some of us detested the idea that the best thing people could turn their minds to was cutting deals with the guards while fleecing fellow prisoners, but others thought it was an admirable example of entrepreneurial spirit.

Wars are a good time for people to focus on what they must do to win, and just as industries such as coal and steel had to effectively be nationalized in Britain as part of the war effort, so we kriegies decided that trading in the new camp should be run to benefit everyone rather than making a few operators rich. We needed to bribe the guards, and that meant we could not afford great lurches in the value of cigarettes or chocolate. We also needed the profit created by the trade to be available for the "purchase" of what we needed for escape—ranging from bits of German uniform to parts for radios and the all-important travel papers.

As usual with such cultural changes, it did not happen without a bit of a struggle, and it probably would not have happened at all had it not been that we were in a new camp where we could start from scratch. Most of all, it would not have happened were it not for the remarkable persuasive powers of Jimmy Deans.

A few of the would-be tycoons objected to the curtailment of their pursuit of riches, and one young guy, recently arrived, complained bitterly about his rights being trampled on. Jimmy was a generally low-key and quiet man, but he had a real authority, and on this one occasion at least, he turned himself up to full volume. He roared at the grumbler, "Rights? The only bloody right you have is to eighteen inches in the ranks!" referring to the statutory width allowed to each man when lined up on parade. "Good men are out there getting killed in the air every night and other good men are in here risking their lives trying to escape, and you talk about rights? Get out of my sight!"

After that, there were no more problems. A flamboyant character called Nat Leaman ran the trading side of things from then on, with all proceeds being funneled into escape activities and the general welfare of the camp. From this arrangement grew a sort of prisoners' store known as Foodaco which used cigarettes as currency, and once again, profits went to where they would do most good for escapes, rather than into a few bulging pockets. Those who just wanted to make a fast buck transferred their energies to gambling for vast amounts of back pay on cards or roulette. Luckily for them, Eddy Asselin was still fleecing all comers back in Luft III; otherwise they would have been lucky to walk away still wearing their uniforms.

Apart from that one justifiable outburst, Jimmy Deans's presence was a constant calming factor in the camp. He enjoyed a rare break from the endless decision making and problem solving with a walk around the camp each day, usually with his pal Ron Mogg, who was another enthusiastic member of the escaping fraternity.

As with the other camps, the Dear John letters or Mespots continued to roll in, increasing in number as the war dragged on and the periods of forced separation between prisoners and their loved ones grew longer, often many times longer than the time they had spent together in the first place. One day a young man had just pinned his sad rejection letter from home to the notice board for all to see. Just as Edwards had done at Schubin, the man ran out and crossed the death wire and started to climb the fence. Jimmy Deans gambled that the guards in the machine-gun towers would recognize him and hesitate to pull the triggers. He shouted at them not to shoot and then marched across the death wire himself. Arms raised, he walked slowly across to the man, who was now sobbing, clinging to the barbed-wire, and waiting for the bullet that would put him out of his misery. Instead, he heard the quiet, calm Scottish voice of Dixie Deans, who gently disentangled him from the wire and led him back to safety, their every step covered by half a dozen nervous guards with fingers on their triggers. The man was handed over to Paddy Pollock, a great Irish doctor and another unsung hero of the camp. After that, Jimmy simply continued his walk with Mogg and went back to talking about camp laundry arrangements.

There were times when being a man of few words was definitely in Jimmy's interest. As our tunnel grew, and became what some people claim was one of the finest to be dug in the course of the war, reaching over 150 feet, Jimmy was summoned to the commandant's office. The commandant had heard there was a tunnel and forged documents in the camp and asked Deans if he knew anything about them. A few hours earlier, Jimmy had been on a secret inspection of our earthworks and had congratulated us on our progress. He looked the commandant in the eye and chose his words carefully, saying he did not know of anything in the camp that should not be there.

A week later we were invaded by the local Gestapo, who joined forces with the guards in the most thorough raid and search we ever experienced. Rooms were ransacked, floorboards ripped up, and hiding places unearthed. They captured maps, papers, compasses, clothing, but in their jubilation at such an impressive haul, one of the Gestapo men momentarily rested his briefcase on a table. When he turned around, it was gone, never to be seen again. From the briefcase we got new documents and a lot of useful information that consoled us on the loss of so much hard-earned equipment. Their frantic searches and threats of reprisals failed to unearth it or its contents.

Despite the loss of the briefcase, which they probably did not even report for fear of being shot by their superiors, the searchers departed happy. They had a good haul of escape equipment, and if there had been a tunnel, they were sure they would have found it. The truth was they had missed it as they inspected the laundry room and prodded the contents of a bubbling wash boiler loaded with clothes.

Those of us on the surface breathed a sigh of relief, but the next day, on the way to a shift at the face of the tunnel, I was surprised to hear a faint rumble growing louder. Sometimes we heard the booming of the long-range Russian artillery on the Eastern Front, but this was more of a low, rolling rumble. Then there was a slight tremor and the grumble turned to a rumble and then a roar. Out from behind some buildings came one of the most eager ferrets, looking pleased with himself and mounted on a huge steamroller that belched smoke as it trundled around the perimeter.

It transpired that the commandant was less convinced than the Gestapo that no tunnel existed just because they had not found it. He was no doubt conscious that being a commandant of one of our camps, whether in Germany, Poland, or Lithuania, seemed like a one-way ticket to the Russian Front. The only way to avoid this fate was to keep us on the inside of the wire. Now he had devised a novel way of deterring tunneling, by driving a steamroller back and forth over all the open ground under which a tunnel might lurk.

I held my breath and spared a thought for the crew who were underground digging as the vast machine rolled directly over the top of our tunnel route. When the coast had cleared, we hurriedly extinguished the boiler fire and were delighted to find not only our comrades unscathed but the tunnel roof holding solidly throughout. But the combination of the searches and the attempts to collapse all our months of hard work did have an effect. Our tunnel had already reached out beyond the perimeter fence, but was not yet at the line of trees that would give us shelter as we emerged. Half of the tunnelers felt that we should risk breaking out into the open as soon as possible rather than wait for the next search to get lucky. The other half wanted to wait for the cover of the trees, even if it meant enduring the increasing possibility of the tunnel being discovered in the weeks it would take us to reach them.

The escape committee met to discuss the matter. Jock Alexander was strongly against the early break, while there were others equally passionate in its favor. I tended to lean toward those who wanted to dig the tunnel straight up and get out as soon as possible. We argued back and forth long into the day, and eventually we decided that we would recommend that the digging continue despite the risk of discovery, but that we would leave the decision to a vote by those who were on the escape. I was one of the few people who was on both the escape committee and the escape, and the sense of urgency in the debate among the escapers was, if anything, higher. Again the arguments ranged back and forth on the growing risk of discovery against the chance that going off half-cocked would lead to disaster.

By now there was a real tension in the air, and one of my reasons for leaning toward an early breakout was that I now had enough experience to know that this actually increased the chances of discovery. It is hard to quantify, but somehow the tension prior to a jailbreak is like an invisible wave of static electricity that spreads through a camp, and somehow the ferrets often seemed to sense it, just as some people or animals can sense a storm coming long before the first cloud has appeared on the horizon.

We took a vote on it, and this time the majority was in favor of a breakout as soon as possible into the open ground on the other side of the wire. Immediately the decision was made, everyone, no matter how they had argued earlier, threw themselves completely into making the escape a success. Frantic work on clothing, maps, and papers aboveground was accompanied by energetic vertical digging down below. The NCO camp, from their election of a sergeant as their leader to their determination to have a vote, even on escaping, was one of the most democratic structures I have ever been in.

The great length of our tunnel enabled us to get fifty men and all their kit inside it on the night of the breakout. Aboveground, the camp was a hotbed of activity. In case there was a snap search, an elaborate series of ruses was devised to ensure that the guards did not notice fifty empty beds. Numerous papier-mâché dummies, adorned with real hair, were tucked into unoccupied bunks. They had been made by many prisoners under cover of the art classes that were meant to keep their minds off escaping. Some were more realistic than others, but all could pass for a dozing prisoner under a blanket in the dark. At the same time, holes were bashed in walls to allow people to be counted in one room, then slip away to another empty bed to be counted again. In every man in the huts who waited and listened, some part of him must have yearned to be one of the fifty in that tunnel, while another part of him thanked his stars he was not.

In the tunnel, I found myself once again at the front, but this time with the added apprehension that we would be breaking out into the open just a few yards from the wire on a regular patrol route. Our normal wonderful air-conditioning could not be used because the fire that made the draft could not be lit at night when we were supposedly all locked up and sleeping peacefully in our barracks. Soon the atmosphere in the tunnel was suffocating, and the closer one was to the tunnel face, the worse the air got. One of the most claustrophobic feelings in the world is being in a space two feet square, jammed up against a wall of earth, and knowing that if there is a collapse, with fifty bodies lined up head to toe behind you, it will take half an hour to reverse up the tunnel one at a time. At the head of the line I would have long since suffocated.

On the other hand, as first man out, I had the delight of digging through after so many months working underground and feeling that great first icy blast of air when we broke through. It rushed and whistled along the tunnel and I could hear the gasps of delight as the icy taste of potential freedom allowed them to breathe once again.

We had been pleased earlier at the signs that it was likely to be a windy, rainy night, during which we hoped the sentries would be less keen on prowling around than usual, and we also made sure that our break was in the dark phase of the moon. By the time I poked my head aboveground the rain had stopped, the wind had died down, and everything seemed bright and still. I ducked down as the guard passed by so close I could hear each footfall. Then it was a quick, silent scramble to the surface and an endless, terrible crawl toward the cover of the trees. Each inch of those ten yards in the open felt like a mile, and I waited for the shout, gunshot, or bayonet that would tell me I had been seen.

Amazingly, I made it to the trees undiscovered. I waited for the next man and helped to get the escape chain going, with each person emerging after the guard had passed and making a dash for the trees. Then I made my own escape, off and running through the darkness into the woods. This time I had decided to travel on my own. I had a homemade compass and some half-baked notion of heading east rather than west as the Germans would expect, in order to hook up with the advancing Russians or maybe a group of partisans. Since the entire continent of occupied Europe lay between me and a good meal in London, the lure of heading toward Germany was not all that strong.

Minutes later, sirens wailed and searchlights flashed on. I could hear gunfire back at the tunnel. Seven of us had slipped out before the law of averages caught up with us. The eighth man out had bolted too soon and the passing sentry had turned back to see him emerging from the tunnel mouth. The guard fired warning shots, and the unfortunate escapee stood with his hands up, paralyzed with fear. The soldiers swarmed over the escape area and fired down into the tunnel to discourage any further visitors from the underworld. Luckily, the steep angle of the rushed tunnel exit meant that most of the bullets dug harmlessly into the tunnel floor, though others helped to bring down part of the roof as the remaining forty or so would-be escapers did their best to reverse hastily toward the entrance chamber.

Suddenly the woods were alive with shouting guards and snarling Alsatian guard dogs. I remember thinking about my childhood pet Alsatian Danny in Texas, whom I had grown up with from the age of five and who taught me what I know about dignity. But these distant Teutonic cousins were unlikely to be impressed by my previous alliance with a German shepherd, and this time I thought they were equally unlikely to be satisfied with a few handfuls of the Mixture. But just as I heard the barking and shouting getting closer, I came to the edge of a small river that ran along one side of the camp. I swam across the icy water and managed to lose the dogs, who continued to sniff and search on the far bank. I ran into the eerie luminous half-light of a Lithuanian dawn and did not stop until I could no longer hear or see any trace of my pursuers.

Years later, I heard about what happened back in the camp as I was running across Lithuanian swampland, sucking in great, damp lungfuls of freedom. As the captured prisoners were marched off to the cooler, they managed to get word to those in the barracks without the guards overhearing that seven had escaped. Minutes later the host of guards, ferrets, and officers descended on the barracks to make a headcount. They were convinced that the man they had caught on the surface was the first one out and were jubilant that they had foiled such a spectacular escape attempt. As the guards went from hut to hut counting, they found numerous dummies slumbering peacefully in the beds. They added up the number of prisoners they had caught, and it exactly matched the number of missing captives. The guards went to bed delighted. While they slept, dreaming of medals for their good work, the men in the camp allowed themselves a quiet smile. They had removed all but seven dummies before the search. Consequently, with the camp satisfied that everyone was either tucked up or locked up, the outside world was not notified of the escape until the following day, by which time most of us were as far away as our spindly legs would carry us.

Next morning in the camp the Tallyho Club managed to ensure that the number counted tallied with the usual camp complement, with seven men engineering things to be counted twice. All was well until one of the seven escapees was captured that morning and brought back to the cooler, which incidentally was now so crowded with those from the tunnel that the guards had to bring in double-decker bunks so that the prisoners could be kept in not very solitary confinement. Major Peschel stared in horror at the extra prisoner and immediately ordered a recount, but the mathematical wizards of the camp were one step ahead of them, and on this second count they ensured that only six men were covered for. The counters went away satisfied, though a little bemused at how they got it wrong the first time.

Another escapee was caught and returned the following day, and once again the prisoners managed to rig the count, this time by five. By now the German officers were getting baffled. They always seemed to have the right number of prisoners, and yet more kept coming back from the outside world. A telephone call on the third day, announcing the capture of a third escaper more than fifty miles from the camp, caused the unfortunate Major Peschel to come close to bursting with rage, confusion, and general apoplexy. He was going to check each man in the camp against his identity card, and he was not going to stop until he knew exactly who and where every prisoner was.

The guards, terrified of Peschel in a rage, marched meekly from their administration building carrying boxes of identity cards, and they set up shop, in orderly Germanic style, starting in A Block of Building A1. Peschel called his men around him in a huddle to give them exact orders on how to identify and count the prisoners, who seemed able to expand and contract their numbers at will. For the two minutes that he took to brief them, a box of the identity cards had been left resting on a table behind them. Unseen hands lifted the box and passed it behind the backs of innocent-looking prisoners until it reached the stove at the end of the building. Up went the stove lid and in went 450 identity cards as a Burnt Offering. In other rooms smaller numbers were filched and the photos steamed off to use on forged documents in the future.

By this time the guards were so demoralized that they slunk off to form another plan. Soon the prisoners were all lined up on the parade ground. Count after count was made, right into the night, when the kriegies were illuminated by searchlight. As the guards' frustration turned to anger and the risk rose that someone would be shot for not knowing when to stop goon-baiting, Jimmy Deans was there to calm things down. The commandant had a new plan. He had six guards bring three ladders and set them up as a sort of chute of the type used to count penned sheep.

A chorus of bleating erupted from the ranks, and prisoners shouted out random numbers in German as they were counted in the hope of putting the counters off. Despite their best efforts, the guards had forgotten to put a guard on the outside wings of the parade ground, so as some prisoners were counted they would sneak back to join the uncounted herd. When they had eventually counted everybody, the guards went into another huddle and declared that they had almost twice as many prisoners as they should have. Some optimistic characters urged them to let half of the prisoners go so their numbers would add up, but instead the guards herded the men back to their huts. The next day, they finally managed to count properly, by which time most of the escapers had been recaptured, but I was still wandering around Lithuania.

The days that followed my escape remain closer to a dream than a waking reality in my mind. A combination of the poor rations, too many trips to the cooler on bread and water, then weeks of tough physical work on the tunnel, followed by the exertions of escape, swimming rivers and sleeping rough in wet clothes, had left me in pretty bad shape. I found myself dizzy and sometimes short of breath, wanting desperately to sleep, yet, when sleep came, finding myself startled awake by the strange noises of the countryside.

But that was only half the story. The other half was the strange, almost supernatural landscape through which I was traveling. That part of Lithuania was like something out of a Grimm's fairy tale. Strange bayou-like marshes and swamplands rose up on all sides, interspersed with ancient woods of tall silver birches. Their narrow silver trunks and almost luminous green leaves seemed to glow from the inside in the perpetual twilight of dawn and dusk.

For a number of days I wandered the countryside, using up my escape supplies and getting more tired and hungry by the day, but managing to avoid capture. This may have partly been because I was heading east, in the general direction of the Russian Front, while any soldiers looking for me would have concentrated on the Baltic coast to the west, which is probably what I should have been doing, too.

I waded through strange marshy meadows and bogs, avoiding quicksand by following the goat paths and places where I saw livestock grazing.

On the third night after my escape, I camped on the banks of a small lake of impenetrably dark water and fell into a fitful, feverish sleep. The water was so black and still it seemed like some huge dark mirror in a fairy tale, and my dreams were filled with nightmarish faces staring back at me from the black depths of the water. When I awoke, it was still dark, but the entire bank of the lake seemed to have been circled by silent German troops. I could not make them out, but I could see the light from their flashlamps tracing the sky and dancing in reflection at the far side of the silent lake. Stranger still, their lights were all different colors— blue, red, orange, and green. I shook my head trying to get the vision to go away, but it just got worse. The silent soldiers now seemed to be throwing their torches in the air, and they would twist and flicker upward before they disappeared altogether.

Slowly my brain started to put facts together. There was no noise, and nothing to break the stillness of the night. There were no German soldiers. The flashlamps were a strange natural phenomenon I had never seen before or since, swamp fires, or *ignis fatuus*—the real-life explanation for such superstitions as the will-o'-the-wisp. Gases would gradually seep from the depths of the swamp and briefly ignite when they reached the surface, creating a small wall of flickering flames around the edge of the lake. Even with this rational explanation, the middle of the Lithuanian night for a sick, hungry runaway could be an eerie place, and I broke camp and stumbled on in the darkness.

On the next night, bathed in that same eerie moonlight, I found myself circling around a large old mansion, cutting through its rambling grounds. I stood for a moment in the center of a vast, beautifully kept Italianate garden, with manicured lawns and topiary hedges clipped in the shape of birds and animals. I stumbled along flagstone paths, past ornate fountains, and rested for a few minutes beside decaying statues of angels and cherubs. All this in the middle of nowhere at the heart of a misty swamp.

Finally, too exhausted to go farther, and feeling like I was wandering around in someone else's dream, I found an outbuild-

ing in a ramshackle farm and fell asleep on the straw. I was woken
by being prodded with a pitchfork. A group of Lithuanian peasants crowded around me, staring distrustfully. The farm patriarch prodded me again and demanded in Lithuanian to know
who I was.

At this point I knew I was probably in big trouble. The history
of Lithuania is one of being rolled over by its larger neighbors.
Some hated the Germans. Others loathed the Russians, and many
regarded anyone not from their village as some form of potential
enemy. While those who hated the occupiers might offer help, in
other areas an escaped prisoner was just as likely to be handed
over or shot.

It took me and the farm patriarch some time to communicate,
using smatterings of German and Russian—none of which either
of us seemed to know. He asked me if I was Russian, I shook my
head no. He spat on the ground and uttered what was probably a
fairly heavy-duty curse, which I presumed indicated that he was
not too fond of Russians.

The others crowded around and nodded belligerently. I nodded too, disloyally. Next he asked if I was Deutscher. I vehe-
mently denied this, hoping that because they hated the Russians,
they did not like the Germans by default. He spat again and came
out with an even more bucolic Lithuanian oath against the Germans and all their works. His followers nodded and glared at me,
just in case.

Was I British? No, I wasn't British, and I didn't fancy attempting to explain about the vague relationship between America,
Britain, and the Royal Canadian Air Force. He seemed pleased
that I was not British and turned to the others to make a gesture
that implied the British were all stuck-up aristocrats. The others

smiled menacing gap-toothed grins and clutched their scythes and pitchforks even more threateningly.

Exasperated, he asked me a question I did not understand, but I guessed that it boiled down to "Then just what the hell *are* you, and why are you in my barn?" I thought about saying I was American, but assumed they were no more fond of Americans than anyone else they had ever heard of, so I pointed at my chest proudly and explained that I was a Texan. The patriarch thought about this and chewed the strange word over in his mouth several times. "Texan . . . Texan. Hmmmm." He turned to the others questioningly, but they all shrugged or looked blank. They had never heard of Texas either. The patriarch made his mind up. He extended a hand of welcome and pulled me to my feet. They did not have anything against Texans—yet—so I could stay. He shoved the pitchfork at me, blunt end first this time. I took it and he pointed out into the fields.

Thus it was that I found myself starting a new life as a Lithuanian peasant. If a German patrol went by, I would stop and gawp with the rest of the farmworkers, then turn back to shoveling whatever was on the end of my pitchfork. It was harvest time, and we worked from dawn to dusk, but at least I was getting fed and staying away from the Germans.

This went on for several days, but ultimately I could not see myself spending the rest of the war as a Lithuanian peasant, so I discussed my plans with the other workers, mostly in sign language. One explained by drawing in the dirt with a stick that there was what looked like boathouses on the shores of the Baltic where I might be able to break in and steal a small boat to head in the general direction of neutral Sweden across the Baltic Sea.

The next day, I was back on the road, heading west this time, toward the coast. I bade farewell to my new farm friends, and they seemed mildly sorry to see me go, loading me up with some vegetables for the road. I had not given them long enough to start disliking Texans yet.

After a few days of avoiding inhabited areas, often traveling at night or in the early morning, I did reach the coast. There, spread out in front of me and shrouded in mist was the whole Baltic Sea. Just as described, I discovered a line of boathouses, containing small sailing vessels locked up for the duration of the war. I slid down a bank and approached them from behind. When the coast was clear, I broke a lock and examined the vessel inside. It was a small sailboat, that might be possible to sail single-handed, though I knew virtually nothing about boats, and my last experience of one had been being sick belowdecks on a huge troopship on my way from Canada to England. But if I was going to make it to Sweden, I needed something that floated, and this seemed like the best bet.

The only problem was that there were several yards of beach and slipway between the Good Ship Ash and the water. I pulled at the boat, then tried hauling it with a rope and pushing it like a reluctant mule. But it would not budge. In my heart I knew that it would take four or five men to have any hope of shifting it. Trusting strangers in Lithuania was a risky business. While some of them hated the Germans, others had sided with them to get rid of the Russians and others still had formed the basis of several Baltic divisions of the SS. On the other hand the farmworkers had helped me.

Ultimately, if I wanted the boat to budge, I had no choice. I looked up and down the coastline and spotted several men in overalls digging in a field. I had managed to convince one group of peasants that Texans were really not all that bad, so I decided to give it a go again. I walked over and gave them a cheery greeting, but they just glanced up, then went back to tending their vegetables. I had been planning to give them some story about why I wanted my boat out of its house in the middle of the war, but since it sounded so improbable even to me, I decided honesty was the best policy. I took a deep breath, and in my best Texan, supported by rather theatrical mime gestures, explained that I was an escaped American pilot, shot down by the Luftwaffe, and that I was trying to get the boat out to go to Sweden.

The diggers exchanged glances and then one wearily stopped digging and rested his hands on the top of his spade, eyeing me with something approaching pity. He spoke rather good if heavily accented English.

"Yes, we would love to help you, but we are soldiers of the German army, and you are standing on our cabbages."

And that is how I quickly found myself handcuffed in the back of a big black car full of silent guards, heading for the town of Hydekrug. Once I got there I was a bit dismayed when instead of turning off in the direction of the POW camp, I was dropped off at a building in the town that boasted a large swastika over the entrance. It was the headquarters of the local Gestapo.

13. Gestapo Revisited

At Hydekrug Gestapo branch office, I gave my name, rank, and serial number—still using my stage name of Don Fair. They fingerprinted me and threw me in a cell for a few days. When they came to get me out, I was very impressed by the size of my escort. I had started out from France a few years earlier with just two bored guards. Now I was in the company of an officer and six armed soldiers. They marched me to the train station and got on with me. This meant that I would not be returning to the Hydekrug camp, which would have been a short drive away.

I assumed that they were taking me back to Stalag Luft III. Somewhere in their tidy heads they seemed to recognize that if I was recaptured and somehow had escaped being shot, the right place to deposit me was back in Luft III, with orders that I should not pass Go, and should not collect $200. Instead, I should miss at least six goes while they put me in the cooler and threw away the key.

The train rumbled on and on, and my guards did not seem to feel much like chatting. I looked out the windows at the devastation caused by war—a world of refugees from the east and bomber raids from the west. Some parts looked like lunar landscapes. Ragged children watched the train roll by from shells of burnt buildings. This was not a war which would let anyone escape from its horrors.

After what seemed like an endless journey, the train started to pull into a big city heavily pockmarked with bomb-damaged buildings. As the train hissed to a stop in the station and I saw its name, my blood froze. I was in Berlin.

I told my guards that they seemed to have taken the wrong train. One smiled grimly and said that it was certainly the wrong train for me. They marched me through the teeming central station. On either side I was flanked by huge blown-up pictures of Hitler and Himmler, so vast that they reached from the floor to the rooftops.

A black Gestapo car was waiting and as I rode in the back, heavily guarded, I felt a terrible sinking fear of what was to come. All my efforts, all the digging and starving had come to this— back in the hands of the Gestapo, this time in Berlin, the heart of Hitler's darkness. I had been lucky once, but doubted I would be so lucky this time.

The car took me to a big dark building that looked like either a prison or a courthouse and turned out to be both. There I was interrogated yet again and did my best to put on a brave face. A Gestapo man with small, clever eyes distorted though thick little glasses peered at the slim file of one Don Fair, who it seemed had behaved himself up to the point that he developed a Texan accent and started a break-out spree in sleepy Lithuania. My interrogator then lifted the phone and called for another file. An assistant came in with a much more weighty volume. This turned out to be the correspondence relating to one William Ash, a serial escapologist who had gone somewhat quiet lately.

It turned out that the meticulous Gestapo had checked my fingerprints after my capture in Lithuania. It did not take them long to gain my confirmation that I was indeed the prisoner formerly known as "Tex" Ash, even though I never really liked the nickname.

The Gestapo man was inquisitive. "What do you think will happen to you?" he inquired. I recalled that the last time one of his Gestapo colleagues had asked me that question in Paris, the correct answer was judged to be that I would be shot forthwith, but I persisted in the illusion that all was well. I suggested that I was a prisoner of war and should be sent back to Stalag Luft III, which was clearly where I belonged, since they kept bringing me back there.

Unfortunately, the Gestapo man disagreed. Somewhere in the spree of breakouts a paranoid subsection of the Gestapo had been plotting my movements across France, Germany, Poland, and Lithuania. Then came the realization that I was operating under an assumed identity and a new name. There was only one possible conclusion. I leaned in, intrigued to find out what I had been up to for the last few years.

The interrogator revealed his theory in triumph. Bill Ash—or whatever my real name happened to be—was not an ordinary prisoner of war, but a professionally trained escapologist. I had been parachuted in with a cover story about crashing in the Pas de Calais before I was picked up in civilian clothes in Paris. Then I had fomented more than half a dozen escapes in Germany, Poland, and Lithuania, some of which had tied up thousands of German troops for weeks. I had assumed a false identity and moved from country to country training other eager POWs in the black arts of escapology.

I listened transfixed at this brilliantly woven story, and it seemed almost a shame to disagree, but I felt I had to set him straight. "That's a splendid theory," I observed. "But didn't it ever strike you that I might just be very good at escaping, but terrible at getting away?"

He confided that he had not, and would not, consider such a preposterous theory. I was to be put on trial, and once it was confirmed that I was a professional escapologist sent to train others, I would no longer be protected by the Geneva Convention as a prisoner of war and could be shot with impunity. Without even trying to beat further secrets out of me, they threw me in a dungeon cell to await my fate.

It is a strange thing about the Nazi psychology that as they were obliterating innocent lives over an entire continent, they always liked doing so under the rule of law. If they did not have a law that said they could torture or execute you, they would rustle one up and have it on the statute books just so that they could kill you in a tidy manner.

My trial fitted in perfectly with that odd way of thinking. I was not allowed to attend myself, but each day a small glum German officer would come and tell me what had been going on, virtually none of which I understood. Then he would ask me a few perfunctory questions to prepare for the next day's hearing. He told me he was my defending officer, and I asked him what my chances were like. He said he was extremely confident—unfortunately, confident that my trial would run its course and I would be shot as planned, thus full-stopping an untidy footnote in Gestapo history.

This went on for some weeks, and if the Third Reich had been in better health, I would no doubt have been duly convicted and shot, but at the close of 1943, things were not looking good for the Axis cause. They had been defeated by the Russians at the great tank battle of Kursk, and had been kicked out of North Africa; their erstwhile friends in Italy had surrendered as the Allies fought their way toward Rome. Closer to home the Allies had intensified daylight bombing of German cities. In one day alone that winter they dropped 1,800 tons of bombs on Berlin.

Among the many buildings destroyed were records offices and parts of the Nazi judiciary. Since I was locked in a dingy basement, I had little way of knowing that my RAF and USAAF friends had blown up any of my own records. All I could do in my dungeon cell was listen to the thuds and shudders as the buildings above me took yet another pounding from the Allied bombers. Fires raged in the streets, as they had in London a few years earlier. All I knew for sure was that the reports by my supposed defender became less and less regular, until one day he came in looking even more glum than usual. I feared the worst and asked him to give it to me straight. "Terrible news," he confided. "The judges have decided that with things as they are, your case must be postponed. Until we get a new trial date, you will be sent back to Stalag Luft III."

I tried to look crestfallen at being robbed of the full majesty of Nazi justice and not tidily shot at the end of the proceedings. "You do understand," he tried to console me, "that under present circumstances, your case could not have much priority." I told them I sympathized fully with their harrowing workload and urged them to take their time before getting back to Little Me.

I had survived into a new year. Returning to Stalag Luft III by train in early 1944, I continued to sprout ever more impressive detachments of guards as escorts. I thought if only the war would go on long enough I could probably solve the whole thing by having an entire German army shuttling with me from one camp to the next, leaving only a few Nazi Boy Scouts to defend France, Italy, and the Russian Front. If my spirits had plummeted as I fell back into the hands of the Gestapo, they soared like an eagle at the thought of getting back to Luft III. I knew it was a bit ironic to be so keen to get back to somewhere I had spent most of the last few years trying to get away from, but the threat of imminent death always gives an interesting perspective on less immediate problems.

I was greeted to a great homecoming and felt like a proud parent looking at my offspring. The camp had now grown almost beyond belief, to house up to ten thousand prisoners. I was put back in my old East Compound, which had changed from being the main compound to just being a relatively small one at the edge of a vast and sprawling complex. It and the other British camp, North Compound, were heaving with shot-down humanity and the American Central and South Compounds were full to bursting, mostly with fresh-faced bomber crews. While I was delighted to be back in East Compound, I soon found out that this separated me from most of my old escaping comrades such as Paddy Barthropp, Tom Kirby-Green, and Roger Bushell, all of whom had been moved to the bigger new North Compound, where they were busy working on the tunnels Tom, Dick, and Harry that were to be used for the Great Escape.

But just as I was about to get used to being back in East Compound, the authorities remembered that I had left camp by swapping identities and had at least half a dozen escape attempts for their punishment to catch up with. I was thrown in the cooler.

Despite the isolation, it was good to be back. The regimen, even in the cooler, was still more civilized than those I had experienced elsewhere, and considerably better than waiting to be shot in Berlin or flattened as collateral damage in the bombing raids there.

I was in the cooler for a long, long time.

Deprived of conversation, company, and anything to read, I found that I had time to think. Never before or since have I had such a sustained period to think about myself, the world, and the actions of those around me. I had seen heroism and treachery, selfless generosity and animal selfishness. This riot of experiences and emotions kindled in me a lifelong interest in philosophy and politics, which are both examples of tiny people in a world several sizes too big for them struggling to make sense of it all. Politically, I came to conclusions which were to stay with me all my life, about the value of real democracy, of the importance of people working together to improve life for everyone, and lastly the necessity to stand up to bullies, exploiters, or dictators as forcefully as possible, as early as possible.

There were some Russian pilot prisoners used around the cooler for jobs like cleaning the latrines, and the guards treated them terribly. I could occasionally snatch a conversation with them if I was allowed out for exercise and became friendly with one of them called Artum.

Artum and I swapped stories from earlier in the war. He told me about possibly the most amazing escape from death in the entire conflict. A pilot friend of his was hit at 30,000 feet over the

Eastern Front, and as his plane was engulfed in flames, he baled out. He pulled frantically at the rip cord of his parachute, but nothing happened as it failed to open. He plummeted for what seemed like an eternity toward certain death, yet landed, in the depths of a Russian winter, on the side of the mountain in a huge drift of powdery snow perhaps a dozen feet deep. He went crashing into the snow, making an impressive imprint and descending a few yards as a giant human snowball, but it broke his fall without killing him. When he had finally stopped rolling, he clambered out of the drift with nothing more than severe bruising and was able to rejoin his unit.

The Germans gave Artum and his fellow Russians the worst jobs and the worst rations. If they attempted an escape, they were shot out of hand. One day Artum and I were cleaning out latrines together. (I think I was being punished for some minor infraction.) The camp loudspeaker used to blare out the news, usually of the latest German triumph, but on this occasion the news was different. The German Sixth Army had been surrounded and destroyed at Stalingrad some months earlier, blunting the Axis offensive in the East. Now the news was even better: Hitler's invincible panzer army had been stopped quite literally in its tracks at the great Battle of Kursk. The tide had turned. Artum translated for me, and we both dropped our cleaning mops and started dancing a jig of triumph and crowing "Russkis kommen" to the world. Normally this activity would have got Artum shot and me a long spell in the cooler at least, but the guards just stood silently staring at us, so shell-shocked were they by the news and the inevitable implication that would reach its conclusion in a Berlin bunker some two years later.

The Nazi treatment of their Russian prisoners is possibly the least known of all the great atrocities of the war. Because I got to know Artum as a person, I was able to get a sense of the enormity of the Nazis' crimes. He was a big, blond Slav with a warm heart and the ability to smile and feel joy at any small victory, even in the heart of darkness into which we had fallen. But there were many Artums. Reliable estimates put the number of Russians taken prisoner in the course of the war at more than five million. Of these more than three million are thought to have died in Nazi captivity, a death count that ranks alongside the unimaginable destruction of the Jews and Gypsies, but which attracted far less investigation or outrage in the West after the war as the cold war descended almost immediately and our allies were suddenly supposed to be our enemies. Two million of them died in prisoner-of-war or concentration camps, while another million died in unspecified German custody, many en route from their capture to the camps.

The death toll from starvation among Russian prisoners in the first years of the German offensive was greatly accelerated by the inhuman conditions in the Russian camps. While we Westerners were kept in cold, flea-infested huts, hundreds of thousands of the Russian prisoners were simply shoved into huge, open barbed-wire corrals where they lived and died, exposed to the elements twenty-four hours a day. In the wintertime with temperatures dropping far below zero, they huddled together in the snow and ice. They died by the thousands from typhus.

RAF officers were treated most of the time according to the Geneva Convention, while the Russians were dealt with as *Untermenschen*, or subhumans, throughout the war. Their rations were about a quarter of what we got, and this is excluding the Red Cross parcels, which they did not get, but which actually sustained us far better than the official ration. The daily German diet for us was based on the minimum nutrition needed to keep a person alive, and the Nazis deliberately fed the Russians on a quarter of this until they starved to death or succumbed to the diseases that accompany starvation.

Back in Schubin camp, there had been a Russian compound beside ours. When we walked on circuits, we could see the Russian prisoners, standing like skeletons, clothed in the gray rags that had once been uniforms. We gave some of our rations to them, but the guards chose to give them only to those who worked. Those who were too sick or starved to work got nothing. When a Russian prisoner died in one of the big, overcrowded huts in which they were kept like animals, the others would keep his body, pretending he was still sick, in order to keep getting his bread ration. The record for keeping a body was rumored to be three weeks.

There were two distinct periods to the Nazi genocide of Russian prisoners. The first and worst came in the aftermath of Operation Barbarossa, in which Hitler's blitzkrieg swept across Russia in 1941, encircling vast numbers of Russian troops. Apologists for the death toll claim that their captors were overwhelmed by their own success and unable to cope with the volume of prisoners, but the Nazis' own documentation proves that they knew they were systematically starving their prisoners to death. More than two million Russian prisoners of war died in enemy hands in just eight months in 1941–42.

The second period followed, in which most of the Russian prisoners were used as forced labor. The death rate continued, and thousands died as slaves in German mines and factories, but at least the slaughter slowed down. At Hydekrug I had talked to

British soldiers who had ended up working in some of the same mines. If a roof collapsed on a side seam leaving Russian prisoners trapped at the coal face, the guards would just seal it off. Why dig out Russians when there were so many more to kill?

By the end of the war the Russian people had lost some twenty million of their number, but after the remarkable defense of Stalingrad, the Wehrmacht knew that their days in the East were numbered. Artum's victory dance at the news of the Germans' rout at Kursk marked the beginning of the end, and the guards knew it. They shuddered, knowing that when the Russians arrived on German soil, the actions of their countrymen in Russia and in the camps would be neither forgiven nor forgotten.

When I emerged from my long spell in the cooler—I think it was by then February 1944—the other prisoners made a great fuss over me, and I discovered that in the year I had been away, my requests to a Swiss organization that supplied books to prisoners had achieved remarkable results. It seemed that the organization only supplied what it regarded as "good books" such as the classics, and while I regretted the lack of cowboy novels, I was greeted by a veritable library that had arrived over the months. There was Descartes, Spinoza, and Leibnitz, Pascal's *Pensées*, and the complete works of Plato in French. Apparently they had a vast store of such books, but I was just about the only prisoner in the western hemisphere who had expressed any interest.

I was quietly glad of the chance to sit still and read. While I still burned to get out, I knew that the next time I fell into Gestapo hands would undoubtedly be my last, and after so much solitary confinement on iron rations, I was ready for a bit of a rest. I was very thin and had been living on my nerves for more than three years. To fill the time I would normally have spent escaping, I decided to write a novel. In order to gather enough paper to write it down, I used to save my chocolate ration and trade it for notebooks.

I don't remember much about the novel now, other than the slightly pretentious title *Happy in Ulabrae*, which was from one of Horace's odes, no doubt another gift from my genteel new literary friends in Switzerland. Like the ode, it was about being content even when you have nothing very much to be content about.

I worked on it for some months, but missed the life of a serial escapologist. Finally, it was finished—a small neat pile of notebooks kept in my locker beside my bunk.

I went out for a walk to celebrate, and when passing close to the main gates of the camp saw that a truck was parked, waiting to go out with bits of broken engineering equipment that was being replaced. A guard had just searched the truck and was walking away with his back to me. For a split second I hesitated. I felt I still had plenty of bad novels in me, and was enjoying the relative peace and stability of being back in Luft III, surrounded by familiar faces. But there is something very deeply ingrained in me that cannot resist a good escape. Perhaps a psychoanalyst could some day test me for a previously unknown disorder called the Houdini Syndrome.

Like someone who cannot resist peeking at the last page of a book to see how it turns out, I jumped into the back of the truck and it motored off.

I got all the way to the next set of gates, crouched in the back, before being discovered. This was possibly my shortest and most badly planned escape of them all. I always envied the characters who spent years learning fluent German, preparing immaculate forged papers, passes, and first-class railway tickets, while pretending to be Danish butter salesmen on the way home from a successful business trip. My approach on the other hand was more fundamental: Get on the other side of the wire and run like hell. As I was frog-marched back to my barracks in order to pick up a few basics on my way to the cooler, I pondered that the reality was that most of the would-be Danish butter salesmen also got caught, and that at least my style of escaping was based on quantity if not always quality.

While I collected my things from my room, the Abwehr officer escorting me glanced around and his eye fell on the small stack of notebooks in my locker. He started to look at them suspiciously, and I did my best to tell them that it was a story about people who lived a very long time ago, and any resemblance to the current world war or anyone in it was purely coincidental. He lifted the first notebook and started to tear it very carefully into tiny pieces, followed by the next and the next. By the time he had shredded the last one, there was an impressive little pile of bits of paper beside his shiny jackboots. He ordered one of the guards to sweep it up and burn it, just in case some future generation should painstakingly decide to reconstruct my lost masterpiece from ten thousand tiny pieces.

As I lay alone in the cell, I decided that, rather than start another novel, I should perhaps get back to some more serious escaping. At least my work there seemed to be appreciated both by my fellow prisoners and—admittedly in a more abstract way—by the Gestapo.

One of the highlights of that trip to the cooler was the sound of the sirens that heralded the Germans' realization that the largest prison break in the history of the war had just got under way in the nearby North Compound. After nearly a year of planning and months of tunneling, my old colleagues over there were up and off in all directions. The sirens wailed, as if bemoaning that so many had gone. The Great Escape had begun.

14. The Scent of Freedom

When I emerged from the cooler some weeks later, in April 1944, I was terribly thin, but was once again raring to go, full of plans for tunnels, trucks, wire cutters, and cross-country escape tactics. I attended my first parade-ground muster after my release, and it felt strange to be in the middle of so many people again after the seclusion of the cooler.

As we stood in neat rows, an ashen-faced Luftwaffe officer read out a list. Fifty of the pilots who got out during the Great Escape had been "shot while resisting arrest." There were fifty dead and none wounded. A great gasp went up from all the men in ranks. Even by the standards of this dirty and vicious war, this was a brutal deed. Everyone knew that the escapers had been re-captured and then executed by the Gestapo. As the officer read out the list of the fifty, it read like a roll call of men who were as close to me as family: Roger Bushell, Tom Kirby-Green, Ian Cross, Danny Krol. Others were still unaccounted for, including Wings Day and John Dodge from the Schubin escape.

My memory of the rest of the parade that announced the murders is hazy from shock. I remember someone staggering forward out of the lines and guards raising their guns, as if they feared a full-scale riot, but the truth is, we were too stunned to even react. The guards, too, were appalled at the actions of the Gestapo. The senior German officer, looking ashamed, dismissed the parade. For a while we just stood there, frozen in shock, but gradually people drifted away. I remember being left on my own in the vastness of the parade area, feeling small and alone.

Yet that was exactly the feeling my friends had set out to challenge. The Great Escape was one of the biggest, boldest, and most brilliantly organized collective ventures of the war. Discussions had started about it before we left for Schubin. Jimmy Buckley had recognized Bushell's organizational genius and appointed him as his number two. We talked about the strategy of mass escape to tie up vast amounts of enemy time and resources, using escape as a weapon of war. We knew that only a big, bold tunnel, supported by hundreds of people making civilian outfits and passes, would be capable of supporting such a plan. Then a great many of us, including Buckley, had been sent to Schubin, where we tried to put those plans into operation through the Asselin tunnel escape on which Buckley died, while those who stayed in Luft III, including Bushell, aimed to build another tunnel to be reckoned with.

It was Bushell's combination of implacable enmity to the Nazis and his great leadership skills that resulted in the unique plan behind the Great Escape. He would lead an escape with 250 fully equipped escapees, fully trained and heading in every direction. They would tie the enemy in knots and make such a splash that their actions would be in every newspaper, both in Germany and at home. Instead of being passive victims, waiting for the war to end, the prisoners would take the war to the enemy in the heart of their homeland.

Roger Bushell's hatred of the Nazis had been sealed even before he reached Stalag Luft III when they executed an entire Czech family who had been hiding him in Prague during a previous escape, following which he himself was tortured by the Gestapo. He had a scar above one eye from a prewar skiing accident, and when he turned his tough face on any fellow prisoner, demanding the impossible in the interests of the escape, there never seemed any possibility other than making it happen. He was one of the greatest natural leaders I ever met. Roger, originally from South Africa, had little time for any distinction between the more civilized Luftwaffe and the degenerate Gestapo. As far as he was concerned they were all *The Enemy*, and his weapon was the tunnel.

As soon as he and some of the others were moved to the newly opened North Compound, he had ordered three tunnels to be started—Tom, Dick, and Harry. They were to be the longest, most ambitious, and best engineered of the war, thanks to a Canadian tunnel engineer, Wally Floody, who in my own wanderings I never met, but who by all accounts was a remarkably hardworking and inventive individual. The entrances to two of the tunnels went straight through the concrete foundations below two huts and were concealed beneath wood-burning stoves. Digging in the soft sand of Sagan proved dangerous, and a great deal of shoring was needed. More than 4,000 bed boards were donated or requisitioned along the way, leaving most of the compound sleeping on thin air and string.

The longer the tunnels got, the greater was the number of people in the compound needed, not just for security and stooging operations, but to manufacture enough clothes and passes for a small army of escapees.

When Tom was promoted within the Great Escape organization to the post of security officer, he worked alongside a remarkable American called George Harsh, who had the dubious distinction of having spent twelve years on a Georgia chain gang for murder before becoming a rear gunner in a bomber and ending up in a German POW camp. Together the two of them devised a security system that allowed three vast tunnels to be dug under the very noses of the ferrets, with hundreds of tons of tunnel dirt being disposed of and almost daily searches being foiled for more than six months as tunneling, tailoring, forging, and escape catering continued apace on a grand scale.

Tom was the opposite of Roger in many ways, but just as brave and just as intelligent. He was a tall, suave, and very well-educated young man who had shared my love of books and also my allergy to bullies. Some people found him a bit eccentric, which may explain why we got on so well. We talked about politics and people around the world, from Andorra to Zululand. In many ways he was a bohemian, quite ahead of his time. He had been born of a colonial family in Malawi, Africa, and had attempted to join up to fight the fascists in the Spanish Civil War, but had ended up fighting them in a world war instead. He became one of the youngest squadron leaders in RAF Bomber Command, at the ripe old age of twenty-three.

Anyone who thought of Kirby-Green as just a colorful character who brightened our drab lives with a love of salsa music and by padding around in carpet slippers and a kaftan did not know much about his record either before or after being shot down. In the early days of the bomber war, anyone who managed more than ten raids was regarded as a rarity. Tom was shot down in October 1941 on his thirty-seventh raid. The Nazis regarded him as such a prize that his capture was announced on German propaganda radio by their chief announcer, Lord Haw-Haw, who was later hanged as a collaborator. As an escape artist, Tom was equally valuable. He used his knowledge of Spain to build intelligence for those who wanted to try reaching there or Gibraltar on their escapes.

Jimmy Buckley's old Fleet Air Arm friend Peter "Hornblower" Fanshawe had invented the "penguin" method of soil disposal. Pouches hidden inside the trousers of wandering prisoners allowed the tunnel spoil to be dropped and dispersed by prisoners as they walked.

The list of those murdered also included one other good friend, Squadron Leader Ian Cross, or Crossie, who had been in charge of one of the two dispersal teams that got rid of tons of tunnel soil under the very noses of the guards without ever arousing suspicion. Crossie had controlled a team of eighty men, including the soil dispersal Penguins. To give just a glimpse of Crossie's achievement, the Great Escape tunnels produced a ton of sand for every twenty cubic feet of tunnel, and it all had to disappear. The tunnel usually progressed at the rate of about three feet a day and the most dirt that could be easily concealed by any one prisoner was sixteen pounds. In the buildup to the Great Escape that meant 18,000 individual journeys to get rid of sand went undetected. The record for the dispersal team run by

Crossie and another Great Escaper, Jimmy James, was getting rid of 3,600 pounds of sand in one hour.

While one tunnel, Dick, was shut when the forest it was meant to surface in became a treeless area earmarked for yet another compound, the other two pressed on. The abandoned tunnel was even used as a handy hole to dispose of sand from the other two. The second tunnel, Tom, was almost at the wire in summer 1943 when its entrance was discovered by a keen-eyed ferret, but the escapees turned all the energy to their one remaining hope. Harry.

Eventually Harry stretched for 336 feet, and on the night of March 24, 1944, my friends made their break for it. Due to an error in surveying, the tunnel came up short of the woods, in the open and not far from a watchtower. Each escaper had to make it across the open ground to the cover of the trees. Remarkably, seventy-four made it out before someone mistook a "stay-put" tug on a signal cord they had set up between the tunnel and the trees for a "go-ahead." A prisoner popped up and was immediately spotted. Firing started, the sirens wailed, and the men inside the tunnel tried to reverse hastily.

So successful was this massive escape that a state of national alert was declared and thousands of troops and home guards had been tied up searching for them at a time when Germany needed every man it could get to shore up their failing, flailing war machine. My only relief came from learning that my friend Paddy Barthropp was safe. He had not yet emerged from the tunnel when the alarm was sounded and had managed to make it back to the hut. I also found out later that a few of my comrades from the Schubin escape, Wings Day and John Dodge, had managed to survive the Gestapo massacre but spent the rest of the war in Sachsenhausen concentration camp.

Three of the seventy-six got all the way back to England. Fifty were shot on the direct orders of Hitler as a warning to the rest of us, and the remainder were either returned to the camp or sent to other prisons. Now, instead of fifty of those brave men digging through the unyielding earth, the soil of Germany was covering them forever.

Yet I just could not think of Crossie or the others as dead. I pictured him smiling as he was marched off to the cooler earlier in the war, in an incident that seemed to come from another lifetime. He had hidden in a truck full of pine branches that was being driven out of the camp. A guard must have spotted him getting in, and the truck was deliberately driven at high speed over the roughest possible ground for a long time. Finally one of the German officers stopped it and asked politely for Herr Cross to come out, assuring him that the walk to the cooler was much less bumpy.

One of the saddest things about the war was thinking about the remarkable contribution some of the men who died would have made had they got home. While the men in prison covered every shade of political opinion, there seemed to be an interesting connection between those of us who shared a fanatical desire to escape and a desire for a better world in the future than the one we had left behind. At one stage, alongside an international debating society, someone had set up a mock parliament to discuss the future after the war. Roger Bushell appointed himself deputy prime minister of the Labour Party and announced the immediate nationalization of all major industries, to be operated for the public good rather than profit. Tom Kirby-Green proposed that there should be a new attitude to Britain's colonies, which would recognize the rights of the black majority rather than treating them as servants or subjects. If these two had survived, the world would have been a more interesting place.

The aftermath of the Great Escape was serious for the Luftwaffe as well as for us. Commandant Von Lindeiner was relieved of duty and arrested, ironically becoming a prisoner himself but escaping a firing squad. He had always tried to run the camp on the basis of the Geneva Convention, and he generally had our respect if rarely our obedience.

Things were to change after that. The Great Escape was recognized by the Gestapo as their chance to make a grab for all prisoners, including the pilots. Soon all the camps, including Stalag Luft III, came under Gestapo and SS jurisdiction, headed by Heinrich Himmler. Leaflets were printed and posted saying bluntly that anyone caught planning an escape or on one would be shot. At the back of the Gestapo moves was the constant but never stated plan to use us as hostages in some negotiated surrender at the end of the war. Himmler intended to survive the war and make peace with the West, and he knew that we prisoners collectively represented a mighty bargaining chip. While our day-to-day existence within the camps did not change much with the change of administration to SS and Gestapo and the guards remained the same, there was no doubt that the repercussions if we were caught escaping would be very different.

Perhaps it was good that we did not know too much. SS General Berger, who was in direct charge of all POWs, claimed later that he was bawled out by Hitler at the Wolf's Lair stronghold for not shooting more of us and for not destroying all Red Cross parcels. It is certain that Hitler and Josef Goebbels toyed with the idea of shooting one of us for each civilian killed in the bombing of his cities, but were dissuaded by representatives of the army and navy.

Back in East Compound, oblivious of such grand schemes, Aidan Crawley, Joe Kayll, and I, along with one or two others, made up the escape committee. Joe was a quiet, gentle man of remarkable courage—one of the pioneers of the technique of chopping up an enemy plane with your propeller when out of ammo. He brought down a German bomber that way before he ended up in the bag. He was quite a fighter pilot. He had brought down nine enemy aircraft and won the DSO before the Battle of Britain even started. On his last sortie in June 1941 he had been flying as wingman for the ebullient Harry Broadhurst, who was in charge at Hornchurch. They ran into a high-level formation of more than twenty enemy aircraft that started to peel off and dive down in an attempt to get behind the raiders, attacking them from out of the sun. Every few minutes the pair had to turn back in to face an attack head-on, firing short bursts in reply to save ammunition. This happened five or six times, and Broady managed to finally get away over the Channel at sea level. Joe was not so lucky.

Like my own experience in a Spitfire about a year later, Joe ended up with an engine full of holes, which he switched off to avoid fire. He hoped to glide as far across the Channel as possible before ditching, to increase his chances of being picked up by a British boat, but he was losing altitude so rapidly that he had to turn back and land in France to start a new career as a prisoner of war and a quiet but ardent escape artist. His record within the camps was equally impressive, and he was one of the organizers of the remarkable Wooden Horse escape in which three prisoners dug a tunnel from under a wooden gymnastics horse while others practiced vaulting over it for hours on end. The Wooden

Horse escapers had made a Home Run—all the way to London, while Joe stayed to organize further escapes.

But there were not too many like Joe at this later stage in the war. The new threat of death upon capture and the shock waves from the murder of our fifty comrades had made escaping an even less attractive option for most of the prisoners, and then came news that was to make it a definite minority pursuit.

In order to keep things going, we had been considering a joint escape attempt with Americans in the compound next to us but we needed to communicate to coordinate. I was chosen for the mission to visit their compound for several reasons. First, I had succeeded in the double-hurdle dash over the barbed-wire fences once before when I had swapped identity with Don Fair and gone off to Hydekrug camp with the sergeants. An even more compelling reason for my new trip in the eyes of my colleagues was that I "spoke American." Most compelling of all was that I was the only one mad enough to go.

Once again, both compounds arranged distractions for both of the machine gunners in the nearest towers, and I vaulted the fences in broad daylight, greeting another blurry figure who was hurtling in the opposite direction. He turned out to be the US-AAF colonel with whom I was swapping places, but there was not much time to salute.

My time with the Americans was made even more enjoyable by a surprise reunion with old friends from my school days in the Lone Star State. They even had good Texas names, such as Buck Wilson and Bulldog Macmillan, and while the thoughts of escaping appealed only to a minority in the American compound, the fact that many of them had been "in the bag" for a shorter period of time seemed to leave some of them at least with a continued, gutsy willingness to risk escape.

The atmosphere in the American compound was also more boisterous, from horseplay to goon-baiting, something that had annoyed some of my more stuffy English friends in the days before we were split up into different nationalities. Personally, I found their energy very refreshing. I enjoyed my strange reunion with these good-natured rumbustious guys in a place none of us ever thought we would end up. When my friends went back to their nearby hut for the night, I stayed with some of the escape committee to go over more plans. Later, as I dozed off in a strange bed, I heard an incredible row and racket coming from the nearby American hut. It sounded like a full-fledged battle, but as the guards investigated, everything went quiet again.

Next morning, as I nervously prepared to do a repeat reverse performance of my high-wire act to get back to my own compound, I managed to snatch a few words with one of my pals from the hut next door. I asked him about the ruckus. He smiled sadly and told me it was just an argument about the war.

I was incredulous. Here we all were, volunteers risking our lives in a battle between good and evil, all prisoners of that same enemy and yet they were still arguing about the war? What the hell was there left to argue about? As I moved into position for my hundred-yard dash over the death wire that led to the fence, my American friend called after me, "Not *this* war. The Civil War!"

I was still smiling about this in an attempt to quell my terror when I stepped over the warning wire, climbed over the first fence, nodded at the American colonel hurtling in the opposite direction, then clambered back over our compound's barbed wire, across the danger zone, and hopped the final warning wire to breathe a long sigh of relief as I strolled briskly away. From a practical point of view our swap and intelligence gathering resulted in some general plans for joint action, but these were inconveniently overtaken by minor events in the outside world, such as the D-day landings.

We had one or two wireless sets hidden about the camp, guarded like gold dust and moved when in danger. But one day one of the wireless operators came bursting out of whatever hut it was hidden in, whooping in delight, leaving the others to hastily hide our treasure. The landings in Normandy had started. By the look on some of the guards' faces, they knew that this was the beginning of the end.

Word spread through the camp like wildfire, and the evil homemade hooch concocted from raisins saved from Red Cross parcels or the even more lethal brews distilled from potato peelings came out of hiding.

Even though we were by then in different compounds, I knew that my pal Paddy would be celebrating in style. He was an expert bootlegger, and the skills of creating illicit alcohol and escaping had much in common. Ingenious methods had to be devised, materials prepared, and ways found to stop the constant security searches that were meant to keep the brews from falling into enemy mouths. Many of the stills were made from Klim milk tins soldered together, much as we had done to make air pipes in the tunnels, but such stills were unwieldy and hard to hide. Pondering the magic combination of yeast, water, container, and heat while shaving one morning, Paddy happened to glance up at the feeble twenty-five-watt lightbulb in the fixture above him. In a slightly dangerous stroke of genius, he filled the globular glass bowl with water, added the fermenting ingredients, reassembled the fixture, and switched the light on. From then on, he had a ready supply of alcohol and the satisfaction of knowing that the heat and electricity were being supplied unwittingly by his captors. But as the best television shows say, Don't try this one at home.

After D-day, and for the first time since we were captured, we knew that sooner or later we would be going home. Escape attempts continued very occasionally after that, but it was recognized that the value of running around Germany tying up troops was weakened by the fact that virtually every able-bodied German had been shipped to one or other of the fronts. In this new situation, escapers were more likely to get knifed by a Nazi Boy Scout with a *Jugenddolch* than be chased by a truckload of soldiers. The scales of reason were weighing more and more heavily in favor of staying put.

Luckily, life is not always made up of safe, rational decisions. Those of us who thought that the only possible response to the Nazi threat of execution on capture was to make our escapes more daring and more successful continued to plot and plan. Speaking for myself, I had come into this war on my own terms and was very reluctant to sit meekly waiting for someone to tell me I had permission to leave it.

Even among the small number of hard-case escapologists, doubts were setting in, and we were being whittled away, losing would-be escapers as they tiptoed away one at a time, like jurors in a prison version of *Twelve Angry Men*, changing their verdict at the last minute. It was around this time that a "blitz" tunnel was dug beside our perimeter fence by two of our dwindling number. This was a short tunnel, designed to be dug quickly and used for a lightning escape under the wire, built on the same principle that had worked brilliantly for Ollie Philpot and a couple of others a year earlier in their Wooden Horse escape. But that was all ancient history by this stage in the war, and the two men who had bravely done the dangerous work of digging the new tunnel were now starting to question the wisdom of using it themselves. This was a tunnel in need of escapees.

Perhaps it was my frugal upbringing in Depression-hit Texas coming out again, but I have never liked to see anything go to waste, be it inedible clipfish or a perfectly good tunnel. A spectacularly mad but very brave New Zealander was extremely keen, and my fellow escape committee veteran Aidan Crawley was willing to give it a go. This was particularly plucky of Aidan, since he was determined by then to become a member of Parliament when he got home—an ambition he achieved—but the most likely outcome of this particular mission would be that he would have to be elected posthumously.

As we prepared to break out that night, some of the more timid prisoners became very indignant. They did not much mind us risking our own lives, but they were convinced that there would be reprisals on those still in the camp. I pointed out that if the brave French people who had risked their lives to help me and so many others had thought that way, they would all have collaborated meekly in return for a quiet life full of threats and hostages. Instead, they chose to resist. We were soldiers, so there was even more reason for us to do so.

Undoubtedly, with hindsight, there was truth on both sides of the argument. At some point escaping became less a tactic and more a simple statement of defiance—an unwillingness to crawl in the face of oppression. But equally, the tactical imperative of slowing down the enemy war machine and spreading unrest at the thought of wicked prisoners on the loose had also diminished greatly. The nervous prisoners took their worries to the commanding officer, and he gently but firmly ordered us not to go. The mad New Zealander was outraged. Aidan Crawley was disappointed, and I pretended to be the same—while breathing a large sigh of relief.

With nothing much left to do but wait for either the Russians to reach us from the East, the British and Americans from the West, or the Gestapo to shoot us all if their negotiations did not work out, we settled down to sit it out. I could not be too angry at the more timid prisoners. All of them had gone through some terrible, traumatic crash or parachute experience just to buy their ticket into Stalag Luft III, and after a few years the wire walls could seem strangely comforting in a sea of death and destruction as well as suffocating and oppressive.

The lack of escapes left more time to think and talk, and perhaps the least discussed but most significant part of life inside the prisoner-of-war camps was that they were centers of learning and political debate to rival the best universities. Of course, they did have the drawback that if you broke the rules you were more likely to be sent to solitary than given another essay to write.

Still, for many prisoners, this was the first and only chance in their lives not only to get more of an education, but also to think about what sort of world they wanted after the war. Every camp I had been in had some sort of educational function, perhaps none more so than the NCO camp in Hydekrug. This may have been because there was a smaller percentage of graduates and the NCOs were mainly civilians who were keen to return to regular life outside the services as soon as possible. For whatever reason, the camp set up what was called the Barbed Wire University.

A guy called Eddie Alderton who went on to become a professor at an American university joined up with a group of men who had been lecturers before the war and used Eddie's experience of starting education courses at Luft III to do the same at Hydekrug. These were not isolated teach-ins. At its height, the university boasted fifty-four lecturers covering some forty subjects with a thousand regular students. They even had term times and faculties covering arts, science, medicine, and law. Subjects studied, often with one eye to the future, ranged from hotel management to local government.

When I wasn't trying to escape, I was reading or writing, and the few photos of myself as a prisoner that I managed to keep all seem to picture me with a hefty book tucked under my arm, usually one of the classics, since cowboy novels were in short supply. Despite this and my love of education, I never really got anywhere with the courses. The few I did start on tended to be interrupted by short periods of escape and then by long periods in the cooler. Still, it was an excellent excuse for not doing homework.

Sometimes I wondered if much of the educational activity was a distraction from escaping, and there were certainly some prisoners who regarded escapes and the clampdowns that inevitably followed them as an outrageous intrusion into their studying time, but most kriegies had a more balanced attitude. Active escaping was always going to be something of a minority pursuit, so the majority of prisoners had to find something else to do with their time. Some found it in sports, others in a remarkably well-developed theatrical community, writing and producing plays every few weeks in virtually every camp. It is true that the leading "ladies" usually had five-o'clock shadow, but apart from that, the performances were often remarkably good and served to keep morale up.

In the army prisoner-of-war nonofficer camps, the men did not have this choice. They were forced to work for the German war effort in factories and mines, often in terrible conditions. But the Geneva Convention ensured that officer prisoners were not required to work. Consequently, a vast sea of empty time loomed before every prisoner in our camps. He could choose to lie on his bunk, moaning about his fate—and some did just that—or he could choose to do something about his own life. That choice often boiled down to doing something about it in the short term, which meant escaping, or possibly the cooler or an early grave, or planning something more long-term, which usually involved thinking about or studying for the day when the war would be over.

All of this study, debate, and occasional friction between restless escapers and those who wanted a quiet life contributed to some of the best political discussions I've ever heard. As prisoners, when not tunneling or scrounging food, we had several years to ponder what sort of future we wanted, and what we were unwilling to return to. Most of our prison-camp debates centered on what sort of world we wanted to build after the war. We talked about what life had been like before the war, about mass unemployment and children going to bed hungry. We talked about democracy and how we could avoid being back in another war in twenty or sixty years' time that a future generation might have to fight. We argued the various merits of socialism and social democracy, and above all we planned for a better future.

The same sort of debates had been going on during the war back in Britain. Before I was shot down I had visited some aircraft factories on a morale-boosting mission with other pilots, and after the usual platitudes—for instance, if it was a factory making propellers we were expected to tell the workers just how much better our planes flew if they had propellers—we would often talk about the future. This was no vague notion about "a land fit for heroes" but a specific determination that if we were fighting and risking our lives, either at the front or on the equally dangerous home front, we were going to have a say in what followed.

This may help some people understand why Winston Churchill, the greatest of all wartime leaders, whom we all respected as such, was rather promptly and soundly defeated at the ballot box immediately after the war, booted out of power and replaced with a more socially progressive government.

From a copy of one of the camp newspapers, the *Daily Recco*, produced by POWs first at Luft III, then at Hydekrug in the NCO camp, it is easy to see how much a part of this movement for progress some of us felt.

The paper was a handwritten one-page newssheet produced under the toughest of conditions by a bunch of prisoners and was eagerly awaited each day by a captive population starved of news, apart from our furtive listening to the BBC via a secret radio. The *Daily Recco* of Wednesday, March 8, 1944—"head office Hut B9, branch off Hut A3"—had a typical mix of news. One story reported that German radio claimed 140 Allied planes were downed in bombing raids over Berlin, while another story reported that the influx of new USAAF prisoners were settling in and getting used to the strange way the locals spoke. But one article sticks out. Under the biggest headline of the day is a story entitled "The People's Government—It Depends on You." The article exhorted kriegies to take part in the debate about what sort of future they wanted when they got home. It ended: "It isn't a question of politics—a government of a country is elected to carry out the wishes of the people—make that wish felt, then perhaps we may get closer to government of the people, by the people, for the people."

The circulation of the *Daily Recco* was somewhat limited by our imprisonment—there was only one handwritten copy produced each day—but it is interesting to note that millions of other people were coming to the same conclusions at home, both those in uniform and civilians.

Somewhere along the line, the politics of escaping and the aspirations for a better world merged in my mind. For those of us who had known that tremendous feeling of being on the outside, or who had at least tried to do so, the debate was about more than short-term pros and cons. Running for your life but knowing that it was your own decision to be there is the most liberating experience imaginable. Every step on the outside was a way of telling the world that freedom was the most important thing in the world, not just as some abstract notion, but personally, collectively, and even at risk of life itself.

The camp newssheets, including the *Daily Recco*, can claim a noble place in literature and politics, even if normally there was only one handwritten copy pinned up for all to see, but it is probably just as well that such a significant article was not intended to appear on April 2, 1943. A notice for that day reads: "The *Daily Recco*—Due to the bad weather conditions yesterday, Issue No. 40 was blown over the wire."

15. The Winter March

That winter of 1944-45 was one of the coldest in living memory. All but the most fanatical Nazis knew that the game was up, but none of them knew how to extricate themselves from the carnage they had helped to create. Like a Greek tragedy lumbering toward its inevitable conclusion, the war dragged on.

Some of the senior Nazis, including Göring and Himmler, still harbored hopes that a separate peace with Britain and America might yet be brokered and that in any such negotiation ten thousand pilot officers would be a handy bargaining chip. They could be returned intact or in pieces, depending on the West's willingness to play ball on minor details such as overlooking war crimes.

For most of the winter we had been on half rations, each prisoner getting half a Red Cross parcel a week, but during January 1945 there was a substantial shipment, and we were put back on full rations, which left us just hungry, rather than ravenous.

Each day we waited for news, but the Western Front had been bogged down by German counteroffensives and our premature overoptimism that D-day would be followed by rapid capitulation had given way for many to caution and doubt following the defeat at Arnhem in September 1944. In the chaos of a bombed-out Germany as the winter began to bite, feeding and sheltering Luftgangsters was far from a high priority, and we clung to hope of liberation as a source of inner warmth.

But if progress in the West was slow, the red tide was sweeping in from the East at a phenomenal rate, and we knew that Stalag Luft III was right in the path of the unstoppable Russian advance. We listened to the German broadcasts and did our best to sift out the reality from the propaganda. Despite their best efforts, the announcers had to mention specific place names where there was fighting, so we were able to rush from the loudspeakers to the map in the library hut where people jostled for position to try plotting the Allies' progress.

We continued to listen to the BBC each day, relayed to us throughout the war thanks to the efforts of radio specialists and shorthand journalists and retold under the cover of other "lessons." This being wartime, we also took some of the BBC's more optimistic announcements with a pinch of salt, but between them, Lord Haw-Haw, and our own horse sense, we had a good idea that the end could not now be too far away.

The camp's rumor mill went into overdrive. Every few days there were contradictory rumors, always expounded with the absolute certainty that the teller's rumor was infinitely superior to the others, and "a sure thing" rather than "duff gen." First we were going to be evacuated. Next we were all going to be shot. Then we were going to be evacuated again. Next we were going to be abandoned in the camp to wait for the Russians.

Those of us who had been active escapees started to try to get a little bit fit, with the thought that we might have to break out or possibly even fight our way out. Members of the escape committee started to make plans. If the SS decided to try mowing us down, we would make an attempt to storm their compound, grab guns, and take some of them with us. In every compound men trained in case they were called on for some last desperate defense or breakout.

By January 1945 we could hear the Russian guns booming, getting louder each day. Marshal Konev's Soviet forces had broken through in a spearhead and were reportedly less than fifty miles from the camp. On the twenty-first a group of Russian T-34 tanks had burst through the German lines and crossed the River Oder just north of Breslau. Even though they were forced to retreat by a German counterattack, we knew that it was now just a matter of time until the camp was overrun.

Farther north, the Russian advance swept over my former prison home at Schubin in Poland, and they had no doubt overrun Hydekrug, too. We heard rumors that the American prisoners who had replaced us at Schubin had been liberated. Yet strangely, despite the excitement, camp life went on much as before. People studied their lines for plays. Others played cricket. The courses in everything from mathematics to law continued, though perhaps without very many attentive students. But the normality was an illusion. Just outside the gates of the camp a human tide of refugees was sweeping eastward. The nearby little town was bursting under the strain of five times its normal population, and the stress was beginning to show on our guards, who wanted to know if they could get their own families out of the area, but they were told no more than me.

The truth was that the German military command was already starting to disintegrate. Lines of communication were being cut. The High Command would make one decision, and a general on the ground would make another. Hitler, increasingly isolated and frantic in his Berlin bunker, would issue some insane order that contradicted their plans. Sometimes his orders were obeyed, since those who disobeyed could expect a bullet in the head from some fanatical SS man who had already burned all his bridges and was simply taking as many fainthearts with him as possible. But more often such mad orders were quietly lost amid the mountain of paperwork, much of which was being shoveled into fires to stop its falling into the hands of the Allies.

We prepared as best we could for the possibility of evacuation. As I walked through the camp, it started to resemble some vast, disorganized workshop. Some prisoners were building sleds to carry their provisions and possessions. Others concentrated on repairing our threadbare clothing for a march that promised to be long and cold. I did not do as much as I should have. For many of the men this would be their first venture outside the wire, but for me it seemed more like the continuation of a nonstop journey that had lasted three years. I was already wearing most of the clothes I owned to keep out the cold, and had a stash of the Mixture left over from the waning popularity of escapology. I was ready to go.

Each day we waited for the Russians to arrive, but in the end it was more German troops who swarmed in. An emphatic order for us to remain in the camp was countermanded later the same day. We were then given an hour or so to collect our few possessions before we were herded out onto the road in a forced march back into Germany, to keep us out of the hands of the Russians. I found out later that the order to keep the pilots of Stalag Luft III as hostages came directly from Adolf Hitler at his 4:30 staff meeting in his Berlin bunker on January 27, 1945.

By that evening, the compounds were still operating normally, but with liberation so close we could almost taste it. In the neighboring South Compound that housed most of the Americans, those who believed the show must go on at all costs were soldiering through the second act of a comedy performed by fellow prisoners called *You Can't Take It with You*, when there was a surprise extra actor on the stage. The senior U.S. officer, Colonel Charles Goodrich gave a short but memorable performance. He told the audience that they had half an hour to pack and prepare for a forced march.

The same message was going out in our own compounds. In under an hour, we put on as many layers of clothing as we could in hopes of keeping out the worst of the snow and cold. We started to look slightly comical, with thin hands and feet sticking out of puffed-up bodies that consisted of ten layers of clothing in all shapes and colors, but lacking flesh. At the same time, every stove in the camp was going full blast. We could only take what we could carry, and every scrap of food, carefully hoarded for weeks or even years, was now being wolfed down. Wonderful cooking smells wafted around the camp. It was an insane scene. Things that were precious, from tins of food to boxes of cigarettes, were suddenly left on tables for others to help themselves, as their owners, cheeks bulging like hamsters and pockets bursting like nomadic misers, could accommodate no more. The stores were raided, and I saw a group of prisoners staggering off with what looked like half a cow.

As people started to realize that they would barely be able to stagger out the gates with their heavy packs, never mind marching for what might be hundreds of miles in the snow, they abandoned cherished possessions. Suddenly wood was more important than food. Bed boards that would once have formed the roof of a tunnel were now requisitioned to make sleds. Our entire value system was turned upside down. Beloved books were thrown away. Some estimates say that more than a million books were abandoned in the camp complex. Ornaments lovingly, painstakingly carved and kept for years as planned souvenirs were abandoned.

At the gates every man was given more to carry—the Red Cross parcels that had been so rare and so precious were suddenly devalued. Every man could have as much as he could carry, and yet there would still be huge amounts left over. I heard afterward that when we left there were still 23,000 Red Cross parcels in the store along with 2.5 million cigarettes.

On our way out the gate as the snow swirled around us in the darkness, we found ourselves treading on half-opened and abandoned Red Cross parcels, looted only of the lightest items, like chocolate. Looking at the ground, strewn with wasted food, I thought about all the debates about commodity trading, the value of key items like cigarettes and chocolate. Suddenly these items were only worth the remaining space in a pocket, even though we might be starving in a few days. The German guards prodded us on, joining a line of marching prisoners from the other compounds. The new reality was that the only thing that mattered now was a good pair of boots and the ability to put one foot in front of the other. By the time the last man left the camp, the column stretched for twenty miles.

As we marched past the food store in the East Compound on the way out, we passed close to where the sixty or so Russian prisoners were kept. There was Artum and his comrades waving us farewell. They were being left for their countrymen to discover. For the course of the war they had suffered more hunger and humiliations than any of the other nationalities, but they now knew that liberation by their own people was close. They were half-starved, and several of us bent down to pick up the countless cans from the abandoned Red Cross packets. I grabbed a tin of Klim milk and lobbed it into their compound. Others did likewise, and soon it was raining food on the delighted Russians. Cheese, butter, and bully beef poured from the sky as the overburdened guards tried to shove us along. The only casualty was a Russian who took an accidental direct hit from a tin of ham. Artum and his countrymen lined the wire and waved farewell. He was a brave man, and as usual he was smiling. I never saw him again.

In this vast human exodus, ten thousand strong, discarded cans and parcels were pounced upon by the ration-starved German women who had worked in the camp, many of them at censoring letters. They bent like gleaners of the fields, gathering what they could to feed their families and then hurried back to their cellars to await with dread the arrival of the Russians.

The column started by heading west, back into Germany and away from the advancing Russians. In the coming days we traveled west, south, and north, with little apparent logic—any way but east. As we marched off to an uncertain destination and an even more uncertain fate, there was one bright spot on the bleak white horizon—all three compounds were emptied out into one giant, struggling, straggling mass of humanity, ten thousand in all. The American compounds left first at one o'clock on the morning of Sunday, January 28, 1945. Our compound did not leave until some time nearer four in the morning.

The mixing up of all the compounds on the march gave me the chance to be reunited for the first time in over a year with my old comrades from the north compound. Soon I found myself marching alongside Paddy Barthropp. It was wonderful to see him again and just like old times. The long line of troops made quite a spectacle—thin men looking fat, bumping into old friends as we lurched along in almost a foot of snow that turned to icy mud with the churning of thousands of marching feet.

But the companionship of meeting old friends could not serve to keep out the cold as we marched for hours, then days, in the ice. The guards had been given orders to shoot anyone who got out of line, and at the back of the column was a pack of vicious, snarling guard dogs ready to fall on anyone who lagged behind. Some of the guards were so dejected they ignored any infractions as long as their officers were not looking. One elderly guard, plodding along miserably, was screamed at by an officer who discovered he was letting a prisoner carry his rifle because his shoulder hurt. Demoralized guards, numb prisoners, and exhausted refugees all headed south and west, like debris floating on an incoming tide.

By the end of the war, even the dogs were confused. One small group of prisoners had fallen out because they had to repack their makeshift sled after the linen strips of bedsheet they were using in lieu of rope gave way. They were repacking their Red Cross food and trying to eat some of it rather than abandon it when one of the more vicious guards stormed up with two Alsatians straining at the leash. He yelled at the prisoners to get going, but they continued to take their time, munching and packing, like a bizarre picnic at the gates of hell. The guard decided to unleash the dogs, and roaring a command for them to do their worst, he set them on the prisoners. Despite their years of training, the dogs trotted up to the prisoners wagging their tails and begging for some food. They were rewarded for their disloyalty with corned beef and chocolate and settled in for a feast while their handler roared, yelled, and hopped up and down to no avail. I liked to think that maybe they were some of the guard dogs I had tried to bribe with a few handfuls of the Mixture over my years in the camps.

The entire march was broken up into numerous columns, and the experiences of each one could be quite different, depending on the nature of the guards in the immediate vicinity and what happened to them along the way. By the end of the war, prisoners in the Luft III march had ended up in at least three camps, hundreds of miles apart and at opposite ends of the country.

The Americans at the front of the column had been force-marched for thirty miles on the first day to make room for those coming along behind. The rest of us traveled shorter distances, but over more days, which gradually wore us down. Sometimes the snow stopped, and at others it whipped itself into a blizzard. I stopped to share a drink from a canteen with Paddy, and as I poured the water into a cup with a shivering hand, it froze solid before we had the chance to drink it. When the guards, laden down by full packs, became as exhausted as we were, there was an order given to halt.

We slumped in the snow for ten minutes, delighted for the chance to rest, but minute by minute the cold seeped into my bones. By the end of ten minutes I could hardly get going again. It seemed a good idea just to lie there and look at the white German sky. Paddy cursed me and hauled me to my feet. We stumbled on. At the next break, when it seemed to him a good idea just to lie there and let the snow cover us, I did the same for him.

By now, every prisoner was wearing virtually every stitch of clothing he owned, and any semblance of an army had been replaced with an endless procession of people dressed in outlandish combinations of army, navy, air force, and civilian gear from head to foot.

When our water ran out and the thirst got too much, we melted some snow to drink and tried to keep our spirits up in the bitter cold by telling bad jokes. At various times both Paddy and I were on our last legs from exhaustion, and when one dropped in the snow, the other one would dissuade him from going to sleep, which seemed to be an excellent idea, but would have meant never waking up again.

On the first night, my fellow travelers and I were almost dropping from exhaustion as we arrived in some small village, which I think may have been Friedwaldau, west of Sagan. We hoped for shelter in some school halls or barns, but the village headman turned out to be a Nazi. He seemed not to have noticed that the war was nearly over. He snarled and ranted at us, outraged at the thought of his village being contaminated by these Luftgangsters and did his best to be unhelpful to us and to the guards who were trying to negotiate us a place to sleep. As they argued, the Russian guns rumbled like thunder in the background, as if attempting to remind them of the impending doom of the Third Reich. We stood for hours in the snow, and some prisoners as well as a few of the guards started to develop frostbite in their feet, hands, and faces, a problem that would get worse in the coming days.

Eventually, some people found billets in the village, while others of us were marched another few miles down the road to another hamlet, where we were crammed into a huge barn, too exhausted to do anything but find a few feet of ground between the bodies of our comrades on which to collapse and sleep.

The next morning, as the sun thawed our bones and we wiped the grimy straw off our clothes, the guards attempted to make a count of the prisoners. Eventually they gave up, and we just pulled out to continue to march through another small town, where we halted and haggled for food.

As the journey wore on, it became clear that the German High Command, insofar as it still existed, had not made any plans to feed or house us. The supplies we had been able to carry dwindled, and we grew more hungry and thirsty as the day wore on. All the marching in the snow took its toll, and my mind started to wander back to that mountain of Red Cross food we had been forced to leave behind. I saw visions of the thousands of packets and cans strewn in the snow at the gates of the camp, but at least we still had the more portable supplies, such as chocolate and cigarettes, and we started to barter with the villagers and farmers we passed. We cursed the fact that we had left so much coffee behind. It was more valuable for trading even than cigarettes.

As we struggled westward the column merged with and separated from all the displaced humanity of the war. Proud Germans stood beside their houses looking at the elderly men and moon-faced boys who were all that seemed to be left of the Third Reich, preparing to meet the Russian onslaught that would follow in our wake. Some cursed at us, but most just stared in amazement that it had come to this or in terror at what would follow us.

Yet ten minutes later we would be forced off the road by columns of trucks moving east, the way we had come. They were full of tough, experienced-looking soldiers heading for the front. In some places the SS were trying to hold a nonexistent line in terms of morale and still had the power to threaten or intimidate the locals away from our column. The local children playing in the snow soon found out they could swap their sleds for more chocolate than they had ever seen, while their parents tried to barter basic foodstuffs for our more exotic fare. The responses of the German people, soldiers and civilians, by that stage were as confused as our own.

At first the guards tried to stop us haggling with the locals, but as the cold got to them, they just ignored the transactions, only shooing us along if we stopped to haggle for too long and started to fall behind. They also got very zealous whenever a senior German officer was around. On one occasion a farmer, standing by the roadside watching the endless cavalcade of ragged humanity passing by, was attempting to negotiate with me over the swap of a circular loaf of bread for about forty cigarettes. Just as we were nearing agreement after a protracted haggle, a German officer strutted past and a guard who had been stumbling along dejectedly rushed over and shooed the farmer away. I was just starting to think of a few choice names to call him when he waited for the officer to disappear ahead, and then he ran back, found the farmer, and brought him back to me to complete the transaction. He accepted a hunk of bread for his role as middleman, a tiny gesture confirming that the world we had all known was crumbling around us.

A new economy developed. Once again the camp currencies of cigarettes and chocolate came into their own. Prisoners grumbled if they were too far back in the column that those farther ahead were offering too many cigarettes for a loaf and so were "spoiling the market." But not everyone was interested in buying and selling. One German couple fed a great huddle of us some thin, hot soup and would not take anything in return. Eventually the wife agreed to take some bars of soap, another of the simple everyday objects that takes on a real value in time of war. At that point a Prussian officer, who had not been able to get his head around the fact that all was lost, came up and shouted at the couple, pushing the prisoners onward on the march. The old man cowered, but his wife stood up to the officer, saying that her son was a prisoner in England, who had said in his letters that he was well treated, so she would do the same for us whether the officer liked it or not.

I remembered back to the letter my own mother had sent with the same sentiments earlier in the war, and I was glad that, even at this late hour, some feelings of humanity were creeping back into the open in Germany. A few years earlier such defiance might have cost the old lady her life, but now the officer just spluttered and kicked the nearly empty soup bucket over into the snow, where the contents melted the ice and formed a sad little puddle, like a miniature sea of humanity in a vast, frozen world. The officer shouted abuse at the couple and at us prisoners and then stormed off to find someone less difficult to bully.

Days and nights merged into a nightmare of frozen travel, huddling, bartering, shivering, and stumbling ever on. A day or so later, staggering with exhaustion, we reached a little town called

Muskau, though the temperatures felt more like Moscow. At times on the march it fell to minus ten degrees and we sought what little shelter we could find along the way, so Muskau felt like an oasis. It was normally a picturesque little town, wrapped around a stately home belonging to the Arnhim family, one of whom had been a German general in North Africa. The locals had been old-fashioned and never overly keen on Hitler, so they treated us relatively well. Some of the luckier prisoners were put up in the stables of the stately home where they had hot and cold running water and as much straw as they could eat. Previously the stables had been one of Europe's best stud farms, and it seemed that the horses had had a better time over the last few years than we had.

Soon we were on the march again. The weather seemed more bitter than ever as we marched straight into the teeth of a biting wind, heads bent, backs arched, pulling sleds or helping those too sick to go on alone. Paddy and I staggered along, talking about nonsense when we had the energy to keep us from slipping back into icy oblivion. As we walked, the temperature dropped below zero again and the snow swirled around us once more. I tried to concentrate on what Paddy was saying as he stumbled along beside me. He was outlining his latest plan to escape from the column. As far as I could tell over the noise of our chattering teeth, his plan was simple and elegant.

"We just keep walking along as we are now," he confided. I leaned in to catch his words. "Then, when we have lulled them into a false sense of security, all of a sudden and without any warning, we die on them."

I agreed with him that this was one foolproof way to escape

the people who had held us prisoner for so long, but suggested we might save the last part of the plan for a little later.

By that evening many prisoners and some of the guards were suffering from severe frostbite and could not go on. Some were left with locals to await assistance from whoever came along next, but others were in too bad a way to wait. One German guard was close to death from frostbite and gangrene. His only hope was to have his foot amputated. This operation was done with no proper instruments or anesthetic by a prisoner called Digby Young, who had to rely on some medical training as a student before the war. All he had to work with was some alcohol and a few kitchen knives. It was a terrible thing, but he managed to save the man's life.

Paddy and I ended up with dozens of others huddled in a vast glass and brick factory where some of the furnaces were still working. The place used French slave labor, but by the time we arrived in the evening it was deserted. Luckily, the furnaces had to be kept at white heat all the time, and we went into the vast central hall of the works with as much delight as tourists in a cathedral. I put my sodden prison-issue boots next to the furnace to dry out, and we huddled around the ovens, basking in the warmth.

Just as I was nodding off, a rumor circulated that there was food to be had. We dragged ourselves up, while leaving a few comrades to guard our precious place by the boiler. The French prisoners and some of the local women started a soup kitchen, working with infinite patience to fill a thousand tin cups and billycans held in our outstretched hands. Teeth chattered, and frostbitten fingers curled around cups as we tasted the first warmth in what felt like a lifetime. Back by the boilers there was more cooking going on, with every kind of Red Cross tin being arranged around the furnaces, warming nicely. As I fell asleep, I hoped we might be able to stay in Muskau forever, or at least until the Russians arrived.

In a corner office, some of the radio operators who had kept us informed through their secret receivers in the camp were setting up shop. They had lovingly carried their homemade contraptions with them, and they strung up a wire aerial, then hunched over with their headphones and listened to the BBC telling us that the war was almost over. There was little concrete news, and the truth was that few people, whether Russian or German, prisoner or civilian, had very much idea what was happening, other than the unavoidable observation that Germany was getting smaller by the day. As my comrades discussed the latest news and rumors, I fell into a deep, dark, sleep—warm for the first time in days.

When I woke, stiff but snug, the factory was a seething mass of activity. I hurried to get dressed. We were pulling out, and when I went to put my nice warm boots on, I found that they had been a bit too close to the oven and were cooked to perfection. As the order came to march on and I pulled them on, the soles came away from the crumbling tops. I wrapped what was left of them in rags and continued forward like a shambling wild man as the cold seeped through the cloth into my feet and threatened frostbite.

But the weather seemed to have broken. Sleet was replaced by rain, and the wind was a little less biting than the days before. While we were grateful not to be frozen to death, we started worrying about drowning in mud. The hundreds of wooden sleds that had saved our lives by allowing us to carry enough supplies to survive were now almost useless, bumping along on the mud and rocks. Just as we were leaving, some of the men managed to persuade the French prisoners to operate one of the giant lathes in the glass factory, and a helpful engineer produced several pairs of little wooden wheels, turning some of our sleds into wagons.

For another two days we staggered on, heading west and north, farther into the dying heart of Germany, with only the food and water we had carried or what we could get by bartering. At one point an Allied plane swooped low over another part of the endless column and some men dived to either side of the road, fearing we would be strafed. A few trigger-happy guards thought it was a mass breakout and started firing. Several wounded men, so close to freedom, was the result.

As we trudged along, we sometimes passed other groups of prisoners being marched for no apparent reason in the opposite direction. When we passed a column of Russian prisoners we saw how comparatively well-off we were. They were all skeleton thin, with brave, sunken eyes burning out of skull-like faces covered in full, ragged beards. Their fanatical SS guards treated them like animals, herding them along with whips and rifle butts.

We could do very little, but one of us threw over some cigarettes. Then somebody else threw some chocolate. Soon there was a small, silent bombardment going on as the Russians smiled and clutched at this act as much for its humanity as for the much needed food. One pack of cigarettes fell short and a Russian prisoner eagerly reached out for it. One of the SS guards lifted his rifle and smashed it into the Russian's head as he stooped to pick up the cigarettes. When the man fell under the blow, the SS man screamed at him and continued to smash him in the face and kick him like a dog. A collective roar of rage went up from our side of the road and several hundred Allied prisoners stopped and moved a few dangerous inches toward the Russian column.

The SS man giving the beating turned around and looked in total astonishment as if it never occurred to him anyone might object to his actions. Other SS guards fingered their weapons nervously, not knowing whether to turn their backs on the Russians or on us. It was a very dangerous moment. Some of our guards, seeing what had happened, ran over to the SS guard and shoved him on. His grateful colleagues were glad to move on rather than face a riot in which they might have killed a lot of us but would have ensured a few of them were torn to pieces, too. The battered Russian managed to get back in line, and even managed a smile through the blood as he picked up the packet of cigarettes. The Russians knew that the Red Army was coming, and they would neither forgive nor forget.

When the column reached the town of Spremberg on our seemingly endless westward retreat, we huddled in the railway yards and were eventually loaded into cattle cars, much as so many innocent Jewish people were sent to their doom. At the time, we had no idea of our destination and wondered if we were moving closer to safety or closer to a bullet in the last act of Hitler's demented rule. Possibly the worst thing about the march was not the cold, or the sickness, or the thirst, but the simple lack of a destination. Rumors that we were to be shot rippled up and down the lines every day, and when we saw the empty cattle cars waiting to take us to destinations unknown, there were few of us who did not at least wonder if it would be our last journey.

The cattle cars were so crowded that it was impossible to sit down, and even for those who managed it, or fell down, the floors were still covered in cattle dung, and many of the men were throwing up, suffering from a dozen different illnesses. Even before the train pulled out, conditions were almost unbearable. By the time we had been rolling along for the best part of a day it was like being in hell.

We were starting to suffocate in the cattle cars and were desperate for a drink of water. The guards refused to stop, and eventually, in desperation, after we had shared what little water we had, we looked for another solution. Some bright spark noticed that we were sharing our journey with one of the padres. We suggested that it was time to liberate his bottle of holy water. At first he was not very keen on the idea, but when it became apparent that not only was it the right thing to do, but that if he didn't he was probably going to be a good candidate for instant martyrdom, he reluctantly agreed. We passed the water and got a sip each. Later, some other smart thinker thought to drain one of the steam engine cisterns so we got another mouthful of muddy warm water to keep us going.

The cattle cars rolled on and stopped somewhere between Bremen and Hamburg. I was beginning to feel pretty grim by this point. By now we were all swarming with lice and fleas, and as I almost keeled over, I realized I was already suffering from a bad case of jaundice. I was dumped off with other prisoners who were mostly in an even worse state than me, some suffering from frostbite, others with dysentery.

By now, with a bad case of jaundice and having spent so much time in punishment cells over the previous three years—maybe six months if you added it all up—I was close to dropping. As the fitter prisoners were moved on, a medic took one look at me and ordered me to remain with those too sick to travel.

I bade a quick farewell to Paddy and my other mates. It was a war of unexpected reunions and sudden partings. The chance meetings, from the choice of which door to knock on in a French village to which pilot would be shoved into a cell beside me, had shaped my life. Perhaps I was lucky that the people I met were the bravest, funniest souls you could hope to have as friends. But maybe behind almost every door there lurks someone with the potential to be remarkable. I thought of all the hurried farewells—the smile and wink from Jimmy Buckley as he scooted out of that tunnel back in Schubin, never to be seen again; the simple good night I had said to Josef and Giselle in a Paris apartment hours before the Gestapo had burst in and taken us in opposite directions forever. These and a thousand other farewells crowded my increasingly fevered brain, but as usual I and my friends just laughed and arranged to meet up in some warm London pub, not too far from Piccadilly, someday.

A minute later and they were all gone, continuing the grueling journey that lasted thirty-six hours on that hell-train to a Marlag, or navy prison camp, farther north, where the conditions were even worse in terms of overcrowding and starvation. Paddy and many of my other friends were liberated near the end of the war, and in true Paddy style he traveled home part of the way in a stolen fire engine. He is still my friend and comrade, sixty years later.

Incredible as it may seem, those of us coming from Stalag Luft III had it easier than the men from some of the other eastern camps, such as Schubin, Hydekrug, and Stalag Luft II, all of which were similarly being evacuated away from the advancing Russians. They were marched in ragged columns similar to ours for up to six weeks, east and west, first one way and then doubling back in the opposite direction as the front lines twisted and turned in the death throes of the Third Reich. Many had even less warning of their departure than we had, and were given little rest, food, or water along the way. Day after day, their guards tried to avoid capture first by the Russians, then by the Americans. My old sergeant friends from Hydekrug had a terrible time, marched to no one knew where for weeks, but they were fortunate to still be under the leadership of that quiet tough man Jimmy Deans.

Dixie had managed to purloin a bicycle and rode up and down the lines, negotiating with the guards and helping his men, strung out in different columns as they walked more than a hundred miles in no particular direction. He was ever present, organizing barns in which to sleep, getting medical attention for the sick, and helping his men to avoid the SS detachments that were then roaming the country looking for anyone, Allied or German, whom they could find an excuse to shoot. On one occasion, cycling in full British uniform, he was caught alone between two columns of his men. An angry German officer wanted to shoot him on the spot, but Dixie just told him off in his excellent German and cycled off, quietly hoping he would not get a bullet in the back of the head.

But there were some things even Dixie could do nothing about. One day, from out of the white winter sky, four RAF Typhoons mistook his ragged columns of prisoners for retreating German soldiers. So-called friendly fire, possibly the biggest euphemism ever coined, was a problem in this war just as much as in the more recent ones. As the planes fired rockets and strafed the column, bullets chewed up the ground and men dived for cover, but thirty were killed, just weeks from liberation.

Dixie did something truly remarkable. He went to the German commander and asked for permission to cross through the battle lines to tell the Allies that the marching columns were prisoners from their own side, not enemy soldiers. The German officers by now knew that, sergeant or not, he was a remarkable leader, and they agreed, either out of honor or to preserve themselves in the trials that they knew would take place after the war.

Dixie made the incredibly dangerous journey through the German defenses and then through the Allied battle lines, where bullets whizzed over his tattered white flag. He made it and debriefed a senior British commander to ensure his men would not be attacked again. The commander was a bit bemused that a mere sergeant was in such a senior position and was even more amazed when Dixie refused to be evacuated back to Britain. Instead, he retraced his dangerous journey across the battlefront to rejoin his men. He may have "only" been a sergeant, but in the eyes of those of us who knew him, James Dixie Deans was a five-star general.

Back in my own particular road to ruin, now far to the west of our starting point, I was taken with the other sick prisoners to an encampment somewhere outside Bremen. It was a crude hospital camp with no facilities, teeming with men suffering from dysentery, gangrene, malnutrition, and frostbite, or, like me, from jaundice. That ailment by this stage pretty neatly summed up my feelings about the Third Reich as it went through its long-overdue demise. I just hoped that my own end would not coincide with that of the Reich as the days turned into weeks, and still the war dragged on.

I felt so sick I could barely move as I lay in an overcrowded compound dotted with tents, waiting to be liberated and thoroughly disgusted with myself for not escaping under my own steam. All the efforts, all the adventures had come to this—a bone-thin creature lying in a sickbed waiting to be shot or saved. I felt one last burst of outrage burn up inside me, like the last flaring and flickering of a candle before it goes out. Then I heard the rumble of mechanized infantry and self-propelled guns. I got a new lease of life and stood up, wobbly on my feet, to greet the Allies. At least I was alive. At least . . . But it wasn't the Allies.

Row upon row of white-clad German soldiers from a crack mountain division poured into the camp and started setting up their self-propelled guns. Behind them, some well-camouflaged Tiger tanks rumbled into the compound and were strategically placed. These were tough troops who had been through five years of victory and defeats, and they were digging in for one last stand on their home turf.

Their commanding officer had chosen the camp with some idea that the Allies would not shell their own prisoners, but as the first shells from the advancing British forces whistled in from the west, both I and the German soldiers knew that this battlefield was not going to be safe for any of us. The alpine troops put up a fierce resistance with small-arms fire, as the boom of their self-propelled guns was joined by the roar of the cannons on the Tiger tanks.

Rockets screamed over our heads, shells burst around us, and shrapnel showered down like rain. I did not feel particularly afraid, but my body seemed to disagree, my knees began to shake so violently that I had trouble staying erect. Then there was a cry for help. The shelling at the top of the camp had become so intense that we either had to watch those in the camp hospital die in a hail of shells and ragged shrapnel or else evacuate them to somewhere less immediately dangerous. All of a sudden my legs decided they were working again. All they needed was something to do. I and some other prisoners who were still well enough to walk started to evacuate the sick bay. Those too ill to walk we carried on our own thin backs.

If anything, the shell fire, both incoming and outgoing, intensified. These battle-hardened soldiers had nowhere left to run, and they were making a real fight of it. Like the English during the Battle of Britain, these men were fighting for their home soil, and the rights and wrongs of the war were forgotten in one last fierce, senseless battle.

I knew that the hundreds of sick prisoners were continuing to get the worst of it, unable to move to safety, and I thought here at last was something I could do to make myself useful in the war. I would stage one last escape and try to reach the Allied troops. I drew a mental map of the locations of the prisoners, the enemy guns, and the concealed Tiger tanks, and then I slipped out of the compound and across the desolation of the battlefield.

I should not make out that my motives were altogether heroic. I did want to help my fellow prisoners, and as always I found myself on the side of the underdog, attempting to protect those who were unable to protect themselves. But I also had simpler, more human motives. One was pride: I had come into this war on my own terms and I was going to leave it that way. I would rather risk a bullet in the back than cower under a hail of shells, wondering if the next incoming round would finish me off or liberate me.

Lastly, I still had the old ticking clock, deep within me, that simply saw the chance for one last escape. It would not be a Great Escape, like that of my fifty friends and comrades who died on that magnificent breakout less than a year earlier and who were now at rest under the cold clay, but it would be a great escape for me. After a wartime of escaping and being recaptured, this time I was going all the way. This time for better or worse, life or death, would be my last escape—my Home Run.

As I dived and dodged though the wire, then through craters and around perimeter defenses, with tracer fire zipping around and the air thick with shrapnel, I had that old feeling again. I was eight years old, back in Texas, and I was off and running again, with ten cents in my pocket and a world to explore.

The chaos of the battle seemed to fade, and in my mind I was running through the green fields of France, looking for and finding a friendly face to hide me. Next I was struggling though the mud of Poland, then swimming the black, deep rivers of Lithuania. And finally I was back at the edge of a field in western Germany as the battle raged behind me. I dived through a hedge and found myself on a small road. I ran down it, running like half the guard dogs in Germany were snapping at my heels. Or maybe it was just Danny, my beloved Alsatian in Texas, running beside a fiddle-footed five-year-old to make sure he did not fall down.

Ahead of me I could see a tank and some raised guns. I slowed down, but I kept moving forward. Rifles clicked at the ready. "Don't shoot!" someone shouted. "He's British!" I replied: "Actually I'm American. And Canadian. And British. It's long story."

But the story would have to wait. I passed on the position of the enemy tanks and guns, and my new acquaintances, the Guards Armored Division, were able to direct their fire at the key enemy positions and away from the prisoners as best they could. After another intense exchange of fire the Allied armor advanced and the white-clad warriors finally threw down their weapons and surrendered.

My new friends in the Guards made a great fuss of their unexpected American catch, getting me to a medic while attempting to ply me with cigarettes, chocolate, and field rations. One week later I was on a plane bound for England from Lüneberg Heath, soon to be the scene of Germany's formal surrender, heading back to an airfield near London, and from there to a hotel on the south coast where a man could eat his fill and still know where his next meal was coming from.

Victory in Europe, VE Day was approaching. I had entered the war on my own terms, crossing over from the Depression and the Hungry Man Diner in Detroit on a bridge that led to a lot more than just Canada. I was ending the journey in the company of strangers, several thousand miles from home, yet I felt this was where I belonged.

Europe lay in ruins. Under the rubble, or at peace in country churchyards, lay about twenty men and women whom I was lucky enough to call friends. Their faces tumbled over each other in my mind, from the young trainee unable to escape his blazing Spitfire, to Victor Beamish, winking as he set off on yet another sortie over the sea; from brave French men and women whom I loved but whose names I never even knew, to men like Jimmy Buckley, George Grimson, and Roger Bushell, quietly determined as they emerged from the darkness of yet another tunnel. All gone, along with sixty million other people who had families, hopes, and dreams like the rest of us. Too many names and too many faces, heaped up in a mental monument to the waste of war, but also to courage and shared humanity.

Yet I was back in England and back on solid ground—the same ground I had flown over and fought for just a few years and what felt like a lifetime earlier. From up there in the cockpit of a Spitfire with the sun at my back, the land below had all looked peaceful, permanent, and still, whether following the timeless curves of the river Thames, the medieval spires of Lincoln Cathedral, or the ancient monolithic circles at Stonehenge. It was a rich prize, and worth fighting for, but the real prize had been the people, an entire generation from all parts of the globe who had taken quiet, personal decisions that had shaped their future and sometimes cost their lives. Together they had decided that the world deserves better than fear, stupidity, and greed. People can soar as well as any Spitfire.

Postscript

More than sixty years later, Bill Ash is still living in London, aged eighty-seven. After the war he was awarded the MBE (Member of the Order of the British Empire), one of Britain's highest honors, by King George VI for his escape activities. He went on to become many things—a student at Oxford University, a revolutionary, a representative for the BBC in India, and, finally, a writer and past president of the Writers' Guild of Great Britain.

Acknowledgments

Most of the events in this book took place between sixty and seventy years ago, so I hope readers will forgive Brendan and me if we have tried to capture the spirit of the time rather than the letter of it.

While I retreat behind the splendid excuse of old age, which I've been using since I turned seven, Brendan, with only the flimsy pretext that he wasn't born at the time, has had the unenviable task of proving that some of the people I remembered really did exist, including me.

To everyone who helped us with recollections and photos, our sincere thanks and apologies if the following list leaves anyone out. Special thanks to two good friends who shared some of these adventures and are still around—the ever-helpful Bill Stapleton and the irrepressible Paddy Barthropp. We also want to thank the

Haley Memorial Library for the photo of outlaw George Coe; George Frame and his grandson, Chris, for the picture of the good ship *Georgic*; John Asmussen for the photo of the *Scharnhorst*; the always generous Richard Smith for a photo of Wilfred Duncan-Smith, who saved my life with good advice; Nicole Asselin in Canada for the picture of my Schubin tunnel partner, her flamboyant father Eddy; Charles Rollings, John Beard, and Penny Cooper for photos of the brave, elusive Jimmy Buckley, who died on the Schubin escape along with Jørgen Thalbitzer, whose life story was translated from Danish for us by Pernille Schulz; fellow Hydekrug inmates Alfred Jenner and Cal Younger for photos of James "Dixie" Deans; Serge Holoduke and Ron Richardson for the RCAF 411 Squadron photos; and William Newmiller of the US Air Force Academy and the staff of the Imperial War Museum for pictures of the camps.

We were also blessed with wonderful editors—Simon Taylor at Transworld Publishing in London and Sean Desmond of St. Martin's Press in New York, plus Robert Kirby at PFD, Scott Waxman at the Waxman Agency, Justin Manask of IPG, and Jasper Smith of General Public Entertainment, who all helped to make it happen.

On the home front, Brendan's thanks to Shelly and mine to Ranjana for their constant love, friendship, and encouragement.

William Ash, MBE

INDEX